THE CULT OF YOUTH IN MIDDLE-CLASS AMERICA

PROBLEMS IN AMERICAN CIVILIZATION

THE CULT OF YOUTH IN MIDDLE-CLASS AMERICA

EDITED AND WITH AN INTRODUCTION BY

Richard L. Rapson

UNIVERSITY OF HAWAII

D. C. HEATH AND COMPANY

Lexington, Massachusetts · Toronto · London

To Richard Hofstadter
1916–1970

Published simultaneously in Canada.

Printed in the United States of America.

Library of Congress Catalog Card Number: 74–146876

CONTENTS

INTRODUCTION

WHEN this volume was first conceived, America's colleges and universities had not yet erupted. The outbreak of student unrest in the late 1960's has focused new attention on the peculiar role of the young in America and the attitude toward them. The unrest has also reminded us of the differences between white radicalism and black militancy, between the white upper-middle-class hippies and the wary, uncertain children of Puerto Rican, Irish, Polish, Italian workers. Crucial ethnic, racial, and social distinctions must be made when one speaks of American "youth."

The extraordinary outspokenness of students—in protest against the war in Vietnam; in defiance of the Chicago police force; in the call for sexual liberty; in the emergence of a drug culture; in their always dramatic gestures of idealism and destructiveness, love and fury, total commitment and total withdrawal—has stimulated a torrent of writing about America's young. If one may generalize about such an imposing quantity of words, this recent literature has been characterized by a certain bravery and confusion. The widest variety of propositions have been offered to account for the meaning, causes, and consequences of youthful assertiveness. It is not clear whether it is a new phenomenon or part of a recurring condition in American life. Nearly all the analyses concentrate exclusively on contemporary developments as though the past did not exist. Both the bravery and the confusion stem from an ignorance of the position of childhood, youth, and the family in the American past; an understanding of the child in the past could contribute impressively to an understanding of current activities.

This lack of perspective upon which to build an analysis of today's turmoil cannot be blamed on the writers who are actively wrestling with that problem. American historians have, however, virtually neglected the study of the American child and his family to an astonishing degree. Such neglect is as serious as any in the writing of American history; it is also unexpected. In the United States (which in this introduction is shorthand for white middle-class America), children are expected to be heard as well as seen; our schools, churches, communities, and parents encourage the child to participate actively, even in the adult world. American culture is youth-oriented and has been so for some time. Our thoughts are toward the future and innovation rather than toward the past and tradition. Our families are egalitarian rather than authoritarian. Our schools have long been regarded by Americans as constituting the best hope in the world. To a great extent life in middle-class America centers on the child.

Even if research in American history were hidebound, formal, and narrow, the nature of youth-oriented American civilization would force the historian to analyze and understand the role of the family and the child perhaps as much as he does politics. But the study of American history has not, in general, been narrow; it has been explorative, innovative, expanding. Especially in the last few decades, with the rise of American Studies and with the catalyzing influence of the social sciences on intellectual and cultural and social history, American historians have probed with imagination, energy, and perception into areas of national life previously excluded from formal study. Despite these exciting changes in historical inquiry, no systematic, comprehensive study of the American family has been written in over half a century.

There is no satisfactory explanation for this serious omission. Perhaps historians have been frightened away by the plethora of studies carried on by the sociologists, psychologists, and anthropologists. The social scientists have jumped into the vacuum, recognizing the intimate relationship between child-rearing patterns and the national character. But for all the volume of material they have published, they too have dealt almost exclusively with contemporary conditions. The few social scientists who have explored the American child of the past have not done so well with it, nor should they be expected to do very well. David Riesman's sociology in *The Lonely Crowd* easily surpasses his history; it should not be surprising to discover that he deals more knowledgeably with the twentieth-century child than he does with the youth of the previous century. The frequently stimulating work of the social scientists has thus intensified rather than obviated the need for historical study of childhood in America.

Another explanation for historical neglect of the child deserves mention: the problem of documentation. The historian cannot carry out controlled surveys as the social scientists sometimes can, nor do the conventional documents of historical research—government documents, original manuscripts, philosophical treatises, unpublished letters—help very much. The historian must forage in the chaotic world of popular fiction, travel accounts, autobiographies, popular magazines, and anything else at all promising. But scarce and shadowy though his material may be, the search for it seems justifiable.

This volume puts together some of the more interesting essays that have considered American childhood in order not only to indicate the intrinsic worth of the subject or to increase our understanding of today's youth culture, but also to reveal how much light the study of the child may shed upon major questions concerning the nature of American society itself. All of the selections that follow have been chosen on the basis of whether the author has attempted to relate his findings about American childhood to an understanding of American society. Essays that deal primarily with just the child himself—his psyche, his problems, his abilities—have therefore been excluded from this volume. This eliminates large chunks of writing, mostly recent, in a field dominated by psychologists, educationists, anti-educationists, and journalists. Since the relationship between childhood and society is best made in a time-centered context, most of the articles in this volume were written either by some of the few historians who have ventured into this area or by reformers of the Progressive era who urged, during a period of decisive importance in the history of the nation and of the child, that the most permanent way to improve the quality of American life lay in serving the needs of American youth.

America has *always* been, in the words of Richard Hofstadter, the land of the "overvalued child." Far more than in Europe, the child in America has been exalted; more effort, attention, and hope have been invested in him here than has been done anywhere else in the world. The readings in this volume are not organized around one particular question, nor is the reader asked to choose between one of two alternatives; rather, a number of problems are posed. But perhaps a central question to all of them is whether Americans have, indeed, overvalued, undervalued, or accurately appraised the potential of children. A hard look at American assumptions concerning the natural goodness, innocence, and practically unlimited educability of children will force the analyst to move from large, abstract queries to difficult and specific questions concerning public education, political reform, the American life-style, and social mobility.

The first section of this volume is strictly historical in nature. Five essays by five historians take the long view of the peculiar American attitude toward children. They attempt to define it and to account for it. What was there in the American experience that led to the breakdown of the Old World authoritarian family? What were the consequences in our history of that breakdown? These are not academic questions; the answers to them, as for many well-put historical questions, furnish tangible evidence for questions of value. If the controlling factors that elevated the child in colonial America are no longer operative, for example, the child of today might best be reined in more tightly; however, if the emancipation of the child contributed in a signal way to American achievements at home and abroad, then the free spirit of the child might be allowed more room to soar than ever. Bernard Bailyn looks to the historical experience of the colonists to find the reasons that rendered the centuries-old patrilineal extended-kinship Old World family pattern irrelevant to the New World. Alexis de Tocqueville writes from the perspective of Jacksonian times and, like Bailyn, looks backward to the roots and forward to the actual and potential consequences of a family pattern that stood in sharpest contrast to what he knew in France.

A study by Ruth Miller Elson of nineteenth-century schoolbooks reminds us that though American schools in the nineteenth century may have been more "progressive" than European schools, they were still, by today's standards, quite conservative. This makes a good corrective to an implication in the Bailyn and Tocqueville sections that the glorification of the child had been accomplished painlessly very early in American history. When did we become conscious of the child as a being of unlimited potential? What forces contributed to this consciousness? Answers to these questions, historical in nature, would be revealing indeed.

The fourth selection, by the editor, tries to fill out the picture of the American child by recreating the shock experienced by British travelers to the United States, who as unsuspecting newcomers described their terrifying first encounters with American children. That they did not like what they saw may tell us more about the Britons and their country than about the United States, but their vivid sensations may also help ground this debate a little more solidly in empirical reality. The final essay in the first section, by David Potter, takes an overview of the American past and suggests a series of connections between (a) American abundance, (b) American child-rearing practices, and (c) the American character. These connections appear even more persuasive in light of the nature of recent student unrest.

Although as far back as the seventeenth century childhood was idealized in the New World more than in Europe, it is not clear that Americans were always conscious of this idealization. If, in fact, we shift our perspective from Europe to that of contemporary America, the picture of our children of yesteryear alters. By comparison with today's view of undeniably liberated youth, the picture of the nineteenth-century boy might include unyielding, autocratic fathers patterned after Clarence Day's *Life With Father;* it might contain ordered, disciplined classrooms where the child had to thoroughly learn his lessons or else risk corporal punishment; it might even recall "the Protestant ethic" or "the inner-directed family" wherein American children of the nineteenth century supposedly had to work hard, obey parental strictures, and be toughened up when young so that they might better adapt as adults to an unyielding world. Hence it may be somewhat deceptive to equate too easily the nineteenth-century child with his contemporary counterpart. The turning point in the history of the American child, that has led to his present state, must be chosen with some care.

Whether the years 1890–1920 may be characterized as *the* watershed in that history is open to debate. But without question this period constitutes one very important turning point in the American attitude toward children. These years encompass the general reforms characterized by Populism and by the Progressive movement. More specifically, this period gave birth to the child-study movement, the Social Gospel, child-labor agitation, and, among many other things, the development of what has come to be called progressive education. The middle section of this volume introduces us to this exciting period and to the views on childhood and society of leading participants of the age who, although engaged in different kinds of activities, were united in their fundamental assumptions about America and her young people. Not sharing the enthusiasm and sense of discovery apparent in these essays, the reader may find himself in a sufficiently detached position to ask some critical questions about these assumptions. But in focusing on these few years in connection with developments which really have a longer history and very deep roots, an equally valuable purpose may be served: it may be demonstrated that childhood can shed light upon a historical period as much as does economic change, political structure, intellectual life, or diplomatic maneuvering. If childhood can add to our understanding of the society as a whole, scholars and students may be equipped with another tool to be used in the interdisciplinary strategy by which they try to come to grips with the meaning of the American past.

Perhaps the major manifestation of American consciousness of the unawakened child at the turn of the century was the child-study movement. Its originator, the psychologist G. Stanley Hall, was also, however, a leader in making Americans aware of the psychological and psychocultural problems of adolescence. Some of his observations on the nature of adolescence, a unique and separate part of the life cycle (he believed), open up the second section of this book. The next selection, by the founder of Hull House, Jane Addams, moves the issue from abstraction to social reform. By detailing, dramatically, what life in the city was like for young people, she invited sympathy, uplift, and many specific proposals for change. For Miss Addams, as for many others, sympathy for the put-upon youngster furnished the leverage by which the case for larger measures of social reform could be pleaded. Much of Jacob Riis' famous muckraking account of *How the Other Half Lives,* for example, is concerned with tenement children in New York at the beginning of the twentieth century. To reformers such as Riis and Addams, it was an article of faith that the young were essentially capable and good beings, who, in the proper environment, would be able to cultivate their best qualities. If they behaved badly, bad environment was to blame. Though there was some question as to whether one could rehabilitate older people who had gone astray (with most Progressives contending that it was never too late), there was no question concerning the potential rerouting of young people who were all, by their nature, good.

The strongest proclamation of the cult of youth was formulated by the young Randolph Bourne. In the third essay of the section, an essay which strikes a contemporary note, Bourne strongly calls upon youth to be the innovative, radical, experimental force in twentieth-century America. Between 1890 and 1920 there seemed to be an inextricable link formed between reforms connected with young people—in the tenements, in the factories, above all in the schools—and the general plans for social and moral uplift so dear to the Progressives. The major voice in these years raised in explicit defense of the child and of far-reaching educational change belonged to John Dewey. His name is synonymous with "progressive education," one of the major indirect triumphs of the Progressives. Dewey's name, in many ways, deserves a better fate than to be synonymous with much that passes as progressive education. His famous essay on "education as growth" completes the middle section of this book and allows the reader to get at the source in order to assess more knowledgeably Dewey's assumptions, intentions, and the kind of attitude toward children that dominated American thinking at least until the end of the Second World War, and which is still deeply engrained in our consciousness today.

Since the end of the Second World War, however, an inevitable paradox has set in. The historic celebration of youth has led to the flowering of a very definite, powerful, visible youth culture;

its definiteness, power, and visibility have stimulated, on the other hand, a bitter reaction among large numbers of Americans against young people. As the cult of youth realized its implications in daily life it was bound to open up the assumptions that lay behind it to a most searching inquiry.

The citizen-critics of permissiveness in American life singled out as their chief targets two special villains: John Dewey and Dr. Benjamin Spock. Lawrence Cremin, perhaps the foremost historian of American education, introduces the final section with a survey of challenges to theories of life-adjustment and progressive education (mistakenly associated with the theories of Dewey) that arose in the early 1940's. Cremin describes the series of defeats that were experienced by the "progressive" educationists in the 1940's and 1950's. This is followed by an excerpt from Richard Hofstadter's *Anti-Intellectualism in American Life*. His analysis of Dewey and American childhood is perhaps the most successful portion of that major study. In it, Hofstadter reviews much of the literature and most of the problems with which the student will have met up to this point. His analysis is subtle, complex, and, if the reader will give it his best thought, extremely rewarding and provocative. It will clearly add a new dimension to our understanding of American civilization.

The focus switches to the contemporary scene for the remainder of the book, with a special impetus provided by the campus revolts of the late 1960's and continuing into the 1970's. The writers are asking, as are so many citizens, the questions: What is going on? Why is this happening? Three social scientists—Bruno Bettelheim, Kenneth Keniston, and Edgar Friedenberg—see problems of the generations at the root of things. The difficulties being psychological and institutional, those who write of the generation gap usually do so without a sense of urgency (Friedenberg is an exception). Psychological and institutional difficulties are not amenable to sudden change; they demand understanding, tolerance, patience. The abstract, scientific, plodding prose of many psychologists and sociologists conforms well with their message that there exist generalizable patterns determining behavior for which understanding is our best response.

There is little determinism evident in the final two essays by the professor-radical Theodore Roszak, and the professor-critic Benjamin DeMott. They concentrate on the issues and life-styles that Americans are debating so fiercely. They emphasize choice, change, and particularities rather than patterns, continuities, and abstractions. Their dramatic, immediate prose conforms well with their message that questions of value are at stake and that the individual can and must make very serious choices about his life and his future.

Bettelheim suggests that young people would both benefit by and prefer more direction from their elders. Keniston, although not responding directly to that point, expresses concern about the tendency of adults to idealize youth in America. Edgar Friedenberg, however, is a sociologist who argues implicitly against the dominant theme of this book: that Americans have historically placed a high value on youth; that contemporary events are a logical extension and application in life of that valuation; that the so-called "generation gap" may be traced to growing doubts among some about the wisdom of allowing so much freedom to the young. Friedenberg views youth as an *exploited* class and in so doing he evokes memories of the liberalism of the 1930's. As is frequently the case with sociologists, he chooses to emphasize definite material and legal class conflicts rather than the less tangible attitudinal differences that most of the other essays in this book stress.

Theodore Roszak, an historian a little too old and too intellectual to be counted one with the student radicals, but a little too radical to belong to The Establishment, follows with his intriguing new analysis of the "counter culture" of youth, an analysis that is definitely, but not uncritically, sympathetic to the efforts of the young. The volume concludes with Benjamin DeMott's fascinating suggestion that, although youth may lead the way, "what's happening" is happening to everybody. The newly emerging sense of self and the new definition of "the good life" may be less revolutionary than Roszak's counter culture, but the milder, more widely diffused personal revolution that DeMott describes should stimulate among readers all kinds of intriguing questions.

The most successful sort of historical analysis engages the whole person, his feelings as well as his thoughts. An understanding of the role of childhood and youth in American society may be of historical and analytic value equal to that of more traditional topics precisely because it is more personally perceived than are the more public subjects. We are learning daily how central to an understanding of outward public, national behavior are the circumstances of inner, private life. Family patterns, child-rearing, adult expectations about one's own and other children are, at the outset, such circumstances of inner life. How do they relate to social and historical generalization?

We know today that over half the population is under 25 years of age. We know that youth represents an imposing economic power, consuming in incredible proportions. We know youth can influence our politics and our foreign policy even without the vote. We know that the nation's tastes in fashion, music, language, and perhaps even life-style are shaped, to quite some extent, by teenagers. And our attitudes? Our thinking? Our conception of the good life? How important are fun, attractiveness, "thinking young," and sex in American life? How influential in forging these values is the cult of youth? Where did the cult arise? How did it arise? Where might it be taking us?[1] How important a factor is it in our understanding of the American past and present—and future?

Its importance may be considerable. Let us suggest as an illustration a bald hypothesis: Americans have, for much of their past, defined the high point in an individual life as falling between the ages of about 15 and about 30. (As we enter the 1970's, we may have to shave off three or four years from both ends of the scale.) Such a proposition will not be "proved" here, nor could it ever be. Yet, allowing for stunning oversimplification, evidence is not altogether lacking to lend credence to that idea. The evidence can range from the observations of foreign travelers two centuries ago to a detached look at today's advertisements, TV programs and movies, and patterns of consumer spending. Our heroes are young, our clothes are young, our language is young, our thoughts are young, our banks are young. This theme is implied in the editor's essay in this volume, but indeed

[1] Does the current intense hostility of the "hardhats" and of many middle Americans toward college students signal the end of the cult of youth? I think not, for several reasons. First of all, the so-called "excesses" of young people may be seen as a *consequence* of the cult; combining with affluence and with disgust over the Vietnam war, the traditional American glorification of youth has created what must now seem to many to be a Frankenstein's monster. The bitterness of the reaction against the college students no doubt includes a betrayal factor ("After all we have done for you . . .") along with the more recognizable sense of envy, especially with regard to the apparent sexual freedom of the young. In this sense, the antipathy firmly relates to the American idealization of the young.

Second, many older Americans make a distinction between most American young people and the college students, between the good young Americans and the bad hippie-radicals. Third, the "excesses," I would be willing to predict, are almost certain to taper off. Though it is likely that the profound disaffection with current American values, institutions, and polices will continue, there are signs that much of the violence, the religious values placed on drugs, and the intensity of cultural revolt simply cannot be maintained. Journalists may soon be describing college students in terms similar to those used to describe the "silent generation" of the 1950's, but this would be as silly as some of the now-fashionable apocalyptic proclamations that today's young are totally unique beings in the history of mankind.

Finally, the concept of the cult of youth, as defined in the remainder of this introductory essay, is a broad and far-reaching notion, and should not be confused with the narrower question of whether groups of young people are or are not in favor at a particular moment in time.

it suggests itself in nearly everything in this book or in every analysis about American youth past and present. If one were to suspend disbelief just for a moment and accept this hypothesis about the peculiar American view of the life cycle as containing some kernel of truth, the consequences of this view would be most interesting.

Looked at simply in its psychological aspects, this hypothesis could help account for these commonly observed conditions throughout our history: young children growing up (too?) fast, losing their innocence in both style and behavior early, the famous "hothouse children" of America; teenagers with unparalleled confidence, arrogance, and little interest in tradition, convention, or their elders; adults (feverishly?) acting younger than their age; older people losing their pride, their joy, no longer consulted, rarely burdened with serious social responsibility. The apparent beneficiaries of such a society are the young, who demand and often achieve fulfillment "while they may still enjoy it"; the losers appear to be the elderly. Contrast this pattern with older Oriental societies where young people were expected to postpone gratification and learn from the wisest, most influential members of society—their grandfathers. In that world, life may have grown sweeter as one aged. Psychologists would most likely define the healthiest arrangement as that in which *each* stage of the life cycle is valued for itself. One would neither have to postpone gratification nor feel by-passed with each passing year. As one grew older, there would be compensating gains for each loss. It would not be difficult to fill in the details of this model.

But in moving from the personal to the national level the moral problem grows more complex. Are there civilizations in which each stage of the life cycle is granted equal esteem? Some European nations seem to have come close to this ideal, but most of them are now outdoing one another in efforts to Americanize themselves. The prevalence of personal neurosis in Americans must not be spoken of without mention of the dynamic, creative, productive quality of American life over the past three centuries. American history, with the serious exception of racial matters, has been a success story. And that success has involved not only the growth of awesome power and great wealth, but also radical and humanitarian ideals. The childlike optimism—the feeling that we can do anything—has served America very well in general. Lest we think that Vietnam and the racial difficulties have today finally proved to Americans the limitations of power and of life, let us simply recall the future-oriented rhetoric and self-congratulation expressed upon the first arrival of Americans on the moon. Has the national faith in the qualities and spirit of youthfulness served the United States badly? Will the "philosophy of optimism"—the belief that the future should be understood "in terms of its benignity, its malleability, its compatibility with our hopes and desires"—serve us ill in the future?[2] These are ultimate questions involving the nature of man and of life itself; the answers must be left to the reader.

One need not subscribe totally to the proposition that our appreciation of youth is the chief factor behind the innovating, optimistic, individualistic, practical, and inventive spirit of Americans or that it was chiefly responsible for our conquest of a continent, our enormous prosperity, our egalitarianism, our idealism, our world leadership. Nor need one blame American crudeness, anti-intellectualism, insecurity, recklessness, violence, acquisitiveness, lack of restraint, lack of culture, lack of respect for the elderly, our hurried life, our conformity, our boastfulness and abuse of power on our cult of youth. But that some relationship exists between these socio-historical generalizations and the middle-class American conception of childhood seems likely. Hopefully this introduction to the study of

[2] Robert Heilbroner, *The Future as History* (New York, 1959), p. 175. Heilbroner's book concentrates on what he regards as the terrible dangers of the American philosophy of optimism.

childhood and American society will furnish the reader with a starting point from which he can consider fruitfully what those relationships might be. Hopefully this volume not only will stimulate some productive thinking about the obvious contemporary, psychological, and philosophical matters connected with childhood and youth, but will also suggest some new possibilities for the historical analysis of American culture.

CONFLICT OF OPINION

Has the American past been characterized by a higher regard for children than existed in the Old World? What in our history may have caused it? What have been its social consequences? Have there been changes in the American attitude?

> By the middle of the eighteenth century the classic lineaments of the American family as modern sociologists describe them—the "isolation of the conjugal unit," the "maximum of dispersion of the lines of descent," partible inheritances, and multilineal growth—had appeared. The consequences can hardly be exaggerated. Fundamental aspects of social life were affected.
>
> —BERNARD BAILYN

> American schoolbooks of the nineteenth century take a firm and unanimous stand on matters of basic belief. . . . Ethics do not evolve from particular cultural situations, nor are they to be developed by the individual from his own experience and critical thinking. Nor are they to come from his peers. They are absolute, unchanging, and they come from God. The child is to learn ethics as he learns information about his world, unquestioningly, by rote. His behavior is not to be inner-directed, nor other-directed, but dictated by authority and passively accepted.
>
> —RUTH MILLER ELSON

What is the child's nature? How shall Americans educate him?

> Respect the child. Be not too much his parent. Trespass not on his solitude. . . . The two points in a boy's training are, to keep his *naturel* and train off all but that; to keep his *naturel*, but stop off his uproar, fooling, and horseplay; keep his nature *and arm it with knowledge in the very direction in which it points.*
>
> —RALPH WALDO EMERSON, quoted approvingly by John Dewey

> Since growth is the characteristic of life, education is all one with growing; it has no end beyond itself. The criterion of the value of school education is the extent in which it creates a desire for continued growth and supplies means for making the desire effective in fact.
>
> —JOHN DEWEY

> Growth is a natural, animal process, and education is a social process. Growth in the child, taken literally, goes on automatically, requiring no more than routine care and nourishment; its end is to a large degree predetermined by genetic inheritance, whereas the ends of education have to be supplied. In contemplating a child's education we are free to consider whether he shall learn two languages, but in contemplating his natural growth we cannot consider whether he shall develop two heads.
>
> —RICHARD HOFSTADTER

> Parenthood in America has become a very special thing, and parents see themselves not as giving their children final status and

place, rooting them firmly for life in a dependable social structure, but merely as training them for a race which they will run alone. With this orientation towards a different future for the child comes also the expectation that the child will pass beyond his parents and leave their standards behind him.

—MARGARET MEAD

How may the youthful assertiveness of today be assessed?

[The young rebels are] a charming group of little children who never made it through the toilet-training chapter of Dr. Spock.

—LIZ CARPENTER,
Mrs. Lyndon Johnson's press secretary, quoted in *Newsweek*

[The counter culture of youth] looks to me like all we have to hold against the final consolidation of a technocratic totalitarianism in which we shall find ourselves ingeniously adapted to an existence wholly estranged from everything that has ever made the life of man an interesting adventure.

—THEODORE ROSZAK

I. SOURCES AND DESCRIPTIONS OF THE AMERICAN YOUTH CULT

Bernard Bailyn

EDUCATION IN THE FORMING OF AMERICAN SOCIETY—AN INTERPRETATION

Bernard Bailyn, an historian at Harvard, has produced some of the freshest, most original work in the writing of American colonial history, chief among which are *The New England Merchants in the Seventeenth Century* and *The Ideological Origins of the American Revolution*. His book on *Education in the Forming of American Society* contains two parts, a 49-page interpretive essay on the subject and a 60-page bibliographical essay which describes the kinds of materials likely to prove most promising to future researchers in a relatively untraveled field. The fragment from the brief interpretive essay that follows is thus a first exploration rather than the fruit of years of laborious research, and is meant to be suggestive rather than conclusive.

THE forms of education assumed by the first generation of settlers in America were a direct inheritance from the medieval past. Serving the needs of a homogeneous, slowly changing rural society, they were largely instinctive and traditional, little articulated and little formalized. The most important agency in the transfer of culture was not formal institutions of instruction or public instruments of communication, but the family; and the character of family life in late sixteenth- and early seventeenth-century England is critical for understanding the history of education in colonial America.

The family familiar to the early colonists was a patrilineal group of extended kinship gathered into a single household. By modern standards it was large. Besides children, who often remained in the home well into maturity, it included a wide range of other dependents: nieces and nephews, cousins, and, except for families at the lowest rung of society, servants in filial discipline. In the Elizabethan family the conjugal unit was only the nucleus of a broad kinship community whose outer edges merged almost imperceptibly into the society at large.

The organization of this group reflected and reinforced the general structure of social authority. Control rested with the male head to whom all others were subordinate. His sanctions were powerful; they were rooted deep in the cultural soil. They rested upon tradition that went back beyond the memory of man; on the instinctive sense of order as hierarchy, whether in the cosmic chain of being or in human society; on the processes of law that reduced the female to perpetual dependency and calibrated a detailed scale of male subordination and servitude; and, above all, on the restrictions of the economy, which made the establishment of independent households a difficult enterprise.

It was these patriarchal kinship communities that shouldered most of the burden of education. They were, in the first place, the primary agencies in the socialization of the child. Not only did the family introduce him to the basic forms of civilized living, but it shaped his attitudes, formed his patterns of behavior, endowed him with manners and morals. It introduced him to the world; and in so doing reinforced the structure of its authority. For the world to the child was an intricate, mysterious contrivance in controlling which untutored skills, raw nature, mere vigor counted for less than knowledge and experience. The child's dependence on his elders was not an arbitrary decree of fate; it was not only biologically but socially functional.

But the family's educational role was not restricted to elementary socialization. Within these kinship groupings, skills that provided at least the first step in vocational training were taught and practiced. In a great many cases, as among the agricultural laboring population and small tradesmen who together comprised the overwhelming majority of the population, all the vocational instruction necessary for mature life was provided by the family.

The family's role in vocational training was extended and formalized in a most important institution of education, apprenticeship. Apprenticeship was the contractual exchange of vocational training in an atmosphere of family nurture for absolute personal service over a stated period of years. Like other forms of bonded servitude, it was a condition of dependency, a childlike state of legal incompetence, in which the master's role, and responsibilities, was indistinguishable from the father's, and the servant's obligations were as total, as moral, and as personal as the son's. Servants of almost every degree were included within the family, and it was the family's discipline that most directly enforced the condition of bondage. The master's parental concern for his servants, and especially for apprentices, included care for their moral welfare as well as for their material condition. He was expected and required by law to bring them up in good Christian cultivation, and to see to their proper deportment.

What the family left undone by way of informal education the local community most often completed. It did so in entirely natural ways, for so elaborate was the architecture of family organization and so deeply founded was it in the soil of stable, slowly changing village and town communities in which intermarriage among the same groups had taken place generation after generation, that it was at times difficult for the child to know where the family left off and the greater society began. The external community, comprising with the family a continuous world, naturally extended instruction and discipline in work and in the conduct of life. And it introduced the youth in a most significant way to a further discipline, that of government and the state. So extensive and intricate were the community's involvements with the family and yet so important was its function as a public agency that the youth moved naturally and gradually across the border line that separates the personal from the impersonal world of authority.

More explicit in its educational function than either family or community was the church. Aside from its role as formal educator exercised through institutions of pedagogy which it supported and staffed, in its primary purpose of serving the spiritual welfare and guarding the morals of the community it performed other less obvious but not less important educational functions. It furthered the introduction of the child to society by instructing him in the system of thought and imagery which underlay the culture's values and aims. It provided the highest sanctions for the accepted forms of behavior, and brought the child into close relationship with the intangible loyalties, the ethos and highest principles, of the society in which he lived. In this educational role, organized religion had a powerfully unifying influence. Indistinguishable at the parish level from the local community, agent and ward of the state, it served as a mechanism of social integration. In all its functions, and especially in those that may be called educational, its force was centripetal.

Family, community, and church together accounted for the greater part of the mechanism by which English culture transferred itself across the generations. The instruments of deliberate pedagogy, of explicit, literate education, accounted for a smaller, though indispensable, portion of the process. For all the interest in formal instruction shown in the century after the Reformation in England, and for all the extension of explicitly educational agencies, the span of pedagogy in the entire spectrum of education remained small. The cultural burdens it bore were relatively slight. Formal instruction in elementary and grammar schools, and in the university, was highly utilitarian. Its avowed purpose was the training of the individual for specific social roles. Of the love of letters, knowledge, and science for their own sakes in Elizabethan and Stuart England there was, needless to say, no ucation was not phrased in terms of the lack; but the justification for formal ed- enrichment of the personality and the satisfactions of knowledge. Literacy had its uses required for the daily tasks of an increasing part of the population. Latin grammar and classical literature, far from being then the cultural ornaments they have since become, were practical subjects of instruction: as necessary for the physician as for the architect, as useful to the local functionary as to the statesman. Even the middle classes, for whom classical education had acquired a special meaning as a symbol of social ascent, justified their interest in grammar school training by reference to its moral and social utility. And the universities' function as professional schools had not been transformed by the influx of sons of gentle and noble families; it had merely been broadened to include training for public responsibility.

The sense of utility that dominated formal education was related in a significant way to the occupational structure of the society. Despite a considerable amount of occupational mobility, the normal expectation was that the child would develop along familiar lines, that the divergence of his career from that of his parents' and grandparents' would be limited, and that he could proceed with confidence and security along a well-worn path whose turnings and inclines had long been known and could be dealt with by measures specified by tradition.

Whatever their limitations by modern standards, formal institutions of instruction occupied a strategic place in English life, and they therefore fell within the concern of the state. But the role of the state in formal education, though forceful, was indirect. It was exhortatory, empowering, supervisory, regulatory; it was, with rare exceptions, neither initiating nor sustaining. Support for schools and universities was almost universally from private benefaction, usually in the form of land endowments; public taxation was rare and where it existed, local and temporary. The reliable support from endowment funds gave educational institutions above the elementary level a measure of autonomy, an independence from passing influences which allowed them to function conservatively, retarding rather than furthering change in their freedom from all but the most urgent pressures.

Of these characteristics of education as it existed in late sixteenth- and early seventeenth-century England prospective emigrants to America would hardly have been aware, and not simply because they were not habituated to think in such terms. They had little cause to probe the assumptions and circumstances that underlay their culture's self-perpetuation. The rapid expansion of instructional facilities of which they were witness had not sprung from dissatisfaction with the traditional modes of education, but from the opposite, from confidence, from satisfaction, and from the desire and the capacity to deal more fully, in familiar ways, with familiar social needs. The basis of education lay secure within the continuing traditions of an integrated, unified culture. The future might be uncertain, but the uncertainties were limited. Nothing disturbed the confident expectation that the world of the child's maturity would be the same as that of the parents' youth, and that the past would continue to be an effective guide to the future.

None of the early settlers in English America, not even those who hoped to create in the New World a utopian improvement on the Old, contemplated changes in this configuration of educational processes, this cluster of assumptions, traditions, and institutions. Yet by the end of the colonial period it had been radically transformed. Education had been dislodged from its ancient position in the social order, wrenched loose from the automatic, instinctive workings of society, and cast as a matter for deliberation into the forefront of consciousness. Its functionings had become problematic and controversial. Many were transferred from informal to formal institutions, from agencies to whose major purpose they had been incidental to those, for the most part schools, to which they were primary. Schools and formal schooling had acquired a new importance. They had assumed cultural burdens they had not borne before. Where there had been deeply ingrained habits, unquestioned tradition, automatic responses, security, and confidence there was now awareness, doubt, formality, will, and decision. The whole range of education had become an instrument of deliberate social purpose.

In many ways the most important changes, and certainly the most dramatic, were those that overtook the family in colonial America. In the course of these changes the family's traditional role as the primary agency of cultural transfer was jeopardized, reduced, and partly superseded.

Disruption and transplantation in alien soil transformed the character of traditional English family life. Severe pressures were felt from the first. Normal procedures were upset by the long and acute discomforts of travel; regular functions were necessarily set aside; the ancient discipline slackened. But once re-established in permanent settlements the colonists moved toward recreating the essential institution in its usual form. In this, despite heroic efforts, they failed. At first they laid their failure to moral disorder; but in time they came to recognize its true source in the intractable circumstances of material life.

To all of the settlers the wilderness was strange and forbidding, full of unexpected problems and enervating hardships. To none was there available reliable lore or reserves of knowledge and experience to draw upon in gaining control over the environment: parents no less than children faced the world afresh. In terms of mere effectiveness, in fact, the young—less bound by prescriptive memories, more adaptable, more vigorous—stood often at advantage. Learning faster, they came to see the world more familiarly, to concede more readily to unexpected necessities, to sense more accurately the phasing of a new life. They and not their parents became the effective guides to a new world, and they thereby gained a strange, anomalous authority difficult to accommodate within the ancient structure of family life.

Other circumstances compounded the disorder. Parental prestige was humbled by involvement in the menial labor necessary for survival; it faded altogether when means of support failed in the terrible "starving periods" and large households were forced to sub-divide and re-form in smaller, self-sufficient units. Desperate efforts to enforce a failing authority by law came to little where the law was vaguely known, where courts were rude and irregular, and where means of enforcement were unreliable when they existed at all. And the ultimate sanction of a restrictive economy failed them: where land was abundant and labor at a premium it took little more to create a household than to maintain one. Material independence was sooner or later available to every energetic adult white male, and few failed to break away when they could. Dependent kin, servants, and sons left the patriarchal household, setting up their own reduced establishments which would never grow to the old proportions.

The response was extraordinary. There is no more poignant, dramatic reading than the seventeenth-century laws and admonitions relating to family life. Those of Massachusetts are deservedly best known: they are most profuse and charged with intense Old Testament passion. But they are not different in kind from the others. Within a decade of their founding all of the colonies passed laws demanding obedience from children and specifying penalties for contempt and abuse. Nothing less than capital punishment, it was ruled in Connecticut and Massachusetts, was the fitting punishment for filial disobedience. Relaxation of discipline was universally condemned, and parents and masters were again and again ordered to fulfill their duties as guardians of civil order. But as the laws and pleas elaborated so too did the problems. If guardians failed, it was finally asked, who would guard the guardians? The famous Massachusetts law of 1679 creating tithingmen as censors extraordinary logically concluded the efforts of two generations to recreate the family as the ordered, hierarchical foundation of an ordered, hierarchical society. By the end of the century the surviving elders of the first generation cried out in fearful contemplation of the future. Knowing no other form than the traditional, they could look forward only to the complete dissolution of the family as the primary element of social order. When that happened, when "the rude son should strike the father dead," they knew the elemental chaos that would result:

> What plagues and what portents, what mutiny,
> What raging of the sea, shaking of earth,
> Commotion in the winds, frights, changes, horrors,
> Divert and crack, rend and deracinate
> The unity and married calm of states
> Quite from their fixture. Oh, when degree is shak'd,
> Which is the ladder to all high designs,
> The enterprise is sick.

Degree was shak'd, order within the family badly disturbed; but the conclusion was not chaos. It was a different ordering and a different functioning of the basic social grouping than had been known before.

By the middle of the eighteenth century the classic lineaments of the American family as modern sociologists describe them—the "isolation of the conjugal unit," the "maximum of dispersion of the lines of descent," partible inheritances, and multilineal growth—had appeared. The consequences can hardly be exaggerated. Fundamental aspects of social life were affected. In the reduced, nuclear family, thrown back upon itself, traditional gradations in status tended to fall to the level of necessity. Relationships tended more toward achievement than ascription. The status of women rose; marriage, even in the eyes of the law, tended to become a contract between equals. Above all, the development of the child was affected.

What is perhaps the most fundamental consequence to the development of the child, reaching into his personality and his relations with the world, is the most difficult to establish and interpret. It concerns the process of the child's entry into society. As the family contracted towards a nuclear core, as settlement and re-settlement, especially on the frontier, destroyed what remained of stable community relations, and constant mobility and instability kept new ties from strengthening rapidly, the once elaborate interpenetration of family and community dissolved. The border line between them grew sharper; and the passage of the child from family to society lost its ease, its naturalness, and became abrupt, deliberate, and decisive: open to question, concern, and decision. As a consequence of such a translation into the world, the individual acquired an insulation of consciousness which kept him from naked contact and immediate involvement with the social world about him: it heightened his sense of separateness. It shifted the perspective in which he viewed society: he saw it from without rather than from within; from an unfixed position not organically or unalterably secured. The community, and particularly the embodiment of its coercive power, the state, tended to be seen as external, factitious. It did not command his automatic involvement.

There were other, more evident and more easily established consequences of the pressures exerted on the family during these years. Within a remarkably short time after the beginnings of settlement it was realized that the family was failing in its more obvious educational functions. In the early 1640's both Virginia and Massachusetts officially stated their dissatisfactions in the passage of what have since become known as the first American laws concerning education. The famous Massachusetts statute of 1642, prefaced by its sharp condemnation of "the great neglect of many parents and masters in training up their children in learning and labor," was one of a series of expedients aimed at shoring up the weakening structure of family discipline. It not only reminded parents and masters of their duty to provide for the "calling and implyment of their children" and threatened punishment for irresponsibility, but added to this familiar obligation the extraordinary provision that they see also to the children's "ability to read and understand the principles of religion and the capitall lawes of this country." Virginia's exactly contemporaneous law ordering county officials to "take up" children whose parents "are disabled to maintaine and educate them" reflected the same concern, as did the Duke's Laws of New York in 1665.

Such laws, expressing a sudden awareness, a heightened consciousness of what the family had meant in education, of how much of the burden of imparting civilization to the young it had borne, and of what its loss might mean, were only the first of a century-long series of adjustments. Responses to the fear of a brutish decline, to the threat of a permanent disruption of the family's educational mechanisms, and to the rising self-consciousness in education varied according to local circumstance. In New England a high cultural level, an intense Biblicism, concentrated settlements, and thriving town institutions led to a rapid enhancement of the role of formal schooling. The famous succession of laws passed in Massachusetts and Connecticut after 1647 ordering all towns to maintain teaching institutions, fining recalcitrants, stating and restating the urgencies of the situation, expressed more than a traditional concern with schooling, and more even than a Puritan need for literacy. It flowed from the fear of the imminent loss of cultural standards, of the possibility that civilization itself would be "buried in the grave of our fathers." The Puritans quite deliberately transferred the maimed functions of the family to formal instructional institutions, and in so doing not only endowed schools with a new importance but expanded their purpose beyond pragmatic vocationalism toward vaguer but more basic cultural goals.

In the context of the age the stress placed by the Puritans on formal schooling is astonishing. In the end it proved too great to be evenly sustained. The broad stream of enforcing legislation that flows through the statute books of the seventeenth century thinned out in the eighteenth century as isolated rural communities, out of contact, save for some of their Harvard- and Yale-trained ministers, with the high moral and intellectual concerns of the settling generation, allowed the level to sink to local requirement. But the tradition of the early years was never completely lost, and New England carried into the national period a faith in the benefits of formal schooling and a willingness to perpetuate and enrich it that has not yet been dissipated.

In the south the awareness that only by conscious, deliberate effort would the standards of inherited culture be transmitted into the future was hardly less acute, but there the environment and the pattern of settlement presented more difficult problems than in the north. Lacking the reinforcement of effective town and church institutions, the family in the south was even less resistant to pressures and sustained even greater shocks. The response on the part of the settlers, however much lower their intellectual demands may have been than the Puritans', was equally intense. The seventeenth-century records abound with efforts to rescue the children from an incipient savagery. They took many forms: the importation of servant-teachers, the attempt to establish parish or other local schools, repeated injunctions to parents and masters; but the most common were parental bequests in wills providing for the particular education of the surviving child or children. These are often fascinating, luminous documents. Susan English of York, for example, who could not sign her name, left each of her children one heifer, the male issue of which was to be devoted to the child's education. Samuel Fenn ordered his executors to devote the entire increase of his stock of cattle to the "utmost education" which could be found for his children in Virginia, and John Custis left the labor of fourteen slaves for the preliminary education of his grandson in Virginia, adding a special provision for paying for its completion in England.

The extravagance and often the impracticality of such efforts in Virginia suggest a veritable frenzy of parental concern lest they and their children succumb to the savage environment. All their fearfulness for the consequences of transplantation, their awareness of the strangeness of the present and the perils of the future, seem to have become concentrated in the issue of education. Their efforts in the seventeenth century came to little; the frustrations multiplied. But the impetus was never entirely lost. The transforming effect of the early years carried over into the education of later, more benign times. When in the eighteenth century the reemergence in the south of approximate replicas of Old World family organizations and of stable if scattered communities furnished a new basis for formal education, something of the same broad cultural emphasis notable in New England became noticeable also in these southern institutions.

This whole cluster of developments—the heightening of sensitivity to educational processes as the family's traditional effectiveness declined, the consequent increase in attention to formal education and in the cultural burdens placed upon it—was not confined to the boundaries of the original seventeenth-century settlements. It was a pattern woven of the necessities of life in the colonies, and it repeated itself in every region as the threat of the environment to inherited culture made itself felt.

Alexis de Tocqueville

INFLUENCE OF DEMOCRACY ON THE FAMILY

In his classic commentary, Tocqueville emphasized the loosening of the ties of authority and property in the American family. Yet he also perceived a new trend of cohesiveness in the American family that was based on strong affectional ties. Tocqueville's attempt to relate his observations of the American family to the general hypothesis of *Democracy in America* gives the following selection added significance.

I HAVE just examined the changes which the equality of conditions produces in the mutual relations of the several members of the community among democratic nations, and among the Americans in particular. I would now go deeper and inquire into the closer ties of family; my object here is not to seek for new truths, but to show in what manner facts already known are connected with my subject.

It has been universally remarked that in our time the several members of a family stand upon an entirely new footing towards each other; that the distance which formerly separated a father from his sons has been lessened; and that paternal authority, if not destroyed, is at least impaired.

Something analogous to this, but even more striking, may be observed in the United States. In America the family, in the Roman and aristocratic signification of the word, does not exist. All that remains of it are a few vestiges in the first years of childhood, when the father exercises, without opposition, that absolute domestic authority which the feebleness of his children renders necessary and which their interest, as well as his own incontestable superiority, warrants. But as soon as the young American approaches manhood, the ties of filial obedience are relaxed day by day; master of his thoughts, he is soon master of his conduct. In America there is, strictly speaking, no adolescence: at the close of boyhood the man appears and begins to trace out his own path.

It would be an error to suppose that this is preceded by a domestic struggle in which the son has obtained by a sort of moral violence the liberty that his father refused him. The same habits, the same principles, which impel the one to assert his independence predispose the other to consider the use of that independence as an incontestable right. The former does not exhibit any of those rancorous or irregular passions which disturb men long after they have shaken off an established authority; the latter feels none of that bitter and angry regret which is apt to survive a bygone power. The father foresees the limits of his authority long beforehand, and when the time arrives, he surrenders it without a struggle; the son looks forward to the exact period at which he will be his own master, and he enters upon his freedom without precipitation and without effort, as a possession which is his own and which no one seeks to wrest from him.

It may perhaps be useful to show how these changes which take place in family relations are closely connected with the social and political revolution that is approaching its consummation under our own eyes.

There are certain great social principles that a people either introduces everywhere or tolerates nowhere. In countries which are aristocratically constituted with all the gradations of rank, the government never makes a direct appeal to the mass of the governed; as men are united together, it is enough to

From Alexis de Tocqueville, *Democracy in America* (Boston: John Allyn Publishers, 1882, 2 vols.), Vol. II, pp. 233–240.

lead the foremost; the rest will follow. This is applicable to the family as well as to all aristocracies that have a head. Among aristocratic nations social institutions recognize, in truth, no one in the family but the father; children are received by society at his hands; society governs him, he governs them. Thus the parent not only has a natural right but acquires a political right to command them; he is the author and the support of his family, but he is also its constituted ruler.

In democracies, where the government picks out every individual singly from the mass to make him subservient to the general laws of the community, no such intermediate person is required; a father is there, in the eye of the law, only a member of the community, older and richer than his sons.

When most of the conditions of life are extremely unequal and the inequality of these conditions is permanent, the notion of a superior grows upon the imaginations of men; if the law invested him with no privileges, custom and public opinion would concede them. When, on the contrary, men differ but little from each other and do not always remain in dissimilar conditions of life, the general notion of a superior becomes weaker and less distinct; it is vain for legislation to strive to place him who obeys very much beneath him who commands; the manners of the time bring the two men nearer to one another and draw them daily towards the same level.

Although the legislation of an aristocratic people grants no peculiar privileges to the heads of families, I shall not be the less convinced that their power is more respected and more extensive than in a democracy; for I know that, whatever the laws may be, superiors always appear higher and inferiors lower in aristocracies than among democratic nations.

When men live more for the remembrance of what has been than for the care of what is, and when they are more given to attend to what their ancestors thought than to think themselves, the father is the natural and necessary tie between the past and the present, the link by which the ends of these two chains are connected. In aristocracies, then, the father is not only the civil head of the family, but the organ of its traditions, the expounder of its customs, the arbiter of its manners. He is listened to with deference, he is addressed with respect, and the love that is felt for him is always tempered with fear.

When the condition of society becomes democratic and men adopt as their general principle that it is good and lawful to judge of all things for oneself, using former points of belief not as a rule of faith, but simply as a means of information, the power which the opinions of a father exercise over those of his sons diminishes as well as his legal power.

Perhaps the subdivision of estates that democracy brings about contributes more than anything else to change the relations existing between a father and his children. When the property of the father of a family is scanty, his son and himself constantly live in the same place and share the same occupations; habit and necessity bring them together and force them to hold constant communication. The inevitable consequence is a sort of familiar intimacy, which renders authority less absolute and which can ill be reconciled with the external forms of respect.

Now, in democratic countries the class of those who are possessed of small fortunes is precisely that which gives strength to the notions and a particular direction to the manners of the community. That class makes its opinions preponderate as universally as its will, and even those who are most inclined to resist its commands are carried away in the end by its example. I have known eager opponents of democracy who allowed their children to address them with perfect colloquial equality.

Thus at the same time that the power of aristocracy is declining, the austere, the conventional, and the legal part of parental authority vanishes and a species of equality prevails around the domestic hearth. I do not know, on the whole, whether society loses by the change, but I am inclined to believe that man individually is a gainer by it. I think that in proportion as manners and laws become more democratic, the relation of father and son becomes more intimate and more affectionate; rules and authority are less talked of, confidence and tenderness are often increased, and it would seem that the natural bond is drawn closer in proportion as the social bond is loosened.

In a democratic family the father exercises no other power than that which is granted to the affection and the experience of age; his orders would perhaps be disobeyed, but his advice is for the most part authoritative. Though he is not hedged in with ceremonial respect, his sons at least accost him with confidence; they have no settled form of addressing him, but they speak to him constantly and are ready to consult him every day. The master and the constituted ruler have vanished; the father remains.

Nothing more is needed in order to judge of the difference between the two states of society in this respect than to peruse the family correspondence of aristocratic ages. The style is always correct, ceremonious, stiff, and so cold that the natural warmth of the heart can hardly be felt in the language. In democratic countries, on the contrary, the language addressed by a son to his father is always marked by mingled freedom, familiarity, and affection, which at once show that new relations have sprung up in the bosom of the family.

A similar revolution takes place in the mutual relations of children. In aristocratic families, as well as in aristocratic society, every place is marked out beforehand. Not only does the father occupy a separate rank, in which he enjoys extensive privileges, but even the children are not equal among themselves. The age and sex of each irrevocably determine his rank and secure to him certain privileges. Most of these distinctions are abolished or diminished by democracy.

In aristocratic families the eldest son, inheriting the greater part of the property and almost all the rights of the family, becomes the chief and to a certain extent the master of his brothers. Greatness and power are for him; for them, mediocrity and dependence. But it would be wrong to suppose that among aristocratic nations the privileges of the eldest son are advantageous to himself alone, or that they excite nothing but envy and hatred around him. The eldest son commonly endeavors to procure wealth and power for his brothers, because the general splendor of the house is reflected back on him who represents it; the younger sons seek to back the elder brother in all his undertakings, because the greatness and power of the head of the family better enable him to provide for all its branches. The different members of an aristocratic family are therefore very closely bound together; their interests are connected, their minds agree, but their hearts are seldom in harmony.

Democracy also binds brothers to each other, but by very different means. Under democratic laws all the children are perfectly equal and consequently independent; nothing brings them forcibly together, but nothing keeps them apart; and as they have the same origin, as they are trained under the same roof, as they are treated with the same care, and as no peculiar privilege distinguishes or divides them, the affectionate and frank intimacy of early years easily springs up between them. Scarcely anything can occur to break the tie thus formed at the outset of life, for brotherhood brings them daily together without embarrassing them. It is not, then, by interest, but by common associations and by the free sympathy of opinion and of taste that democracy unites brothers to each other. It divides their inheritance, but allows their hearts and minds to unite.

Such is the charm of these democatic manners that even the partisans of aristocracy are attracted by it; and after having experienced it for some time, they are by no means tempted to revert to the respectful and frigid observances of aristocratic families. They would be glad to retain the domestic habits of democracy if they might throw off its social conditions and its laws; but these elements are indissolubly united, and it is impossible to enjoy the former without enduring the latter.

The remarks I have made on filial love and fraternal affection are applicable to all the passions that emanate spontaneously from human nature itself.

If a certain mode of thought or feeling is the result of some peculiar condition of life, when that condition is altered nothing whatever remains of the thought or feeling. Thus a law may bind two members of the community very closely to each other; but that law being abolished, they stand asunder. Nothing was more strict than the tie that united the vassal to the lord under the feudal system; at the present day the two men do not know each other; the fear, the gratitude, and the affection that formerly connected them have vanished and not a vestige of the tie remains.

Such, however, is not the case with those feelings which are natural to mankind. Whenever a law attempts to tutor these feelings in any particular manner, it seldom fails to weaken them; by attempting to add to their intensity it robs them of some of their elements, for they are never stronger than when left to themselves.

Democracy, which destroys or obscures almost all the old conventional rules of society and which prevents men from readily assenting to new ones, entirely effaces most of the feelings to which these conventional rules have given rise; but it only modifies some others, and frequently imparts to them a degree of energy and sweetness unknown before.

Perhaps it is not impossible to condense into a single proposition the whole purport of this chapter, and of several others that preceded it. Democracy loosens social ties, but tightens natural ones; it brings kindred more closely together, while it throws citizens more apart.

Ruth Miller Elson

THE CHILD OF THE NINETEENTH CENTURY AND HIS SCHOOLBOOKS

The most fervent historiographical debate about America has centered on the question of conflict versus consensus. Do we best understand America by remembering the real and dramatic conflicts between liberals and conservatives, workers and businessmen, frontiersmen and eastern citydwellers? Or should we realize that our conflicts are far less important than our agreements? that we are all Lockeans? that Republicans and Democrats share more assumptions than do Tweedledum and and Tweedledee? that radical and reactionary ideologies rarely thrive in America? One simple answer to this debate has been occurring to more and more historians: compared to the class and ideological rifts that have divided European society, America has indeed had a functioning consensus; but within that consensus there have been real and dramatic domestic conflicts, serious enough to have cost the lives of hundreds of thousands of Americans.

Perhaps the application of this double perspective to the question of how permissive American families and institutions have been toward children can save us valuable time. After reading about egalitarian fami-

Reprinted with permission of the University of Nebraska Press from *Guardians of Tradition* by Ruth Miller Elson, pp. 1–2, 8–11, 337–339. Copyright 1964 by the University of Nebraska Press.

lies in the colonial period (Bailyn) and during Jacksonian days (Tocqueville), some parents may be tempted to dismiss these and the final two essays in this section as balderdash. Haven't we all heard how tough the parents of our parents were? Don't we know how difficult and demanding school used to be? Can't we remember what would have happened to our parents if they did the things we do? These claims are not all fantasy. Before 1890, for example, American schools were not particularly progressive nor were children unleashed—at least by present-day standards. Ruth Elson, in her analysis of the nineteenth-century child and his schoolbooks, gives us a glimpse of that more disciplined world, a world that recalls *Life With Father*. She reminds us that the battles during the Progressive era which are discussed in the middle section of this volume were real battles which could have gone either way. She reminds us that the society has had and can again have different ways of understanding and dealing with childhood than those that emerged from the clamor of the Progressive age, or than those that seem to prevail, though shakily, at the moment. Hence the double perspective: compared to conditions in Europe, American family life has perhaps always been more permissive, with more lavish attention and freedom being granted to young Americans at all periods than to their European peers; but within America, through renewed conflicts and efforts, there has been a steady widening of the sphere granted to young people, and earlier periods of American life were truly more authoritarian than they are now.

Whether or not this growing permissiveness constitutes a form of "progress" remains an open and quite serious question.

THE purpose of nineteenth-century American public schools was to train citizens in character and proper principles. Most textbook writers had an exalted idea of their function; almost all made statements such as the following: "The mind of the child is like the soft wax to receive an impression, but like the rigid marble to retain it." They were much more concerned with the child's moral development than with the development of his mind. The important problem for nineteenth-century American educators was to mold the wax in virtue rather than in learning. Noah Webster advocated the use of his book on the grounds that it would enable teachers "To instil into their [the children's] minds, with the first rudiments of the language, some just ideas of religion, morals and domestic economy." The textbook was to be a compilation of the ideas of the society. In 1789 he stated his purpose in writing a schoolbook: "To refine and establish our language, to facilitate the acquisition of grammatical knowledge and diffuse the principles of virtue and patriotism is the task I have labored to perform." There was no doubt in the minds of the authors that the books used in public schools were important for the future of the Republic. They saw their function as the creation of an American nationality, the formation of a "National Character." Most of them believed that as European educators sponsored children's books which "are calculated to impress on their youthful minds a prejudice in favor of the existing order of things," so American educators must inculcate "American principles." The ideas taught in the nineteenth-century school were not necessarily universal truths, but national truths. It was the national prototype that was to be embodied in American schoolbooks. . . .

The classroom method of the period made the textbook peculiarly important in the school. Because the teachers were relatively untrained, letter-perfect memorization without particular attention to meaning was the basic method of common, or public, school education. Few teachers outside of the large cities had much education beyond that of the schools in which they taught. When examined for the position their moral character was considered more important for teaching than any technical training. A nineteenth-century work on the theory and practice of teaching suggests that teachers be better prepared; the author believed that this could be accomplished if the teacher would read over the textbook before class. Apparently even this would have constituted a reform. The subject of professional training for teachers increasingly absorbed educational leaders from the 1830's on. In 1839 Massachusetts established the first public normal school, but by 1860 there were only twelve such schools in the United States. One half of these were in New England; the others were distributed one in New York (1844), one in Michigan (1849), one in New Jersey (1855), one in Illinois (1857), one in Pennsylvania (1859), and one in Minnesota (1860). Four of the pre-Civil War normal schools were in one state, Massachusetts. These were reinforced by six private normal schools, but it is obvious that although the situation was improving, the day of the teacher trained for his profession was still in the future for most American schools.

The Pestalozzian method, antithetical to memorization, became known here after 1835 with the publication of a translation of Victor Cousin's report to the French government on the schools of Prussia, Calvin Stowe's report in Ohio in 1837 on Prussian schools, and Horace Mann's Seventh Report on European education. The educational journals, particularly those of William Woodbridge, published between 1831 and 1839, and the later ones of Mann and Henry Barnard, introduced their readers to this method. But such reports and journals obviously reached only a small fraction of the teaching population and had relatively little effect on the schools of the nineteenth century.

In many classrooms the memorization technique was reinforced by the monitorial system, whereby older students were designated to hear the recitations of the younger ones. It was a method attractive to taxpayers, since one teacher with the aid of monitors could handle an enormous class of many grades. But the monitor could be trusted only to see whether the student's memorization of the schoolbook was letter perfect. Questions given as teaching aids in the books themselves clearly expect this method. The typical form of question is: "What is said of . . . ?" Memorizing the sentiment or value judgment was quite as often required as memorizing the fact. For example, a textbook in the history of the United States requires that the child: "Mention any other things in our national history which should excite our gratitude." A list of these "other things" appears in the text above.

Such classroom methods required absolute uniformity of texts to make mass recitation or recitation before an untrained teacher possible. This system remained in the realm of the ideal during the first part of the century, because the children used the schoolbooks of their parents, neighbors, or relatives to save money. In 1846 the state of Connecticut discovered that there were two hundred and fifteen different texts in use in its schools, although an official text had been chosen by each district board. But the method apparently conditioned the writers of textbooks effectively. Many of the books were written wholly in the catechism form. In order to assure boards of education that a new issue of an older textbook could be used in the same classroom with the original work, many of the Histories retained the old copyright date and added more recent material at the end of the book. A History ostensibly published in 1881 might include material through 1888. Many gave such assurance of stability as the following: "Teachers may rest assured, that all future editions of this work will be printed page for page with the present." This often produced strange anachronisms: the 1862 and 1865 editions of Mitchell's Geographies follow previous editions so closely that no word of secession or the Civil War appears, although both contain extensive treatments of the Southern states. When a revision of an older text was published, the publisher often made some such promise as the following: "This revision can be used in class with the older edition as the pages correspond throughout." As a result of this effort at uniformity the textbooks were singularly resistant to change.

Furthermore the basic material of many of the textbooks was in previously published schoolbooks; the essential method of composing a schoolbook was often one of compilation and plagiarism. Throughout this study such similarities will be manifest; word order was left unchanged in many cases where no authority was cited, and where the last authority was clearly another textbook author. This is true even in the Geographies, where one would expect recent expert knowledge to be vital. The method of compilation itself, then, produced a startling similarity and time lag. It is well to keep in mind that experts in the particular fields did not enter the textbook writing arena until almost the end of the century, and that even then they accounted for a very small minority of schoolbooks.

Schoolbooks, central to the curriculum of the nineteenth-century school, offered both information and standards of behavior and belief that the adult world expected the child to make his own. . . .

The world created in nineteenth-century schoolbooks is essentially a world of fantasy—a fantasy made up by adults as a guide for their children, but inhabited by no one outside the pages of schoolbooks. It is an ideal world, peopled by ideal villains as well as ideal heroes. Nature is perfectly if sometimes inscrutably planned by God for the good of man, with progress as its first and invariable law. Nothing can hinder this march toward material and moral perfection, a movement particularly visible in the United States. Nature is benign, and the life close to nature inevitably a happy and healthy one. Individuals are to be understood in terms of easily discernible, inherent characteristics of their race and nationality as much as in terms of their individual character. Virtue is always rewarded, vice punished. And one can achieve virtue and avoid vice by following a few simple rules. Assuredly the adult world did not live by this pattern but elected to believe in it as what *should* be true, as the inhabitants of Samuel Butler's *Erewhon* believed in their "musical banks." Wishfully, adults in any age would like to proffer to their children a neatly patterned model of life, however mythical, which the child can accept and, following it, live happily ever after. But inevitably the growing child soon sees that life is not so simple: that the life close to nature may not only be a hard one but unrewarding and frustrating; that virtue is not always rewarded on this earth and that not even his schoolbooks can really know whether there is compensation for this after death; that progress in one area comes at great cost in another, that Catholics may be sincere, Indians gentle, Negroes intelligent, and Jews generous. To live in the real world the child would eventually have to abandon the simple model of his schoolbooks. And, with luck, he will develop experientially, and perhaps experimentally, a more adequate world view.

Perhaps the most fundamental assumption in nineteenth-century schoolbooks is the moral character of the universe—an assumption at the base of American culture in this period. Religion itself is rather a matter of morals than theology. Furthermore, all nature as well as man is invested with morality; animal and plant life both follow moral law. In schoolbooks, when ants store up food they do so as an act of moral responsibility rather than as instinctual behavior. Conversely, the grasshopper's careless ways in not preparing for winter are his own fault, and his hunger in lean times is a richly deserved punishment. Whether a man succeeds in his business is not so much a question of the application of intelligence and energy to the problems of that business, but a result of good character. Success in business is viewed in schoolbooks largely as a by-product of virtue. It is to be sought not for material comforts it will bring, but as a sign of virtue, a status symbol if you will. Similarly, natural resources, location, availability of capital, and labor are minor factors in evaluating the decline and fall of nations; only a moral nation can achieve lasting power. The decline of Spain and the growth of the United States are illustrations of this. Everything in life is to be judged in moral terms. Nineteenth-century intellectuals might view nature as amoral, but the Puritan tradition still provided the basis of popular culture.

Unlike many modern schoolbooks, those of the nineteenth century made no pretense of neutrality. While they evade issues seriously controverted in their day, they take a firm and unanimous stand on matters of basic belief. The value judgment is their stock in trade: love of country, love of God, duty to parents, the necessity to develop habits of thrift, honesty, and hard work in order to accumulate property, the certainty of progress, the perfection of the United States. These are not to be questioned. Nor in this whole country of great external change is there any deviation from these basic values. In pedagogical arrangements the schoolbook of the 1970's is vastly different from that of the 1890's, but the continuum of values is uninterrupted. Neither the Civil War nor the 1890's provide any watershed in basic values. There is no hint here of Darwin's natural selection from chance variations, nor of the Higher Criticism, comparative religion, William James' pluralism, nor of the neutral nature depicted by literary realists. Ethics do not evolve from particular cultural situations, nor are they to be developed by the individual from his own experience and critical thinking. Nor are they to come from his peers. They are absolute, unchanging, and they come from God. The child is to learn ethics as he learns information about his world, unquestioningly, by rote. His behavior is not to be inner-directed, nor other-directed, but depicted by authority and passively accepted.

Richard L. Rapson

THE AMERICAN CHILD AS SEEN BY BRITISH TRAVELERS, 1845–1935

Foreign observers possess a certain advantage over the native in social generalization. They can see what the native often takes for granted; they have a fresh eye and a distant perspective which leads them to notice obvious contrasts with their own homeland which the native, who has not traveled and has no standard of comparison, misses altogether. American children were, to American adults, just children. To the British travelers, American children were strange beasts indeed. This alienation and the insights to which it led are analyzed in the next essay. Because travel literature constitutes one of the best of the few sources available for studying American children, the footnotes have been retained so that the interested student might be directed to some intriguing kinds of materials that are normally too problematical and too inaccessible to justify inclusion in general bibliographies such as the one at the end of this volume.

WHILE British travelers to American shores disagreed with one another on many topics between the years 1845 and 1935, they spoke with practically one voice upon two subjects: American schools and American children.[1] On the whole they thought the public school system admirable; with near unanimity they found the children detestable.

This adds up to a paradox, for if the innovation of free public education was, as most of these visitors contended, the best thing about America, surely some decent effect upon the schools' young charges should have been faintly discernible. Yet the British were not at all charmed by the youngsters, and the foreign observers had very few kind things to say in behalf of American children.

The paradox as stated must leave one unsatisfied. In any nation one should expect the child to stamp his impress upon the climate of the entire society; the detestable child should become the detestable adult. But especially in a nation which the British characterized by the term "youthful"—the epithet more often used in a complimentary rather than a deprecatory fashion—one would with reason expect to find some association between the word and the actual young people of the country.

There was no question as to what quality in the children did most to nettle the Englishmen. As David Macrae said in 1867: "American children are undoubtedly precocious."[2] In the same year, Greville Chester explained a little this theme, which appeared with more monotonous regularity than did any other in these books. "Many of the children in this country," he said, "appear to be painfully precocious—small stuck-up caricatures of men and women, with but little of the fresh ingenuousness and playfulness of childhood."[3]

Again in that same uneventful year of 1867, the Robertsons embellished this developing portrait thus:

[1] The evidence for this article derives from a reading of over 260 published books composed by Britons who wrote of the United States on the basis of visits made here between 1845 and 1935.

[2] Macrae, *The Americans at Home* (New York, 1952), p. 45. (First edition, Edinburgh, 1870).

[3] Chester, *Transatlantic Sketches* (London, 1869), pp. 230–31.

> Their infant lips utter smart sayings, and baby oaths are too often encouraged . . . even by their own parents, whose counsel and restraint they quickly learn wholly to despise. It is not uncommon to see children of ten calling for liquor at the bar, or puffing a cigar in the streets. In the cars we met a youth of respectable and gentlemanly exterior who thought no shame to say that he learned to smoke at eight, got first 'tight' at twelve, and by fourteen had run the whole course of debauchery.[4]

Every year American youth was similarly berated for its precocity. "Precocity" politely expressed the British feeling that American children were pert, impertinent, disrespectful, arrogant brats. But "precocious" meant more than that; it implied that American children weren't children at all. Three British mothers made this point. Therese Yelverton exclaimed that "in the course of my travels I never discovered that there were any American *children.* Diminutive men and women in process of growing into big ones, I have met with; but the child in the full sense attached to that word in England—a child with rosy cheeks and bright joyous laugh, its docile obedience and simplicity, its healthful play and its disciplined work, is a being almost unknown in America."[5]

Daniel Boorstin in the introduction to a new edition of *A Lady's Life in the Rocky Mountains* wrote of how Isabella Bird "saw a society where, in a sense, everyone was young, yet where the most painful sight was 'the extinction of childhood. I have never seen any children, only debased imitations of men and women.' "[6] And Lady Emmeline Stuart-Wortley, before the Civil War, commented: "Little America is unhappily, generally, only grown-up America, seen through a telescope turned the wrong way. The one point, perhaps, in which I must concur with other writers on the United States, is there being no real child-like children here."[7]

Eyre Crowe tells how he and his traveling companion, William Makepeace Thackeray, came across a youngster reading a newspaper, "already devouring the toughest leaders, and mastering the news of the world whilst whiffing his cigar, and not without making shies at a huge expectorator close at hand."[8] The picture of the cigar-smoking cherub flashed recurrently in these accounts.

The visitors did not have to search far for an explanation—at least a superficial explanation—for this disconcerting childhood behavior. Although a few of them remarked at the leniency of the common schools and regretted the lack of corporal punishment handed out there,[9] many more felt that the only doses of discipline ever received by the child were administered, even if in small quantities, in the schoolrooms. No, it was unquestionably in the home that the child was indulged, and indulgence gave him his swagger.

His parents either could not or else chose not to discipline their offspring. To be sure, the school system was not blameless. Many, like Fraser, regarded the school "as an extension of the family," which, by its very effectiveness made matters more difficult for mother and father.[10]

> . . . it must be allowed that schools are robbing parents of the power to control their families. The school has drawn to itself so much of the love and veneration of the young that in the homes missing its spell they grow unruly. Parents are not experts in the management of children, nor have they the moral weight of an institution to back them up, hence they fail to keep up the smooth ascendancy of the school.[11]

[4] William and W. F. Robertson, *Our American Tour* (Edinburgh, 1871), pp. 9–10.

[5] Therese Yelverton, *Teresina in America* (London, 1875), I, 263. She also found them to be "insolent, unruly, and rude." *Ibid.*, p. 269. Oscar Wilde thought that little girls were more charming in their precocity than little boys. *Writings* (New York, 1907), III, 251.

[6] Isabella Lucy Bird, *A Lady's Life in the Rocky Mountains.* The edition by Daniel Boorstin (Norman, Okla., 1960) was used, p. xxii. (First edition, London, 1875).

[7] Stuart-Wortley, *Travels in the United States* (Paris, 1851), p. 67.

[8] Eyre Crowe, *With Thackeray in America* (London, 1893), p. 21.

[9] John Strathesk [John Tod], *Bits About America* (Edinburgh, 1887), p. 149; Richard De-Bary, *The Land of Promise* (London, 1908), p. 131.

[10] James Nelson Fraser, *America, Old and New* (London, 1910), p. 280.

[11] *Ibid.*, p. 282.

P. A. Vaile blamed the American mother: "She is refusing to perform her part of the contract. First she 'went back' on raising her children, now she does not want to have any children at all."[12] Mrs. Humphreys raged at "the conspicuous absence of maternal instinct as a feature of American marriages."[13]

Many others accused fathers, but usually with greater sympathy. After all, the father simply worked too hard all day to have much time, interest or energy to devote to his little ones. "The husband has his occupations, friends, and amusements."[14]

No matter which parent had to bear the burden of guilt, many an Englishman simply felt that home life in the United States just wasn't homelike; it lacked atmosphere, comfort, love, play and warmth. It never became the cozy, friendly hearth which imparted to a family a sense of kinship, identity or oneness. Long after young couples had forsaken the custom of dwelling in boarding houses or hotels and exposing their tiny ones to the dregs of society—a custom deplored by every Englishman—long after this, W. L. George, along with most others, refused to admit that Americans still had any idea as to what constituted a "real" home.

> The hard child [he said] suggests the hard home, which is characteristic of America. I visited many houses in the United States, and, except among the definitely rich, I found them rather uncomfortable. They felt bare, untenanted; they were too neat, too new . . . one missed the comfortable accumulation of broken screens, old fire irons, and seven-year-old volumes of the *Illustrated London News,* which make up the dusty, frowsy feeling of home. The American house is not a place where one lives, but a place where one merely sleeps, eats, sits, works.[15]

George may have been a bit unfair to expect to find "seven-year-old volumes of the *Illustrated London News*" lying about, but he had a right to notice the lack of age; it takes years for a family to implant its brand on a structure of brick and mortar.[16] Perhaps, as many visitors rightly pointed out, Americans were too much on the go, too mobile for them ever to fulfill George's requirements for home-ness.[17] This nonetheless did not excuse the parents from their failure to bring up their children appropriately. Joseph Hatton, in 1881, begged the mothers and fathers to take their responsibilities as parents more seriously than they were and to realize, as any sensible person must, that their overindulgence of the child was "excessive and injurious."[18]

Little Fritz, a pretty little American boy who sat as the subject for one of Philip Burne-Jones' paintings, told his grandmother, in the artist's presence, "I'll kick your head!" After being chided and asked to apologize there was "dead silence on the part of Fritz." Finally, after some more pleading, Fritz relented and uttered "a few perfunctory and scarcely audible sounds, which were generously construed by the family as expressive of contrition and penitence; and Fritz started again with a clear record, for a brief period. His mother had absolutely no influence on him whatever, and she admitted as much."[19]

Other American parents admitted as much also; they were fully aware of their inability to control their little ones, but they just didn't know what to do about it. L. P. Jacks, in 1933, let an American mother speak her heart about her utter helplessness and frustration in a way that was rather revealing and even poignant:

[12] P. A. Vaile, Y., *America's Peril* (London, 1909), p. 111.
[13] Mrs. Desmond Humphreys, *America Through English Eyes* (London, n.d. [1913?]), p. 165.
[14] *Ibid.*, p. 161. Horace Vachell said that in the West at least "you will find fathers and mothers the slaves of their children." *Life and Sport on the Pacific Slope* (New York, 1901), p. 74.
[15] Walter L. George, *Hail Columbia!* (New York, 1921), p. 199.
[16] At least "if ever so humble, the abodes in America are invariably neat and cleanly," claimed Alfred Pairpont in 1890 in *Rambles in America* (Boston, 1891), p. 166.
[17] Said George Steevens, *The Land of the Dollar* (Edinburgh, 1897): "You cannot call a people who will never be happy ten years in the same place . . . home-loving in the English sense." p. 313.
[18] Joseph Hatton, *Today in America* (New York, 1881), p. 7.
[19] Sir Philip Burne-Jones, *Dollars and Democracy* (New York, 1904), p. 36.

We mothers are rapidly losing all influence over our children, and I don't know how we can recover it. We have little or no control over them whether boys or girls. The schools and the colleges take them out of our hands. They give them everything for nothing, and that is what the children expect when they come home. Their standards and their ideals are formed in the school atmosphere, and more by their companions than their teachers. They become more and more intractable to home influence and there is nothing for it but to let them go their own way.[20]

But the majority of the Britons did not accept either the influence of the schools or the social fact of mobility as sufficient explanations for the precocious child; they would have had little justification for disliking the child with the fervor they did and deploring the parents' follies so strongly if these impersonal forces accounted adequately for the situation.

They felt, rather, that causes ran deeper, in more insidious channels. Not only did the parents spoil their children, but they *wanted* to spoil them. Not only did the mothers and fathers put up with more than they should have, but they were actually proud of their babies. The Britons were especially distressed when they decided that parents felt, as a rule, not the least bit guilty over their own efforts or over the way their boys and girls were turning out. The travelers came not to the conclusion that American parents were unable to discipline their sons and daughters, but that they deliberately chose to "let them go their own way." This either infuriated the by now bewildered visitor, or else made him desperate to figure out just how this insanity could possibly reign.

William Howard Russell could not accept the excuse that the schools preempted parental power since "there is nothing in the American [school] system to prevent the teaching of religious and moral duties by parents at home; but it would seem as if very little of that kind of instruction was given by the busy fathers and anxious mothers of the Republic. . . ."[21]

Horace Vachell, as did many others, told a child story that turned into a mother story. It seems that one day the author was in the parlor of a ship filled with ailing people, including the author's own mother who was suffering with a bad headache. Into this sickly assemblage trooped our hero—a small American boy who decided to soothe the aches of all by playing on the bagpipes! "The wildest pibroch ever played in Highland glen was sweet melody compared to the strains produced by this urchin."[22] He naturally continued to play, louder than ever, despite the daggered glances hurled at him from all around the parlor; he stopped only when he tired. Then, instead of permitting sweet peace, "he flung down the pipes, walked to the piano, opened it, sat down, and began to hammer the keys with his feet."[23]

At this turn of events, our long-suffering author had had enough. " 'You play very nicely with your feet,' I ventured to say, as I lifted him from the stool, 'but some of these ladies are suffering with headache, and your music distresses them. Run away, like a good boy, and don't come back again.' "[24]

But Vachell's story did not end here because, in the final analysis, this is more of a mother tale than a child story. "The mother was furious. Had I been Herod the Great, red-handed after the slaughter of the Innocents, she could not have looked more indignant or reproachful. I was interfering with the sacred rights of the American child to do what he pleased, where he pleased, and when he pleased."[25]

Vachell's first conclusion inevitably was that American children were unspeakable monsters, utterly lacking in "sense of duty, reverence, humility, obedience."[26] His second conclusion was, however, more interesting and more im-

[20] L. P. Jacks, *My American Friends* (New York, 1933), p. 149. Notice the young mother's stress on the influence which the peer-group culture held over her children.

[21] William Howard Russell, *Hesperothen: Notes from the West* (London, 1882), II, 156.
[22] Vachell, p. 80.
[23] *Ibid.*, p. 80.
[24] *Ibid.*, p. 80.
[25] *Ibid.*, p. 80.
[26] *Ibid.*, p. 79.

portant, namely that parents actually "encourage the egoism latent in all children, till each becomes an autocrat."[27]

Once this appalling discovery had been verified, it occurred to the more curious of the Britons to raise the appropriate question: how could the American parents be proud of these diminutive devils?

Sir Edwin Arnold presented a question of this sort, in more general form, to one whom he regarded as an expert on this strange *genus Americanus:* Walt Whitman. "'But have you reverence enough among your people?' I asked. 'Do the American children respect and obey their parents sufficiently, and are the common people grateful enough to the best men, their statesmen, leaders, teachers, poets, and "betters" generally?' "[28]

To this most fundamental of all inquiries Whitman responded: "'Allons, comrade!, your old world has been soaked and saturated in reverentiality. We are laying here in America the basements and foundation rooms of a new era. And we are doing it, on the whole, pretty well and substantially. By-and-by, when that job is through, *we will look after the steeples and pinnacles.*' "[29]

Whitman and Arnold included childhood precocity within the larger framework of a new people refusing to pay homage to their betters, refusing to revere their "superiors." Such reverence constitutes one of the necessary ingredients of an aristocratically-oriented society. Lack of that reverence suggests an egalitarian society, and these two distinguished men of letters were implying that the precocious child was symptomatic not merely of weak, stupid, willful parents, but rather of the pervasiveness in American society of the principle of equality. In fact no generalization about America was made more forcefully or repeatedly by the commentators en masse than that the thrust of the American belief in equality (understood as opportunity to rise more than as classlessness) was ubiquitous; it extended into every corner of the daily institutional fabric of American life—into the schools wherein all children had the right to a free education, into politics where all had the right to vote, into the enhanced place of women in American society, into the fluid class structure, into the churches wherein voluntary religion was the rule, and, perhaps most astonishing of all, apparently even into the homes where little boys and little girls were granted unheard-of liberties.

Captain Marryat, as early as 1839, related a well-known example illustrating this last point:

Imagine a child of three years old in England behaving thus:—

> "Johnny, my dear, come here," says his mamma.
>
> "I won't," cries Johnny.
>
> "You must, my love, you are all wet, and you'll catch cold."
>
> "I won't," replies Johnny.
>
> "Come, my sweet, and I've something for you."
>
> "I won't."
>
> "Oh! Mr. —, do, pray make Johnny come in."
>
> "Come in, Johnny," says the father.
>
> "I won't."
>
> "I tell you, come in directly, sir—do you hear?"
>
> "I won't," replies the urchin, taking to his heels.
>
> "A sturdy republican, sir," says his father to me, smiling at the boy's resolute disobedience.[30]

In 1845 Francis Wyse generalized upon incidents like these, placing them in a broad social context. "There is seldom any very great restraint," he noted, "imposed upon the youth of America whose precocious intellect, brought forth and exercised at an early, and somewhat premature age, and otherwise encouraged under the republican institu-

[27] *Ibid.*, p. 79. One should bear in mind at all times the difficulties the travelers had of meeting representative American families since, as W. L. George candidly admitted, "truly representative families generally keep themselves rather to themselves." George, p. viii.

[28] Sir Edwin Arnold, *Seas and Lands* (New York, 1891), pp. 78–79.

[29] *Ibid.*, p. 79.

[30] Quoted in Lawrence A. Cremin, *The American Common School* (New York, 1951), p. 217.

tions of the country, has generally made them impatient of parental authority."[31]

Parental authority did not sensibly differ from any other exercise of power: royal, military, governmental or private. Americans had established their independence in rebellion against authority; they had rejected all artificially imposed forms of superiority; and they had proclaimed the equality of man. Surely these principles should extend to the family. Indeed, Jacks talked aptly of the way in which children had applied (with considerable parental approval) the Declaration of Independence to themselves.[32] And James Fullarton Muirhead, who composed one of the most informative chapters on this topic, formulated the grand generalization thus: "The theory of the equality of man is rampant in the nursery."[33] He referred to the infants as "young republicans," "democratic sucklings," "budding citizens of a free republic."[34]

Here then was another application of the theory of equality—one which even the friendly Muirhead could not get himself to smile upon. It "hardly tends," he patiently tried to explain, "to make the American child an attractive object to the stranger from without. On the contrary, it is very apt to make said stranger long strenuously to spank these budding citizens of a free republic, and to send them to bed *instanter*."[35]

One must, of course, sympathize with the British traveler as he suffered through each encounter with these young specimens of the New World. But their hate affair is as much beside the point as their love affair with the schools. Both child-rearing at home and the nation-wide system of compulsory public education were faithful to the omnipresent force of equality, and the paradox which began this chapter turns out to be no paradox at all. The commentators liked what they saw in the classrooms because authority was being exercised. It was being exercised by teachers who wielded it in the interests of learning and morality. When the visitors confronted the child outside the schools and in the context of home and family they were appalled by what they believed to be the universal and inexcusable betrayal of authority by the parents.

This reversal in the roles of authority vis-à-vis children disoriented the observers to such an extent that many of them never realized that, just a few chapters before their excoriation of the American child, they had been blessing his development in the schoolrooms. Although the traveler frequently sensed that the "success" of the teachers and the indulgent "failures" of the parents were related to each other, and that both stemmed from the same peculiar general assumptions in which American society was rooted, not one of them ever managed to pose squarely the problem of how and whether dual authority *could* be exerted on the child, of just how parent and teacher *should* combine their efforts in child-rearing, given the public school system and the widespread assumption that the child was an equal partner in the family "team."

The origins of this dilemma may be traced back to colonial days when, under the pressure of new conditions, the familiar family pattern brought over from the Old World suffered major transformations affecting both child-rearing practices and the role of education.

The traditional family was the wide kinship group with the source of power vested in the father and extending outward to include not only wife and children, but cousins, other relatives and servants as well. The father was the chief educator, transferring the traditions of his culture and vocational training itself to his sons. But authority and traditionalism were, as revealed in an excellent study by Bernard Bailyn, inadequate for conditions in the New World where problems were new, land abundant, labor scarce and old solutions

[31] *America: Its Realities and Resources* (London, 1846), p. 295.
[32] *My American Friends*, pp. 150–51.
[33] Muirhead, *America, The Land of Contrasts* (London, 1902), p. 64. (First edition, London, 1898).
[34] *Ibid.*, pp. 63, 65.
[35] *Ibid.*, p. 65.

to old problems irrelevant.[36] In these circumstances "the young—less bound by prescriptive memories, more adaptable, more vigorous—stood often at advantage. Learning faster, they came to see the world more familiarly, to concede more readily to unexpected necessities, to sense more accurately the phasing of a new life. They and not their parents became the effective guides to a new world, and they thereby gained a strange, anomalous authority difficult to accommodate within the ancient structure of family life."[37]

While the details need not concern us here, the traditional family and educative pattern could not survive these challenges.

> By the middle of the eighteenth century the classic lineaments of the American family as modern sociologists describe them—the "isolation of the conjugal unit," the "maximum of dispersion of the lines of descent," partible inheritances, and multilineal growth—had appeared. The consequences can hardly be exaggerated. Fundamental aspects of social life were affected. In the reduced, nuclear family, thrown back upon itself, traditional gradations in status tended to fall to the level of necessity. Relationships tended more toward achievement than ascription. The status of women rose; marriage, even in the eyes of the law, tended to become a contract between equals. Above all, the development of the child was affected.[38]

One of the effects on the child cited by Bailyn concerned the passage of the child into society as "the once elaborate interpenetration of family and community dissolved." A result was that "the individual acquired an insulation of consciousness," a "heightened . . . sense of separateness" from society, and particularly from the state which no longer could "command his automatic involvement."[39] Perhaps this is what the British meant by precocity.

A second result came as the Puritans transferred the primary educative responsibilities from "the maimed . . . family to formal instructional institutions, and in so doing not only endowed schools with a new importance but expanded their purpose beyond pragmatic vocationalism toward vaguer but more basic cultural goals."[40] Perhaps this explains why the British abused American parents.

The commentators who believed that parents must exercise authority over children were not pleased by what they saw in American families. In order to muster any kind words it was necessary to revise traditional conceptions of the family and accept a measure of equality in the home, accept the notion that the various family members could be close friends.

Dicey was one who was able to take this step. He concluded one of his volumes in 1863 in praise of "the great charm which surrounds all family relations in the North. Compared with Europe, domestic scandals are unknown; and between parents and their grown-up children, there exists a degree of familiarity and intimacy which one seldom witnesses in this country."[41]

There were other companions besides the parents and grown-up children. Growing boys and their fathers were companions, wrote Zincke in 1868. "In America the father never loses sight of his child, who thus grows up as his companion, and is soon treated as a companion, and as in some sort an equal."[42] Zincke went on to relate a pleasant incident he observed on a train between a fourteen-year-old boy and his father:

> They had long been talking on a footing of equality. . . . At last, to while away the time, they began to sing together. First they accompanied each other. Then they took alternate lines; at last alternate words. In this of course they tripped frequently, each laughing at the other for his mistakes. There was no attempt at keeping up the dignity of a parent, as might have been considered necessary and proper with us. There

[36] Bernard Bailyn, *Education in the Forming of American Society* (Chapel Hill, N.C., 1960).
[37] *Ibid.*, pp. 22–23.
[38] *Ibid.*, pp. 24–25.
[39] *Ibid.*, pp. 25–26.
[40] *Ibid.*, p. 27.
[41] Edward Dicey, *Six Months in the Federal States* (London, 1863), I, 310.
[42] Foster Barham Zincke, *Last Winter in the United States* (London, 1868), pp. 70–71.

was no reserve. They were in a certain sense already on an equal footing of persons of the same age.[43]

Mothers and daughters were companions, Low maintained. "Daughters are much with their mothers, and they become their companions younger than they do in Europe. At an age when the French girl, for instance, is still demurely attending her convent, or the English girl is in the hands of her governess, her more emancipated sister across the Atlantic is calling with her mother on her friends, or assisting her in the drawing-room on her reception days."[44]

Sons and daughters received equal treatment, claimed Saunders. Whereas "in an English family, as a rule, the greatest consideration is shown to the boys," in America, if anything, "the wishes of the girls would be first listened to, and their education provided for." The boy, after all, "is as eager to start life on his own account as is a grey hound to rush after the hare." "In the matter of early independence both sexes are equal."[45]

Even husbands and wives were companions. While the wife "will not consent to being submerged by her children, she gives much of her time to them, and is still able to find time to be with her husband. The average American husband makes a confidante and a companion of his wife. . . ."[46]

The patriarchies and matriarchies of the past had been replaced by a family team composed of equals. The British perceived this family revolution as being directly parallel to the fundamental cultural difference between the New World which blurred distinctions and the Old which honored and preserved them. As Muirhead put it: "The reason—or at any rate one reason—of the normal attitude of the American parent towards his child is not far to seek. It is almost undoubtedly one of the direct consequences of the circumambient spirit of democracy. The American is so accustomed to recognize the essential equality of others that he sometimes carries a good thing to excess. . . . The present child may be described as one of the experiments of democracy."[47]

Americans enthroned their children not merely out of blind obedience to some social ethos which compelled them to do in the home something consonant with what the nation proclaimed to the world as its faith. Americans, as Zincke's story of the singing father and son so nicely shows, were often quite fond of their children, and rather than being harried or intimidated, they were not infrequently joyful parents. In fact, the Americans, according to the British, believed in their young ones in much the same way that they believed in their future. Let the youths' natural spirit triumph and they would not only participate in a grand future, but they would be the chief forgers of that future; the child was the future. Children could be heard as well as seen because they represented hope in "the land of youth." "Nowhere," said Muirhead, "is the child so constantly in evidence; nowhere are his wishes so carefully consulted; nowhere is he allowed to make his mark so strongly on society in general."[48] Richard DeBary chimed in that "America is wholly convinced . . . that the young child can take it all in. The child is given kingship and becomes the king."[49]

Those few Englishmen who thought well of American children praised precisely the same qualities which the detractors abominated. Arnold Bennett, for example, came across one "captivating creature whose society I enjoyed at frequent intervals throughout my stay in

[43] *Ibid.*, p. 71.
[44] A. M. Low, *America at Home* (London, 1905), p. 74.
[45] William Saunders, *Through the Light Continent* (London, 1879), pp. 399–400. Also enlightening on these leveling tendencies in the home are J. Nelson Fraser, p. 246, and Harold Spender, *A Briton in America* (London, 1921), pp. 253–54.
[46] Low, p. 82.
[47] Muirhead, pp. 70–71.
[48] *Ibid.*, p. 63.
[49] DeBary, p. 128. "Young America does not sit at the master's feet and worship; it has definite opinions, which it deems as much deserving of hearing as other people's, and it gives them forth with the bold confidence born of youthful inexperience and immaturity," Emily Faithful, *Three Visits to America* (Edinburgh, 1884), p. 89.

America. . . . [She] was a mirror in which I saw the whole American race of children—their independence, their self-confidence, their adorable charm, and their neat sauciness."[50] The reformer George Holyoake liked "the American habit of training their children to independence" more than he did England's "unwise domestic paternalism, which encourages a costly dependence."[51]

John Strathesk did not employ the term "precocious" in a deprecating manner when he decided that "the girls and boys of America are very frank, even precocious."[52] And Sir Philip Gibbs expanded upon this theme. "The children of America," he said, "have the qualities of their nation, simplicity, common sense, and self-reliance. They are not so bashful as English boys and girls, and they are free from the little constraints of nursery etiquette which make so many English children afraid to open their mouths. They are also free entirely from that juvenile snobbishness which is still cultivated in English society, where boys and girls of well-to-do parents are taught to look down with contempt upon children of the poorer classes."[53]

It may be noticed that the adjectives used to depict the child are similar, whether used in delight or disgust: saucy, self-reliant, wild, spontaneous, immodest, independent, demanding, irreverent. It may furthermore be observed that they bear resemblance to adjectives which some Englishmen thought applicable to the young nation as a whole.[54] Some visitors also found the terms suitable for characterizing American adults as well.

The blurring of lines between young and old in the New World furnished an invitation to some British writers to caricature both American parents and children. But to Margaret Mead this leveling tendency forms an explicable part of a peculiarly national approach to child-rearing which she has called "third-generation American."[55] The American child, contends this anthropologist, is expected to traverse a course very different from his father's, and "with this orientation towards a different future for the child comes also the expectation that the child will pass beyond his parents and leave their standards behind him."[56] Thus "it comes about that American parents lack the sure hand on the rudder which parents in other societies display."[57] Or, approaching the matter from a different perspective than either the historian Bailyn or Miss Mead, Erik Erikson supports their findings when he writes that "the psychoanalysis of the children of immigrants clearly reveals to what extent they, as the first real Americans in their family, become their parents' cultural parents."[58]

As Erikson and many other psychologists have stressed, the high prestige accorded youth, understandable though it may be considering the abundant resources, the scarcity of labor, the virgin conditions, and the rapid pace of change in the egalitarian New World, is not without cost to Americans. The child himself has to pay a price for his exalted place; the compulsion to achieve, to succeed, can be taxing and perhaps ultimately futile. Unlike his Old World counterpart who begins life with a position of ascribed status which he knows is his own, the American child can never let up.

The society, too, has to pay a price for its cult of youth. It is paid not only in the primitive music, the puerile television and the domestic tyranny to which the adult world is exposed at the command of teenagers, and to which the adults meekly succumb. It is paid also in the sacrifice of wisdom, of standards, of permanence, of serenity under the

[50] Arnold Bennett, *Your United States* (New York, 1912), pp. 147–48.
[51] George Jacob Holyoake, *Among the Americans* (Chicago, 1881), p. 183.
[52] Strathesk, p. 149.
[53] Philip Gibbs, *Land of Destiny* (New York, 1920), p. 88.
[54] Even Vachell, who told the story of the boy with the bagpipes, had to confess to the "originality, independence, pluck, and perspicuity" of the children (p. 83).

[55] Margaret Mead, *And Keep Your Powder Dry: An Anthropologist Looks at America* (New York, 1942), p. 45.
[56] *Ibid.*, p. 41.
[57] *Ibid.*, p. 43.
[58] Erik Erikson, *Childhood and Society* (2nd ed.; New York, 1963), p. 294.

frantic injunction to constantly "think young." The quiet contemplation of the past and the present is sacrificed when all must worship at the altar of the future.

The most repeated consensus at which the travelers arrived concerning the "American character" was that that character resembled, at heart, the character of a child. If there were no childlike children, if there were only miniature adults in "the land of youth," then the reverse was equally true—there were few adultlike adults; there were only adults trying to be young. "There are no old in America at all," said George Steevens in 1900.[59] By this he meant two things. First, that adult virtues are uncultivated in the New World; the American "retains all his life a want of discipline, an incapacity for ordered and corporate effort."[60]

Steevens' second meaning centered on the fate of those who were actually aged. "They are shouldered unmercifully out of existence," he claimed. "I found in New York a correspondence on the open question whether the old have any right to respect. Many of the public thought, quite seriously, they had no right even to existence."[61]

The dearest price of all is paid neither by the children nor by the society but by the adults who have to be "boys" at the office, who as parents must "live for their children," who as mature women must forever look and act like eighteen-year-olds, who as elderly must join the other aged in some zippy retirement community quarantined from the rest of mankind.

The cult of youth has perhaps permitted a more spontaneous family life to develop, and it has, no doubt, lent to our national life a special vigor and freshness. But in exalting childhood and early youth to the consummatory positions in life, it follows that maturity and old age should become anti-climactic. Indeed, in America, as one ages, one declines, and the reward of lower movie admission fees for "senior citizens" furnishes rather ineffectual solace. One can only guess at the extent to which the American fixation on the earlier stages of the life cycle is related to our tendency to deny the reality of old age and to put from our minds all thoughts of death. And it is not possible to do more here than to raise the question which then becomes inescapable: what kinds of spiritual reserves might this habit of mind take from the individual as he passes through life?[62]

Thirty years after his 1869 visit to America, the Rev. Mr. Macrae returned and noted that the "independence and precocious intellect of the American children" had not diminished; but he was "less struck with these features this time."[63] The reason he was less struck was precisely the same that made Harold Spender think better of the American children in 1920, twenty years after *his* first visit. "Our English child in the interval," said Spender, substituting his native land for Macrae's Scotland, "has become a little more American."[64] By the early years of the twentieth century, America's startling departure in raising children and in inflating the status of the youngsters in the family hierarchy was, like various other American innovations, becoming more general in the Old World also.

[59] George Steevens, p. 314.
[60] *Ibid.*, p. 314.
[61] *Ibid.*, p. 314.

[62] The seeds of the thoughts in the above paragraph, and in many others in this paper, were planted by Richard Hofstadter, both in conversation and in an early draft of an as-yet unpublished article called "Foreign Observers and American Children"—an article from which Professor Hofstadter was kind enough to let me read.
[63] David Macrae, *America Revisited and Men I Have Met* (Glasgow, 1908), p. 24.
[64] Harold Spender, p. 271.

David M. Potter

ABUNDANCE AND THE FORMATION OF CHARACTER

One of David Potter's goals in *People of Plenty* was to indicate how the historian might benefit from the work of the behavioral scientist and vice versa. He did this by relating one factor in the American past, historical and economic in nature, to a wide variety of American institutions and activities. The factor was abundance; the areas in which it worked itself out included political democracy, the class structure, advertising as a value-making institution in the twentieth century, and foreign policy. However, it was in the final chapter, reproduced below, that Potter most explicitly attempted to sketch the possibilities for relating historical factors to childhood and family life in America. Some of the connections he suggested between child-rearing patterns in the United States, the American character, and the condition of economic plenty which has characterized our past may strike the reader as far-fetched, but the author readily admitted the speculative quality of his essay; his hope was to spark some new thinking.

WHAT, if anything, does the factor of abundance have to do with the process of personality formation (in so far as this process is understood) in the United States? How does the process differ from that in countries where the measure of abundance is not so great?

To these questions, I believe, some highly explicit answers are possible. Let us therefore be entirely concrete. Let us consider the situation of a six-month-old American infant, who is not yet aware that he is a citizen, a taxpayer, and a consumer.

This individual is, to all appearances, just a very young specimen of *Homo sapiens*, with certain needs for protection, care, shelter, and nourishment which may be regarded as the universal biological needs of human infancy rather than specific cultural needs. It would be difficult to prove that the culture has as yet differentiated him from other infants, and, though he is an American, few would argue that he has acquired an American character. Yet abundance and the circumstances arising from abundance have already dictated a whole range of basic conditions which, from his birth, are constantly at work upon this child and which will contribute in the most intimate and basic way to the formation of his character.

To begin with, abundance has already revolutionized the typical mode of his nourishment by providing for him to be fed upon cow's milk rather than upon his mother's milk, taken from the bottle rather than from the breast. Abundance contributes vitally to this transformation, because bottle feeding requires fairly elaborate facilities of refrigeration, heating, sterilization, and temperature control, which only an advanced technology can offer and only an economy of abundance can make widely available. I will not attempt here to resolve the debated question as to the psychological effects, for both mother and child, of bottle feeding as contrasted with breast feeding in infant nurture. But it is clear that the changeover to bottle feeding has encroached somewhat upon the intimacy of the bond between mother and child. The nature of this bond is, of course, one of the most crucial factors in the formation of character. Bottle feeding also must tend to emphasize the separateness of the infant as an individual, and thus it makes, for the first time, a point which the entire culture reiterates constantly throughout the life of the average American. In addition to the psychic influences which may be involved in the manner of taking the food, it is also a matter of capital importance that the bottle-fed baby is, on the whole, better nourished than the breast-fed infant and therefore likely to grow more rapidly, to be more vigorous, and to suffer fewer ailments, with whatever effects these physical conditions may have upon his personality.

It may be argued also that abundance has provided a characteristic mode of housing for the infant and that this mode further emphasizes his separateness as an individual. In societies of scarcity, dwelling units are few and hard to come by, with the result that high proportions of newly married young people make their homes in the parental ménage, thus forming part of an "extended" family, as it is called. Moreover, scarcity provides a low ratio of rooms to individuals, with the consequence that whole families may expect as a matter of course to have but one room for sleeping, where children will go to bed in intimate propinquity to their parents. But abundance prescribes a different regime. By making it economically possible for newly married couples to maintain separate households of their own, it has almost destroyed the extended family as an institution in America and has ordained that the child shall be reared in a "nuclear" family, so-called, where his only intimate associates are his parents and his siblings, with even the latter far fewer now than in families of the past. The housing arrangements of this new-style family are suggested by census data for 1950. In that year there were 45,983,000 dwelling units to accommodate the 38,310,000 families in the United States, and, though the median number of persons in the dwelling unit was 3.1, the median number of rooms in the dwelling unit was 4.6. Eighty-four per cent of all dwelling units reported less than one person per room. By providing the ordinary family with more than one room for sleeping, the economy thus produces a situation in which the child will sleep either in a room alone or in a room shared with his brothers or sisters. Even without allowing for the cases in which children may have separate rooms, these conditions mean that a very substantial percentage of children now sleep in a room alone, for, with the declining birth rate, we have reached a point at which an increasing proportion of families have one child or two children rather than the larger number which was at one time typical. For instance, in the most recent group of mothers who had completed their childbearing phase, according to the census, 19.5 per cent had had one child and 23.4 had had two. Thus almost half of all families with offspring did not have more than two children throughout their duration. In the case of the first group, all the children were "only" children throughout their childhood, and in the second group half of the children were "only" children until the second child was born. To state this in another, and perhaps a more forcible, way, it has been shown that among American women who arrived at age thirty-four during the year 1949 and who had borne children up to that time, 26.7 per cent had borne only one child, and 34.5 per cent had borne only two. If these tendencies persist, it would mean that, among families where there are children, hardly one in three will have more than two children.

The census has, of course, not got around to finding out how the new-style family, in its new-style dwelling unit, adjusts the life-practice to the space situation. But it is significant that America's most widely circulated book on the care of infants advises that "it is preferable that he [the infant] not sleep in his parents' room after he is about 12 months old," offers the opinion that "it's fine for each [child] to have a room of his own, if that's possible," and makes the sweeping assertion that "it's a sensible rule not to take a child into the parents' bed for any reason." It seems clear beyond dispute that the household space provided by the economy of abundance has been used to emphasize the separateness, the apartness, if not the isolation, of the American child.

Not only the nourishment and housing, but also the clothing of the American infant are controlled by American abundance. For one of the most sweeping consequences of our abundance is that, in contrast to other peoples who keep their bodies warm primarily by wearing clothes, Americans keep their bodies warm primarily by a far more expensive and even wasteful method: namely, by heating the buildings in which they are sheltered. Every American who has been abroad knows how much lighter is the clothing—especially the underclothing—of Americans than of people in countries like England and France, where the winters are far less severe than ours, and every American who can remember the conditions of a few decades ago knows how much lighter our clothing is than that of our grandparents. These changes have occurred because clothing is no longer the principal device for securing warmth. The oil furnace has not only displaced the open fireplace; it has also displaced the woolen undergarment and the vest.

This is a matter of considerable significance for adults but of far greater importance to infants, for adults discipline themselves to wear warm garments, submitting, for instance, to woolen underwear more or less voluntarily. But the infant knows no such discipline, and his garments or bedclothes must be kept upon him by forcible means. Hence primitive people, living in outdoor conditions, swaddle the child most rigorously, virtually binding him into his clothes, and breaking him to them almost as a horse is broken to the harness. Civilized peoples mitigate the rigor but still use huge pins or clips to frustrate the baby's efforts to kick off the blankets and free his limbs. In a state of nature, cold means confinement and warmth means freedom, so far as young humans are concerned. But abundance has given the American infant physical freedom by giving him physical warmth in cold weather.

In this connection it may be surmised that abundance has also given him a permissive system of toilet training. If our forebears imposed such training upon the child and we now wait for him to take the initiative in these matters himself, it is not wholly because the former held a grim Calvinistic doctrine of childrearing that is philosophically contrary to ours. The fact was that the circumstances gave them little choice. A mother who was taking care of several babies, keeping them clean, making their clothes, washing their diapers in her own washtub, and doing this, as often as not, while another baby was on the way, had little choice but to hasten their fitness to toilet themselves. Today, on the contrary, the disposable diaper, the diaper service, and most of all the washing machine, not to mention the fact that one baby seldom presses upon the heels of another, make it far easier for the mother to indulge the child in a regime under which he will impose his own toilet controls in his own good time.

Thus the economy of plenty has influenced the feeding of the infant, his regime, and the physical setting within which he lives. These material conditions alone might be regarded as having some bearing upon the formation of his character, but the impact of abundance by no means ends at this point. In so far as it has an influence in determining what specific individuals shall initiate the infant into the ways of man and shall provide him with his formative impressions of the meaning of being a person, it must be regarded as even more vital. When it influences the nature of the relationships between these individuals and the infant, it must be recognized as reaching to the very essence of the process of character formation.

The central figures in the dramatis personae of the American infant's universe are still his parents, and in this respect, of course, there is nothing peculiar either to the American child or to the child of abundance. But abundance has at least provided him with parents who are in certain respects unlike the parents of children born in other countries or born fifty years ago. To begin with, it has given him young parents, for the median age of fathers at the birth of the first child in American marriages (as of 1940) was 25.3 years, and the median age of mothers was 22.6 years. This median age was substantially lower than it had been in the United States in 1890 for both fathers and mothers. Moreover, as the size of families has been reduced and the wife no longer continues to bear a succession of children throughout the period of her fertility, the median age of mothers at the birth of the last child has declined from 32 years (1890) to 27 years (1940). The age of the parents at the birth of both the first child and the last child is far lower than in the case of couples in most European countries. There can be little doubt that abundance has caused this differential, in the case of the first-born by making it economically possible for a high proportion of the population to meet the expenses of homemaking at a fairly early age. In the case of the last-born, it would also appear that one major reason for the earlier cessation of childbearing is a determination by parents to enjoy a high standard of living themselves and to limit their offspring to a number for whom they can maintain a similar standard.

By the very fact of their youth, these parents are more likely to remain alive until the child reaches maturity, thus giving him a better prospect of being reared by his own mother and father. This prospect is further reinforced by increases in the life-span, so that probably no child in history has ever enjoyed so strong a likelihood that his parents will survive to rear him. Abundance has produced this situation by providing optimum conditions for prolonging life. But, on the other hand, abundance has also contributed much to produce an economy in which the mother is no longer markedly dependent upon the father, and this change in the economic relation between the sexes has probably done much to remove obstacles to divorce. The results are all too familiar. During the decade 1940–49 there were 25.8 divorces for every 100 marriages in the United States, which ratio, if projected over a longer period, would mean that one marriage out of four would end in divorce. But our concern here is with a six-month-old child, and the problem is to know whether this factor of divorce involves childless couples predominantly or whether it is likely to touch him. The answer is indicated by the fact that, of all divorces granted in 1948, no less than 42 per cent were to couples with children under eighteen, and a very large proportion of these children were of much younger ages. Hence one might say that the economy of abundance has provided the child with younger parents who chose their role of parenthood deliberately and who are more likely than parents in the past to live until he is grown, but who are substantially less likely to preserve the unbroken family as the environment within which he shall be reared.

In addition to altering the characteristics of the child's parents, it has also altered the quantitative relationship between him and his parents. It has done this, first of all, by offering the father such lucrative opportunities through work outside the home that the old agricultural economy in which children worked alongside their fathers is now obsolete. Yet, on the other hand, the father's new employment gives so much more leisure than his former work that the child may, in fact, receive considerably more of his father's attention. But the most vital transformation is in the case of the mother. In the economy of scarcity which controlled the modes of life that were traditional for many centuries, an upper-class child was reared by a nurse, and all others were normally reared by their mothers. The scarcity economy could not support many nonproductive members, and these mothers, though not "employed," were most decidedly hard workers, busily engaged in cooking, washing, sewing, weaving, preserving, caring for the henhouse, the garden, and perhaps the cow, and in general carrying on the domestic economy of a large family. Somehow they also attended to the needs of a numerous brood of children, but the mother was in no sense a full-time attendant upon any one child. Today, however, the economy of abundance very nearly exempts a very large number of mothers from the requirement of economic productivity in order that they may give an unprecedented share of their time to the care of the one or two young children who are now the usual number in an American family. Within the home, the wide range of labor-saving devices and the assignment of many functions, such as laundering, to service industries have produced this result. Outside the home, employment of women in the labor force has steadily increased, but the incidence of employment falls upon unmarried women, wives without children, and wives with grown children. In fact, married women without children are two and one-half times as likely to be employed as those with children. Thus what amounts to a new dispensation has been established for the child. If he belongs to the upper class, his mother has replaced his nurse as his full-time attendant. The differences in character formation that might result from this change alone could easily be immense. To mention but one possibility, the presence of the nurse must inevitably have made the child somewhat aware of his class status, whereas the presence of the mother would be less likely to have this effect. If the child does not belong to the upper class, mother and child now impinge upon each other in a relationship whose intensity is of an entirely different magnitude from that which prevailed in the past. The mother has fewer physical distractions in the care of the child, but she is more likely to be restive in her maternal role because it takes her away from attractive employment with which it cannot be reconciled.

If abundance has thus altered the relationship of the child with his parent, it has even more drastically altered the rest of his social milieu, for it has changed the identity of the rest of the personnel who induct him into human society. In the extended family of the past, a great array of kinspeople filled his cosmos and guided him to maturity. By nature, he particularly needed association with children of his own age (his "peers," as they are called), and he particularly responded to the values asserted by these peers. Such peers were very often his brothers and sisters, and, since they were all members of his own family, all came under parental control. This is to say that, in a sense, the parents controlled the peer group, and the peer group controlled the child. The point is worth making because we frequently encounter the assertion that parental control of the child has been replaced by peer-group control; but it is arguable that what is really the case is that children were always deeply influenced by the peer group and that parents have now lost their former measure of control over this group, since it is no longer a familial group. Today the nursery school replaces the large family as a peer group, and the social associations, even of young children, undergo the same shift from focused contact with family to diffused contact with a miscellany of people, which John Galsworthy depicted for grown people in the three novels of the *Forsyte Saga*. Again, the effects upon character may very well be extensive.

Abundance, then, has played a critical part in revolutionizing both the physical circumstances and the human associations which surround the American infant and child. These changes alone would warrant the hypothesis that abundance has profoundly affected the formation of character for such a child. But to extend this inquiry one step further, it may be worthwhile to consider how these altered conditions actually impinge upon the individual. Here, of course, is an almost unlimited field for investigation, and I shall only attempt to indicate certain crucial points at which abundance projects conditions that are basic in the life of the child.

One of these points concerns the cohesive force which holds the family together. The family is the one institution which touches all members of society most intimately, and it is perhaps the only social institution which touches young children directly. The sources from which the family draws its strength are, therefore, of basic importance. In the past, these sources were, it would seem, primarily economic. For agrarian society, marriage distinctively involved a division of labor. Where economic opportunity was narrowly restricted, the necessity for considering economic ways and means in connection with marriage led to the arrangement of matches by parents and to the institution of the dowry. The emotional bonds of affection, while always important, were not deemed paramount, and the ideal of romantic love played little or no part in the lives of ordinary people. Where it existed at all, it was as an upper-class luxury. (The very term "courtship" implies this upper-class orientation.) This must inevitably have meant that the partners in the majority of marriages demanded less from one another emotionally than do the partners of romantic love and that the emotional factor was less important to the stability of the marriage. Abundance, however, has played its part in changing this picture. On the American frontier, where capital for dowries was as rare as opportunity for prosperous marriage was plentiful, the dowry became obsolete. Later still, when abundance began to diminish the economic duties imposed upon the housewife, the function of marriage as a division of labor ceased to seem paramount, and the romantic or emotional factor assumed increasing importance. Abundance brought the luxury of romantic love within the reach of all, and, as it did so, emotional harmony became the principal criterion of success in a marriage, while lack of such harmony became a major threat to the existence of the marriage. The statistics of divorce give us a measure of the loss of durability in marriage, but they give us no measure of the factors of instability in the marriages which endure and no measure of the increased focus upon emotional satisfactions in such marriages. The children of enduring marriages, as well as the children of divorce, must inevitably feel the impact of this increased emphasis upon emotional factors, must inevitably sense the difference in the foundations of the institution which holds their universe in place.

In the rearing of a child, it would be difficult to imagine any factors more vital than the distinction between a permissive and an authoritarian regime or more vital than the age at which economic responsibility is imposed. In both these matters the modern American child lives under a very different dispensation from children in the past. We commonly think of these changes as results of our more enlightened or progressive or humanitarian ideas. We may even think of them as results of developments in the specific field of child psychology, as if the changes were simply a matter of our understanding these matters better than our grandparents. But the fact is that the authoritarian discipline of the child, within the authoritarian family, was but an aspect of the authoritarian social system that was linked with the economy of scarcity. Such a regime could never have been significantly relaxed within the family so long as it remained diagnostic in the society. Nor could it have remained unmodified within the family, once society began to abandon it in other spheres.

Inevitably, the qualities which the parents inculcate in a child will depend upon the roles which they occupy themselves. For the ordinary man the economy of scarcity has offered one role, as Simon N. Patten observed many years ago, and the economy of abundance has offered another. Abundance offers "work calling urgently for workmen"; scarcity found the "worker seeking humbly any kind of toil." As a suppliant to his superiors, the worker under scarcity accepted the principle of authority; he accepted his own subordination and the obligation to cultivate the qualities appropriate to his subordination, such as submissiveness, obedience, and deference. Such a man naturally transferred the principle of authority into his own family and, through this principle, instilled into his children the qualities appropriate to people of their kind—submissiveness, obedience, and deference. Many copybook maxims still exist to remind us of the firmness of childhood discipline, while the difference between European and American children—one of the most clearly recognizable of all national differences—serves to emphasize the extent to which Americans have now departed from this firmness.

This new and far more permissive attitude toward children has arisen, significantly, in an economy of abundance, where work has called urgently for the workman. In this situation, no longer a suppliant, the workman found submissiveness no longer a necessity and therefore no longer a virtue. The principle of authority lost some of its majesty, and he was less likely to regard it as the only true criterion of domestic order. In short, he ceased to impose it upon his children. Finding that the most valuable trait in himself was a capacity for independent decision and self-reliant conduct in dealing with the diverse opportunities which abundance offered him, he tended to encourage this quality in his children. The irresponsibility of childhood still called for a measure of authority on one side and obedience on the other, but this became a means to an end and not an end in itself. On the whole, permissive training, to develop independent ability, even though it involves a certain sacrifice of obedience and discipline, is the characteristic mode of childrearing in the one country which most distinctively enjoys an economy of abundance. Here, in a concrete way, one finds something approaching proof for Gerth and Mills's suggestion that the relation of father and child may have its importance not as a primary factor but rather as a "replica of the power relations of society."

If scarcity required men to "seek humbly any kind of toil," it seldom permitted women to seek employment outside the home at all. Consequently, the woman was economically dependent upon, and, accordingly, subordinate to, her husband or her father. Her subordination reinforced the principle of authority within the home. But the same transition which altered the role of the male worker has altered her status as well, for abundance "calling urgently for workmen" makes no distinctions of gender, and, by extending economic independence to women, has enabled them to assume the role of partners rather than of subordinates within the family. Once the relation of voluntarism and equality is introduced between husband and wife, it is, of course, far more readily extended to the relation between parent and child.

If abundance has fostered a more permissive regime for the child, amid circumstances of democratic equality within the family, it has no less certainly altered the entire process of imposing economic responsibility upon the child, hence the process of preparing the child for such responsibility. In the economy of scarcity, as I have remarked above, society could not afford to support any substantial quota of nonproductive members. Consequently, the child went to work when he was as yet young. He attended primary school for a much shorter school year than the child of today; only a minority attended high school; and only the favored few attended college. Even during the brief years of schooling, the child worked, in the home, on the farm, or even in the factory. But today the economy of abundance can afford to maintain a substantial proportion of the population in nonproductive status, and it assigns this role, sometimes against their will, to its younger and its elder members. It protracts the years of schooling, and it defers responsibilities for an unusually long span. It even enforces laws setting minimal ages for leaving school, for going to work, for consenting to sexual intercourse, or for marrying. It extends the jurisdiction of juvenile courts to the eighteenth or the twentieth year of age.

Such exemption from economic responsibility might seem to imply a long and blissful youth free from strain for the child. But the delays in reaching economic maturity are not matched by comparable delays in other phases of growing up. On the contrary, there are many respects in which the child matures earlier. Physically, the child at the lower social level will actually arrive at adolescence a year or so younger than his counterpart a generation ago, because of improvement in standards of health and nutrition. Culturally, the child is made aware of the allurements of sex at an earlier age, partly by his familiarity with the movies, television, and popular magazines, and partly by the practice of "dating" in the early teens. By the standards of his peer group, he is encouraged to demand expensive and mature recreations, similar to those of adults, at a fairly early age. By reason of the desire of his parents that he should excel in the mobility race and give proof during his youth of the qualities which will make him a winner in later life, he is exposed to the stimuli of competition before he leaves the nursery. Thus there is a kind of imbalance between the postponement of responsibility and the quickening of social maturity which may have contributed to make American adolescence a more difficult age than human biology alone would cause it to be. Here, again, there are broad implications for the formation of character, and here, again, abundance is at work on both sides of the equation, for it contributes as much to the hastening of social maturity as it does to the prolongation of economic immaturity.

Some of these aspects of the rearing of children in the United States are as distinctively American, when compared with other countries, as any Yankee traits that have ever been attributed to the American people. In the multiplicity which always complicates social analysis, such aspects of child-rearing might be linked with a number of factors in American life. But one of the more evident and more significant links, it would seem certain, is with the factor of abundance. Such a tie is especially pertinent in this discussion, where the intention of the whole book has been to relate the study of character, as the historian would approach it, to the same subject as it is viewed by the behavioral scientist. In this chapter, especially, the attempt has been made to throw a bridge between the general historical force of economic abundance and the specific behavioral pattern of people's lives. Historical forces are too often considered only in their public and over-all effects, while private lives are interpreted without sufficient reference to the historical determinants which shape them. But no major force at work in society can possibly make itself felt at one of these levels without also having its impact at the other level. In view of this fact, the study of national character should not stand apart, as it has in the past, from the study of the process of character formation in the individual. In view of this fact, also, the effect of economic abundance is especially pertinent. For economic abundance is a factor whose presence and whose force may be clearly and precisely recognized in the most personal and intimate phases of the development of personality in the child. Yet, at the same time, the presence and the force of this factor are recognizable with equal certainty in the whole broad, general range of American experience, American ideals, and American institutions. At both levels, it has exercised a pervasive influence in the shaping of the American character.

II. THE INTENSIFICATION OF THE CULT OF YOUTH, 1890–1920

G. Stanley Hall

ADOLESCENCE AND THE GROWTH OF SOCIAL IDEALS

The first section of this volume (Elson's essay excepted) implies that the cult of youth has been a constant factor in American history. Such is not the case. As in everything else in life, there are ebbs and flows; the long perspective of these essays should not hide the fact there has rarely been unanimous national agreement about the nature of the child, the way he should be brought up, and his place in the society. Reform of "child abuses" or practices that "keep him in his proper place" (the phrase used depending upon one's predilections) have been periodic, and have usually coincided with periods of general reform. One such quickening of activity occurred in the 1830's, when Tocqueville visited America and when Horace Mann spread the gospel of free public education. Another burst of activity, and perhaps of greater significance and duration, came during the Populist-Progressive years from about 1890 to the end of the First World War. In this section we examine various utterances from leading spirits of that latter age and get to see the problem of childhood in the context of real events, tangible issues, and unresolved encounters. In this way, the abstract questions concerning childhood come alive, are linked to a world of historical reality, and become implements for dealing with a variety of social and historical issues.

G. Stanley Hall (1844–1924) was a path-breaking psychologist and a distinguished educator. As the first president of Clark University (Worcester, Massachusetts), as a professor of psychology (Antioch, Harvard, Johns Hopkins), and as a writer, Hall established himself as the leading American educational psychologist of the nineteenth century, whose contributions seem to grow with time. Hall set into motion the "child-study movement," institutionalized as a national association (with local and state societies), composed chiefly of teachers. Some of his major, influential ideas about adolescence as a separate and definable stage in the life cycle are found in the following selection. It can be shown that his various writings about child psychology and adolescence laid the groundwork for much of the intellectual ferment of the *fin de siècle* and some of the political activism generated during the first two decades of the twentieth century.

This selection is reworked from *Adolescence,* Hall's major contribution as a developmental psychologist. It provides some intellectual and scientific underpinnings for the development of a separate teenage culture which has since become such an integral part of the American scene.

From *Youth: Its Education, Regimen, and Hygiene* by G. Stanley Hall (Copyright 1907 by D. Appleton and Company), pp. 207–209, 212–213, 215–221, 223–224, 226–230.

IN A few aspects we are already able to trace the normal psychic outgrowing of the home of childhood as its interests irradiate into an ever enlarging environment. Almost the only duty of small children is habitual and prompt obedience. Our very presence enforces one general law—that of keeping our goodwill and avoiding our displeasure. They respect all we smile at or even notice, and grow to it like the plant toward the light. Their early lies are often saying what they think will please. At bottom, the most restless child admires and loves those who save him from too great fluctuations by coercion, provided the means be rightly chosen and the ascendency extend over heart and mind. But the time comes when parents are often shocked at the lack of respect suddenly shown by the child. They have ceased to be the highest ideals. The period of habituating morality and making it habitual is ceasing; and the passion to realize freedom, to act on personal experience, and to keep a private conscience is in order. To act occasionally with independence from the highest possible ideal motives develops the impulse and the joy of pure obligation, and thus brings some new and original force into the world and makes habitual guidance by the highest and best, or by inner as opposed to outer constraint, the practical rule of life. To bring the richest streams of thought to bear in interpreting the ethical instincts, so that the youth shall cease to live in a moral interregnum, is the real goal of self-knowledge. This is true education of the will and prepares the way for love of overcoming obstacles of difficulty, perhaps even of conflict. This impulse is often the secret of obstinacy. And yet, "at no time in life will a human being respond so heartily if treated by older and wiser people as if he were an equal or even a superior. The attempt to treat a child at adolescence as you would treat an inferior is instantly fatal to good discipline." Parents still think of their offspring as mere children, and tighten the rein when they should loosen it. Many young people feel that they have the best of homes and yet that they will go crazy if they must remain in them. If the training of earlier years has been good, guidance by command may now safely give way to that by ideals, which are sure to be heroic. The one unpardonable thing for the adolescent is dullness, stupidity, lack of life, interest, and enthusiasm in school or teachers, and, perhaps above all, too great stringency. Least of all, at this stage, can the curriculum or school be an ossuary. The child must now be taken into the family councils and find the parents interested in all that interests him. Where this is not done, we have the conditions for the interesting cases of so many youth, who now begin to suspect that father, mother, or both, are not their true parents. Not only is there interest in rapidly widening associations with coevals, but a new lust to push on and up to maturity. One marked trait now is to seek friends and companions older than themselves, or, next to this, to seek those younger. This is in marked contrast with previous years, when they seek associates of their own age. Possibly the merciless teasing instinct, which culminates at about the same time, may have some influence, but certain it is that now interest is transpolarized up and down the age scale. One reason is the new hunger for information, not only concerning reproduction, but a vast variety of other matters, so that there is often an attitude of silent begging for knowledge. In answer to Lancaster's questions on this subject, some sought older associates because they could learn more from them, found them better or more steadfast friends, craved sympathy and found most of it from older and perhaps married people. Some were more interested in their parents' conversation with other adults than with themselves, and were particularly entertained by the chance of hearing things they had no business to. There is often a feeling that adults do not realize this new need of friendship with them and show want of sympathy almost brutal. . . .

On a basis of 1,400 papers answering the question whom, of anyone ever heard or read of, they would like to resemble,

Barnes found that girls' ideals were far more often found in the immediate circle of their acquaintance than boys, and that those within that circle were more often in their own family, but that the tendency to go outside their personal knowledge and choose historical and public characters was greatly augmented at puberty, when also the heroes of philanthropy showed marked gain in prominence. Boys rarely chose women as their ideals; but in America, half the girls at eight and two-thirds at eighteen chose male characters. The range of important women ideals among the girls was surprisingly small. Barnes fears that if from the choice of relatives as ideals, the expansion to remote or world heroes is too fast, it may "lead to disintegration of character and reckless living." "If, on the other hand, it is expanded too slowly we shall have that arrested development which makes good ground in which to grow stupidity, brutality, and drunkenness—the first fruits of a sluggish and self-contained mind." "No one can consider the regularity with which local ideals die out and are replaced by world ideals without feeling that he is in the presence of law-abiding forces," and this emphasizes the fact that the teacher or parent does not work in a world governed by caprice. . . .

L. W. Kline studied by the census method returns from 2,594 children, who were asked what they wished to be and do. He found that in naming both ideals and occupations girls were more conservative than boys, but more likely to give a reason for their choice. In this respect country children resembled boys more than city children. Country boys were more prone to inattention, were more independent and able to care for themselves, suggesting that the home life of the country child is more effective in shaping ideals and character than that of the city child. Industrial occupations are preferred by the younger children, the professional and technical pursuits increasing with age. Judgments of rights and justice with the young are more prone to issue from emotional rather than from intellectual processes. Country children seem more altruistic than those in the city, and while girls are more sympathetic than boys, they are also more easily prejudiced. Many of these returns bear unmistakable marks that in some homes and schools moralization has been excessive and has produced a sentimental type of morality and often a feverish desire to express ethical views instead of trusting to suggestion. Children are very prone to have one code of ideals for themselves and another for others. Boys, too, are more original than girls, and country children more than city children. . . .

Taylor, Young, Hamilton, Chambers, and others, have also collected interesting data on what children and young people hope to be, do, whom they would like to be, or resemble, etc. Only a few at adolescence feel themselves so good or happy that they are content to be themselves. Most show more or less discontent at their lot. From six to eleven or twelve, the number who find their ideals among their acquaintances falls off rapidly, and historical characters rise to a maximum at or before the earliest teens. From eleven or twelve on into the middle teens contemporary ideals increase steadily. London children are more backward in this expansion of ideals than Americans, while girls' chose more acquaintance ideals at all ages than do boys. The expansion, these authors also trace largely to the study of history. The George Washington ideal, which leads all the rest by far and is greatly overworked, in contrast with the many heroes of equal rank found in England, pales soon, as imperfections are seen, and those now making history loom up. This is the normal age to be free from bondage to the immediate present, and this freedom is one measure of education. Bible heroes are chosen as ideals by only a very small percentage, mostly girls, far more characters being from fiction and mythology; where Jesus is chosen, His human is preferred to His divine side. Again, it would seem that teachers would be ideals, especially as many girls intend to teach, but they are generally unpopular as choices. In an ideal system they would be the first step in expansion from home ideals.

Military heroes and inventors play leading rôles in the choices of pubescent boys.

Girls at all school ages and increasingly up the grades prefer foreign ideals, to be the wife of a man of title, as aristocracies offer special opportunities for woman to shine, and life near the source of fashion is very attractive, at least up to sixteen. The saddest fact in these studies is that nearly half our American pubescent girls, or nearly three times as many as in England, choose male ideals, or would be men. Girls, too, have from six to fifteen times as many ideals as boys. In this significant fact we realize how modern woman has cut loose from all old moorings and is drifting with no destination and no anchor aboard. While her sex has multiplied in all lower and high school grades, its ideals are still too masculine. Text-books teach little about women. When a woman's Bible, history, course of study, etc., is proposed, her sex fears it may reduce her to the old servitude. While boys rarely, and then only when very young, choose female ideals, girls' preference for the life of the other sex sometimes reaches sixty and seventy per cent. The divorce between the life preferred and that demanded by the interests of the race is often absolute. Saddest and most unnatural of all is the fact that this state of things increases most rapidly during just those years when ideals of womanhood should be developed and become most dominant, till it seems as if the female character was threatened with disintegration. While statistics are not yet sufficient to be reliable on the subject, there is some indication that woman later slowly reverts toward ideals not only from her own sex but also from the circle of her own acquaintances.

The reasons for the choice of ideals are various and not yet well determined. Civic virtues certainly rise; material and utilitarian considerations do not seem to much, if at all, at adolescence, and in some data decline. Position, fame, honor, and general greatness increase rapidly, but moral qualities rise highest and also fastest just before and near puberty and continue to increase later yet. By these choices both sexes, but girls far most, show increasing admiration of ethical and social qualities. Artistic and intellectual traits also rise quite steadily from ten or eleven onward, but with no such rapidity, and reach no such height as military ability and achievement for boys. Striking in these studies is the rapid increase, especially from eight to fourteen, of the sense of historic time for historic persons. These long since dead are no longer spoken of as now living. Most of these choices are direct expressions of real differences of taste and character.

Property, Kline and France have defined as "anything that the individual may acquire which sustains and prolongs life, favors survival, and gives an advantage over opposing forces." Many animals and even insects store up food both for themselves and for their young. Very early in life children evince signs of ownership. Letourneau says that the notion of private property, which seems to us so natural, dawned late and slowly, and that common ownership was the rule among primitive people. Value is sometimes measured by use and sometimes by the work required to produce it. Before puberty, there is great eagerness to possess things that are of immediate service; but after its dawn, the desire of possession takes another form, and money for its own sake, which is at first rather an abstraction, comes to be respected or regarded as an object of extreme desire, because it is seen to be the embodiment of all values. . . .

SOCIAL JUDGMENT, CRONIES, SOLITUDE

The two following observations afford a glimpse of the development of moral judgments. From 1,000 boys and 1,000 girls of each age from six to sixteen who answered the question as to what should be done to a girl with a new box of paints who beautified the parlor chairs with them with a wish to please her mother, the following conclusion was drawn. Most of the younger children would whip the girl, but from fourteen on the number declines very rapidly. Few of the young children suggest explaining why it was wrong; while at twelve, 181, and at sixteen, 751 would explain. The motive of the younger children in punishment is revenge; with the older ones that of preventing a repetition of the act comes in; and higher and later comes the purpose of reform. With age comes also a marked distinction between the act and its motive and a sense of the girl's ignorance. Only the older children would suggest extracting a promise not to offend again. Thus with puberty comes a change of view-point from judging actions by results to judging by motives, and only the older ones see that wrong can be done if there are no bad consequences. There is also with increased years a great development of the quality of mercy. . . .

FIRST FORMS OF SPONTANEOUS SOCIAL ORGANIZATIONS

Gulick has studied the propensity of boys from thirteen on to consort in gangs, do "dawsies" and stumps, get into scrapes together, and fight and suffer for one another. The manners and customs of the gang are to build shanties or "hunkies," hunt with sling shots, build fires before huts in the woods, cook their squirrels and other game, play Indian, build tree-platforms, where they smoke or troop about some leader, who may have an old revolver. They find or excavate caves, or perhaps roof them over; the barn is a blockhouse or a battle-ship. In the early teens boys begin to use frozen snowballs or put pebbles in them, or perhaps have stone-fights between gangs than which no contiguous African tribes could be more hostile. They become toughs and tantalize policemen and peddlers; "lick" every enemy or even stranger found alone on their grounds; often smash windows; begin to use sticks and brass knuckles in their fights; pelt each other with green apples; carry shillalahs, or perhaps air-rifles. The more plucky arrange fights beforehand; rifle unoccupied houses; set ambushes for gangs with which they are at feud; perhaps have secrets and initiations where new boys are triced up by the legs and butted against trees and rocks. When painted for their Indian fights, they may grow so excited as to perhaps rush into the water or into the school-room yelling; mimic the violence of strikes; kindle dangerous bonfires; pelt policemen, and shout vile nicknames. . . .

From a study of 1,166 children's organizations described as a language lesson in school composition, Mr. Sheldon arrives at some interesting results. American children tend strongly to institutional activities, only about thirty per cent of all not having belonged to some such organization. Imitation plays a very important rôle, and girls take far more kindly than boys to societies organized by adults for their benefit. They are also more governed by adult and altruistic motives in forming their organizations, while boys are nearer to primitive man. Before ten comes the period of free spontaneous imitation of every form of adult institution. The child reproduces sympathetically miniature copies of the life around him. On a farm, his play is raking, threshing, building barns, or on the seashore he makes ships and harbors. In general, he plays family, store, church, and chooses officers simply because adults do. The feeling of caste, almost absent in the young, culminates about ten and declines thereafter. From ten to fourteen, however, associations assume a new character; boys especially cease to imitate adult organizations and tend to form social units characteristic of lower stages of human evolution—pirates, robbers, soldiers, lodges, and other savage reversionary combinations, where the strongest and boldest is the leader. They build huts, wear feathers and tomahawks as badges, carry knives and toy-pistols, make raids and sell the loot. Cowards alone, together they fear nothing. Their imagination is perhaps inflamed by flash literature and "penny-dreadfuls." Such associations often break out in decadent country communities where, with fewer and feebler offspring, lax notions of family discipline prevail and hoodlumism is the direct result of the passing of the rod. These barbaric societies have their place and give vigor; but if unreduced later, as in many unsettled portions of this country, a semi-savage state of society results. At twelve the predatory function is normally subordinated, and if it is not it becomes dangerous, because the members are no longer satisfied with mere play, but are stronger and abler to do harm, and the spice of danger and its fascination may issue in crime. Athleticism is now the form into which these wilder instincts can be best transmuted, and where they find harmless and even wholesome vent. Another change early in adolescence is the increased number of social, literary, and even philanthropic organizations and institutions for mutual help—perhaps against vice, for having a good time, or for holding picnics and parties. Altruism now begins to make itself felt as a motive.

STUDENT LIFE AND ORGANIZATIONS

Student life is perhaps the best of all fields, unworked though it is, for studying the natural history of adolescence. Its modern record is over eight hundred years old and it is marked with the signatures of every age, yet has essential features that do not vary. Cloister and garrison rules have never been enforced even in the hospice, bursa, inn, "house," "hall," or dormitory, and *in loco parentis* practises are impossible, especially with large numbers. The very word "school" means leisure, and in a world of toil and moil suggests paradise. Some have urged that *élite* youth, exempt from the struggle to live and left to the freedom of their own inclinations, might serve as a biological and ethnic compass to point out the goal of human destiny. But the spontaneous expressions of this best age and condition of life, with no other occupation than their own development, have shown reversions as often as progress. The rupture of home ties stimulates every wider vicarious expression of the social instinct. Each taste and trait can find congenial companionship in others and thus be stimulated to more intensity and self-consciousness. Very much that has been hitherto repressed in the adolescent soul is now reënforced by association and may become excessive and even aggressive. While many of the race-correlates of childhood are lost, those of this stage are more accessible in savage and subsavage life. Freedom is the native air and vital breath of student life. The sense of personal liberty is absolutely indispensable for moral maturity; and just as truth can not be found without the possibility of error, so the *posse non peccare* precedes the *non posse peccare*, and professors must make a broad application of the rule *abusus non tollit usum*. The student must have much freedom to be lazy, make his own minor morals, vent his disrespect for what he can see no use in, be among strangers to act himself out and form a personality of his own, be baptized with the revolutionary and skeptical spirit, and go to extremes at the age when excesses teach wisdom with amazing rapidity, if he is to become a true knight of the spirit and his own master. Ziegler frankly told German students that about one-tenth of them would be morally lost in this process, but insisted that on the whole more good was done than by restraint; for, he said, "youth is now in the stage of Schiller's bell when it was molten metal."

Of all safeguards I believe a rightly cultivated sense of honor is the most effective at this age. Sadly as the unwritten code of student honor in all lands needs revision, and partial, freaky, and utterly perverted, tainted and cowardly as it often is, it really means what Kant expressed in the sublime precept, "Thou canst because thou oughtest." Fichte said that *Faulheit, Feigheit,* and *Falschheit* were the three dishonorable things for students. If they would study the history and enter into the spirit of their own fraternities, they would often have keener and broader ideas of honor to which they are happily so sensitive. If professors made it always a point of honor to confess and never to conceal the limitation of their knowledge, would scorn all pretense of it, place credit for originality frankly where it belongs, teach no creeds they do not profoundly believe, or topics in which they are not interested, and withhold nothing from those who want the truth, they could from this vantage with more effect bring students to feel that the laziness that, while outwardly conforming, does no real inner work; that getting a diploma, as a professor lately said, an average student could do, on one hour's study a day; living beyond one's means, and thus imposing a hardship on parents greater than the talent of the son justifies; accepting stipends not needed, especially to the deprivation of those more needy; using dishonest ways of securing rank in studies or positions on teams, or social standing, are, one and all, not only ungentlemanly but cowardly and mean, and the axe would be laid at the root of the tree. Honor should impel students to go nowhere where they conceal their college, their fraternity, or even their name; to keep themselves immaculate from all contact with that class of women which, Ziegler states, brought twenty-five per cent of the students of the University of Berlin in a single year to physicians; to remember that other's sisters are as cherished as their own; to avoid those sins against confiding innocence which cry for vengeance, as did Valentine against Faust, and which strengthen the hate of social classes and make mothers and sisters seem tedious because low ideas of womanhood have been implanted, and which give a taste for mucky authors that reek with suggestiveness; and to avoid the waste of nerve substance and nerve weakness in ways which Ibsen and Tolstoi have described. These things are the darkest blot on the honor of youth.

Jane Addams

YOUTH IN THE CITY

Jane Addams (1860–1935) was the leading female social refomer of her age. She founded Hull-House in 1889. The first settlement house of its kind in America, Hull-House was committed to the improvement of life in the slums of Chicago. Her later career as a pacifist brought her the Nobel Peace Prize in 1931. Her faith that a reform of the city environment would bring about psychic reform among its inhabitants, especially the young ones, is almost touching in its love, gentility, simplicity, and hope. These virtues seem, to many, to belong to an age long ago, and to be no longer suited to the complexity and danger of our own. Then again, has America ever truly attempted to do what Miss Addams and others of her kind proposed?

NOTHING is more certain than that each generation longs for a reassurance as to the value and charm of life, and is secretly afraid lest it lose its sense of the youth of the earth. This is doubtless one reason why it so passionately cherishes its poets and artists who have been able to explore for themselves and to reveal to others the perpetual springs of life's self-renewal.

And yet the average man cannot obtain this desired reassurance through literature, nor yet through glimpses of earth and sky. It can come to him only through the chance embodiment of joy and youth which life itself may throw in his way. It is doubtless true that for the mass of men the message is never so unchallenged and so invincible as when embodied in youth itself. One generation after another has depended upon its young to equip it with gaiety and en-

From *The Spirit of Youth and the City Streets* by Jane Addams, pp. 3–21. Copyright 1909 by The Macmillan Company.

thusiasm, to persuade it that living is a pleasure, until men everywhere have anxiously provided channels through which this wine of life might flow, and be preserved for their delight. The classical city promoted play with careful solicitude, building the theater and stadium as it built the market place and the temple. The Greeks held their games so integral a part of religion and patriotism that they came to expect from their poets the highest utterances at the very moments when the sense of pleasure released the national life. In the medieval city the knights held their tourneys, the guilds their pageants, the people their dances, and the church made festival for its most cherished saints with gay street processions, and presented a drama in which no less a theme than the history of creation became a matter of thrilling interest. Only in the modern city have men concluded that it is no longer necessary for the municipality to provide for the insatiable desire for play. In so far as they have acted upon this conclusion, they have entered upon a most difficult and dangerous experiment; and this at the very moment when the city has become distinctly industrial, and daily labor is continually more monotonous and subdivided. We forget how new the modern city is, and how short the span of time in which we have assumed that we can eliminate public provision for recreation.

A further difficulty lies in the fact that this industrialism has gathered together multitudes of eager young creatures from all quarters of the earth as a labor supply for the countless factories and workshops, upon which the present industrial city is based. Never before in civilization have such numbers of young girls been suddenly released from the protection of the home and permitted to walk unattended upon city streets and to work under alien roofs; for the first time they are being prized more for their labor power than for their innocence, their tender beauty, their ephemeral gaiety. Society cares more for the products they manufacture than for their immemorial ability to reaffirm the charm of existence. Never before have such numbers of young boys earned money independently of the family life, and felt themselves free to spend it as they choose in the midst of vice deliberately disguised as pleasure.

This stupid experiment of organizing work and failing to organize play has, of course, brought about a fine revenge. The love of pleasure will not be denied, and when it has turned into all sorts of malignant and vicious appetites, then we, the middle aged, grow quite distracted and resort to all sorts of restrictive measures. We even try to dam up the sweet fountain itself because we are affrighted by these neglected streams; but almost worse than the restrictive measures is our apparent belief that the city itself has no obligation in the matter, an assumption upon which the modern city turns over to commercialism practically all the provisions for public recreation.

Quite as one set of men has organized the young people into industrial enterprises in order to profit from their toil, so another set of men and also of women, I am sorry to say, have entered the neglected field of recreation and have organized enterprises which make profit out of this invincible love of pleasure. . . .

In every city arise so-called "places"—"gin-palaces," they are called in fiction; in Chicago we euphemistically say merely "places,"—in which alcohol is dispensed, not to allay thirst, but, ostensibly to stimulate gaiety, it is sold really in order to empty pockets. Huge dance halls are opened to which hundreds of young people are attracted, many of whom stand wistfully outside a roped circle, for it requires five cents to procure within it for five minutes the sense of allurement and intoxication which is sold in lieu of innocent pleasure. These coarse and illicit merrymakings remind one of the unrestrained jollities of Restoration London, and they are indeed their direct descendants, properly commercialized, still confusing joy with lust, and gaiety with debauchery. Since the soldiers of Cromwell shut up the people's playhouses and destroyed their pleasure fields, the Anglo-Saxon city has turned over the provision for public recreation to the most evil-minded and the most unscrupulous members of the community. We see thousands of girls walking up and down the streets on a pleasant evening with no chance to catch a sight of pleasure even through a lighted window, save as these lurid places provide it. Apparently the modern city sees in these girls only two possibilities, both of them commercial: first, a chance to utilize by day their new and tender labor power in its factories and shops, and then another chance in the evening to extract from them their petty wages by pandering to their love of pleasure.

As these overworked girls stream along the street, the rest of us see only the self-conscious walk, the giggling speech, the preposterous clothing. And yet through the huge hat, with its wilderness of bedraggled feathers, the girl announces to the world that she is here. She demands attention to the fact of her existence, she states that she is ready to live, to take her place in the world. The most precious moment in human development is the young creature's assertion that he is unlike any other human being, and has an individual contribution to make to the world. The variation from the established type is at the root of all change, the only possible basis for progress, all that keeps life from growing unprofitably stale and repetitious.

Is it only the artists who really see these young creatures as they are—the artists who are themselves endowed with immortal youth? Is it our disregard of the artist's message which makes us so blind and so stupid, or are we so under the influence of our *Zeitgeist* that we can detect only commercial values in the young as well as in the old? It is as if our eyes were holden to the mystic beauty, the redemptive joy, the civic pride which these multitudes of young people might supply to our dingy towns.

The young creatures themselves piteously look all about them in order to find an adequate means of expression for their most precious message: One day a serious young man came to Hull-House with his pretty young sister who, he explained, wanted to go somewhere every single evening, "although she could only give the flimsy excuse that the flat was too little and too stuffy to stay in." In the difficult role of elder brother, he had done his best, stating that he had taken her "to all the missions in the neighborhood, that she had had a chance to listen to some awful good sermons and to some elegant hymns, but that some way she did not seem to care for the society of the best Christian people." The little sister reddened painfully under this cruel indictment and could offer no word of excuse, but a curious thing happened to me. Perhaps it was the phrase "the best Christian people," perhaps it was the delicate color of her flushing cheeks and her swimming eyes, but certain it is, that instantly and vividly there appeared to my mind the delicately tinted piece of wall in a Roman catacomb where the early Christians, through a dozen devices of spring flowers, skipping lambs and a shepherd tenderly guiding the young, had indelibly written down that the Christian message is one of inexpressible joy. Who is responsible for forgetting this message delivered by the "best Christian people" two thousand years ago? Who is to blame that the lambs, the little ewe lambs, have been so caught upon the brambles?

But quite as the modern city wastes this most valuable moment in the life of the girl, and drives into all sorts of absurd and obscure expressions her love and yearning towards the world in which she forecasts her destiny, so it often drives the boy into gambling and drinking in order to find his adventure.

Of Lincoln's enlistment of two and a half million soldiers, a very large number were under twenty-one, some of them under eighteen, and still others were mere children under fifteen. Even in those stirring times when patriotism and high resolve were at the flood, no one responded as did "the boys," and the great soul who yearned over them, who refused to shoot the sentinels who slept the sleep of childhood, knew, as no one else knew, the precious glowing stuff of which his army was made. But what of the millions of boys who are now searching for adventurous action, longing to fulfil the same high purpose?

One of the most pathetic sights in the public dance halls of Chicago is the number of young men, obviously honest young fellows from the country, who stand about vainly hoping to make the acquaintance of some "nice girl." They look eagerly up and down the rows of girls, many of whom are drawn to the hall by the same keen desire for pleasure and social intercourse which the lonely young men themselves feel.

One Sunday night at twelve o'clock I had occasion to go into a large public dance hall. As I was standing by the rail looking for the girl I had come to find, a young man approached me and quite simply asked me to introduce him to some "nice girl," saying that he did not know anyone there. On my replying that a public dance hall was not the best place in which to look for a nice girl, he said: "But I don't know any other place where there is a chance to meet any kind of a girl. I'm awfully lonesome since I came to Chicago." And then he added rather defiantly: "Some nice girls do come here! It's one of the best halls in town." He was voicing the "bitter loneliness" that many city men remember to have experienced during the first years after they had "come up to town." Occasionally the right sort of man and girl meet each other in these dance halls and the romance with such a tawdry beginning ends happily and respectably. But, unfortunately, mingled with the respectable young men seeking to form the acquaintance of young women through the only channel which is available to them, are many young fellows of evil purpose, and among the girls who have left their lonely boarding houses or rigid homes for a "little fling" are likewise women who openly desire to make money from the young men whom they meet, and back of it all is the desire to profit by the sale of intoxicating and "doctored" drinks.

Perhaps never before have the pleasures of the young and mature become so definitely separated as in the modern city. The public dance halls filled with frivolous and irresponsible young people in a feverish search for pleasure, are but a sorry substitute for the old dances on the village green in which all of the older people of the village participated. Chaperonage was not then a social duty but natural and inevitable, and the whole courtship period was guarded by the conventions and restraint which were taken as a matter of course and had developed through years of publicity and simple propriety.

The only marvel is that the stupid attempt to put the fine old wine of traditional country life into the new bottles of the modern town does not lead to disaster oftener than it does, and that the wine so long remains pure and sparkling.

We cannot afford to be ungenerous to the city in which we live without suffering the penalty which lack of fair interpretation always entails. Let us know the modern city in its weakness and wickedness, and then seek to rectify and purify it until it shall be free at least from the grosser temptations which now beset the young people who are living in its tenement houses and working in its factories. The mass of these young people are possessed of good intentions and they are equipped with a certain understanding of city life. This itself could be made a most valuable social instrument toward securing innocent recreation and better social organization. They are already serving the city in so far as it is honeycombed with mutual benefit societies, with "pleasure clubs," with organizations connected with churches and factories which are filling a genuine social need. And yet the whole apparatus for supplying pleasure is wretchedly inadequate and full of danger to whomsoever may approach it. Who is responsible for its inadequacy and dangers? We certainly cannot expect the fathers and mothers who have come to the city from farms or who have emigrated from other lands to appreciate or rectify these dangers. We cannot expect the young people themselves to cling to conventions which are totally unsuited to modern city conditions, nor yet to be equal to the task of forming new conventions through which this more agglomerate social life may express itself. Above all we cannot hope that they will understand the emotional force which seizes them and which, when it does not find the traditional line of domesticity, serves as a cancer in the very tissues of society and as a disrupter of the securest social bonds. No attempt is made to treat the manifestations of this fundamental instinct with dignity or to give it possible social utility. The spontaneous joy, the clamor for pleasure, the desire of the young people to appear finer and better and altogether more lovely than they really are, the idealization not only of each other but of the whole earth which they regard but as a theater for their noble exploits, the unworldly ambitions, the romantic hoax the make-believe world in which they live, if properly utilized, what might they not do to make our sordid cities more beautiful, more companionable? And yet at the present moment every city is full of young people who are utterly bewildered and uninstructed in regard to the basic experiences which must inevitably come to them, and which has varied, remote, and indirect expressions.

Even those who may not agree with the authorities who claim that it is this fundamental sex susceptibility which suffuses the world with its deepest meaning and beauty, and furnishes the momentum towards all art, will perhaps permit me to quote the classical expression of this view as set forth in that ancient and wonderful conversation between Socrates and the wise woman Diotima. Socrates asks: "What are they doing who show all this eagerness and heat which is called love? And what is the object they have in view? Answer me." Diotima replies: "I will teach you. The object which they have in view is birth in beauty, whether of body or soul. . . . For love, Socrates, is not as you imagine the love of the beautiful only . . . but the love of birth in beauty, because to the mortal creature generation is a sort of eternity and immortality."

To emphasize the eternal aspects of love is not of course an easy undertaking, even if we follow the clue afforded by the heart of every generous lover. His experience at least in certain moments tends to pull him on and out from the passion for one to an enthusiasm for that highest beauty and excellence of which the most perfect form is but an inadequate expression. Even the most loutish tenement-house youth vaguely feels this, and at least at rare intervals reveals it in his talk to his "girl." His memory unexpectedly brings hidden treasures to the surface of consciousness and he recalls the more delicate and tender experiences of his childhood and earlier youth. "I remember the time when my little sister died, that I rode out to the cemetery feeling that everybody in Chicago had moved away from the town to make room for that kid's funeral, everything was so darned lonesome and yet it was kind of peaceful too." Or, "I never had a chance to go into the country when I was a kid, but I remember one day when I had to deliver a package way out on the West Side, that I saw a flock of sheep in Douglas Park. I had never thought that a sheep could be anywhere but in a picture, and when I saw those big white spots on the green grass beginning to move and to turn into sheep, I felt exactly as if Saint Cecilia had come out of her frame over the organ and was walking in the park." Such moments come into the life of the most prosaic youth living in the most crowded quarters of the cities. What do we do to encourage and to solidify those moments, to make them come true in our dingy towns, to give them expression in forms of art?

We not only fail in this undertaking but even debase existing forms of art. We are informed by high authority that there is nothing in the environment to which youth so keenly responds as to music, and yet the streets, the vaudeville shows, the five-cent theaters are full of the most blatant and vulgar songs. The trivial and obscene words, the meaningless and flippant airs run through the heads of hundreds of young people for hours at a time while they are engaged in monotonous factory work. We totally ignore that ancient connection between music and morals which was so long insisted upon by philosophers as well as poets. The street music has quite broken away from all control, both of the educator and the patriot, and we have grown singularly careless in regard to its influence upon young people. Although we legislate against it in saloons because of its dangerous influence there, we constantly permit music on the street to incite that which should be controlled, to degrade that which should be exalted, to make sensuous that which might be lifted into the realm of the higher imagination.

Our attitude towards music is typical of our carelessness towards all those things which make for common joy and for the restraints of higher civilization on the streets. It is as if our cities had not yet developed a sense of responsibility in regard to the life of the streets, and continually forget that recreation is stronger than vice, and that recreation alone can stifle the lust for vice.

Perhaps we need to take a page from the philosophy of the Greeks to whom the world of fact was also the world of the ideal, and to whom the realization of what ought to be, involved not the destruction of what was, but merely its perfecting upon its own lines. To the Greeks virtue was not a hard conformity to a law felt as alien to the natural character, but a free expression of the inner life. To treat thus the fundamental susceptibility of sex which now so bewilders the street life and drives young people themselves into all sorts of difficulties, would mean to loosen it from the things of sense and to link it to the affairs of the imagination. It would mean to fit to this gross and heavy stuff the wings of the mind, to scatter from it "the clinging mud of banality and vulgarity," and to speed it on through our city streets amid spontaneous laughter, snatches of lyric song, the recovered forms of old dances, and the traditional rondels of merry games. It would thus bring charm and beauty to the prosaic city and connect it subtly with the arts of the past as well as with the vigor and renewed life of the future.

Randolph Bourne

YOUTH AND LIFE

Youth and Life was published when its author, Randolph Bourne (1886–1918), was in his mid-twenties. His short, intense life was ended by an attack of influenza brought back by soldiers returning from the World War he so detested. Bourne's major contribution was as an essayist, and *Youth and Life* was his first volume of essays. He was on the staff of *New Republic* from its birth in 1914. He fought for John Dewey's educational ideas, for peace, for radicalism and experimentation, and above all for faith in the possibilities of youth. In youth, he was sure, would come the reconstitution of society which he felt was desperately needed. Too radical for his own time, he could very easily become a culture-hero to some of the young people of the 1970's.

HOW shall I describe Youth, the time of contradictions and anomalies? The fiercest radicalisms, the most dogged conservatisms, irrepressible gayety, bitter melancholy,—all these moods are equally part of that showery springtime of life. One thing, at least, it clearly is: a great, rich rush and flood of energy. It is as if the store of life had been accumulating through the slow, placid years of childhood, and suddenly the dam had broken and the waters rushed out, furious and uncontrolled, before settling down into the quieter channels of middle life. The youth is suddenly seized with a poignant consciousness of being alive, which is quite wanting to the naïve unquestioning existence of the child. He finds himself overpoweringly urged toward self-expression. Just as the baby, born into a "great, blooming, buzzing confusion," and attracted by every movement, every color, every sound, kicks madly in response in all directions, and only gradually gets his movements co-ordinated into the orderly and precise movements of his elders,—so the youth suddenly born into a confusion of ideas and appeals and traditions responds in the most chaotic way to this new spiritual world, and only gradually learns to find his way about in it, and get his thoughts and feelings into some kind of order.

Fortunate the young man who does not make his entrance into too wide a world. And upon the width and depth of that new world will depend very much whether his temperament is to be radical or conservative, adventurous or conventional. For it is one of the surprising things about youth that it can so easily be the most conservative of all ages. Why do we suppose that youth is always radical? At no age are social properties more strictly observed, and Church, State, law, and order, more rigorously defended. But I like to think that youth is conservative only when its spiritual force has been spent too early, or when the new world it enters into is found, for some reason, to be rather narrow and shallow. It is so often the urgent world of pleasure that first catches the eye of youth; its flood of life is drawn off in that direction; the boy may fritter away his precious birthright in pure lightness of heart and animal spirits. And it is only too true that this type of youth is transitory. Pleasure contrives to burn itself out very quickly, and youth finds itself left prematurely with the ashes of middle age. But if, in some way, the flood of life is checked in the direction of pleasure, then it bursts forth in another,—in the direction of ideals; then we say that the boy is radical. Youth is always turbulent, but the momentous difference is whether it shall be turbulent in passion or in enthusiasm. Nothing is so pathetic as the young man who spends his spiritual force too early, so that when the world of ideals is presented to him, his force being spent, he can only grasp at second-hand ideals and mouldy formulas.

This is the great divergence which sets youth not only against old age, but against youth itself: the undying spirit of youth that seems to be fed by an unquenchable fire, that does not burn itself out but seems to grow steadier and steadier as life goes on, against the fragile, quickly tarnished type that passes relentlessly into middle life. At twenty-five I find myself full of the wildest radicalisms, and look with dismay at my childhood friends who are already settled down, have achieved babies and responsibilities, and have somehow got ten years beyond me in a day. And this divergence shows itself in a thousand different ways. It may be a temptation to a world of pleasure, it may be a sheltering from the stimulus of ideas, or even a sluggish temperament, that separates traditional and adventurous youth, but fundamentally it is a question of how youth takes the world. And here I find that I can no longer drag the traditional youth along with me in this paper. There are many of him, I know, but I do not like him, and I know nothing about him. Let us rather look at the way radical youth grows into and meets the world.

From the state of "the little child, to whom the sky is a roof of blue, the world a screen of opaque and disconnected facts, the home a thing eternal, and 'being good' just simple obedience to unquestioned authority," one steps suddenly into that "vast world of adult perception, pierced deep by flaring searchlights of partial understanding."

The child has an utter sense of security; childhood is unconscious even that it is alive. It has neither fears nor anxieties, because it is incorrigibly poetical. It idealizes everything that it touches. It is unfair, perhaps, to blame parents and teachers, as we sometimes do in youth, for consciously biasing our child-minds in a falsely idealistic direction; for the child will infallibly idealize even his poorest of experiences. His broken glimpses and anticipations of his own future show him everything that is orderly, happy, and beautifully fit. He sees his grown-up life as old age, itself a sort of reversed childhood, sees its youth. The passing of childhood into youth is, therefore, like suddenly being turned from the cosy comfort of a warm fireside to shift for one's self in the world. Life becomes in a moment a process of seeking and searching. It appears as a series of blind alleys, all equally and magnificently alluring, all equally real and possible. Youth's thirst for experience is simply that it wants to be everything, do everything and have everything that is presented to its imagination. Youth has suddenly become conscious of life. It has eaten of the tree of the knowledge of good and evil.

As the world breaks in on a boy with its crashing thunder, he has a feeling of expansion, of sudden wisdom and sudden care. The atoms of things seem to be disintegrating around him. Then come the tearings and the grindings and the wrenchings, and in that conflict the radical or the poet is made. If the youth takes the struggle easily, or if his guardian angels have arranged things so that there is no struggle, then he becomes of that conservative stripe that we have renounced above. But if he takes it hard,—if his struggles are not only with outward material conditions, but also with inner spiritual ones,—then he is likely to achieve that gift of the gods, perpetual youth. The great paradox is that it is the sleek and easy who are prematurely and permanently old. Struggle brings youth rather than old age.

In this struggle, thus beset with problems and crises, all calling for immediate solution, youth battles its way into a sort of rationalization. Out of its inchoateness emerges a sort of order; the disturbing currents of impulse are gradually resolved into a character. But it is essential that that resolution be a natural and not a forced one. I always have a suspicion of boys who talk of "planning their lives." I feel that they have won a precocious maturity in some illegitimate way. For to most of us youth is so imperious that those who can escape the hurly-burly and make a sudden leap into the prudent, quiet waters of life seem to have missed youth altogether. And I do not mean here the hurly-burly of passion so much as of ideals. It seems so much better, as well as more natural, to expose one's self to the full fury of the spiritual elements, keeping only one purpose in view,—to be strong and sincere,—than to pick one's way cautiously along.

The old saying is the truest philosophy of youth: "Seek ye first the Kingdom of God, and all these things shall be added unto you." How impossible for a youth who is really young to plan his life consciously! This process that one sometimes sees of cautiously becoming acquainted with various ideas and systems, and then choosing deliberately those that will be best adapted to a concerted plan, is almost uncanny. This confidence in one's immunity to ideas that would tend to disarrange the harmony of the scheme is mystifying and irritating. Youth talks of "getting" or "accepting" ideas! But youth does not get ideas,—ideas get him! He may try to keep himself in a state of spiritual health, but that is the only immunity he can rely upon. He cannot really tell what idea or appeal is going to seize upon him next and make off with him.

We speak as if falling in love were a unique phase in the life of youth. It is rather the pattern and symbol of a youth's whole life. This sudden, irresistible seizure of enthusiasm that he cannot explain, that he does not want to explain, what is it but the aspect of all his experience? The youth sees a pretty face, reads a noble book, hears a stirring appeal for a cause, meets a charming friend, gets fired with the concept of science, or of social progress, becomes attracted to a profession,—the emotion that fixes his enthusiasm and lets out a flood of emotion in that direction, and lifts him into another world, is the same in every case. Youth glories in the sudden servitude, is content to let the new master lead wherever he will; and is as surprised as any one at the momentous and startling results. Youth is vulnerable at every point. Prudence is really a hateful thing in youth. A prudent youth is prematurely old. It is infinitely better, I repeat, for a boy to start ahead in life in a spirit of moral adventure, trusting for sustenance to what he may find by the wayside, than to lay in laboriously, before starting, a stock of principles for life, and burden himself so heavily for the journey that he dare not, and indeed cannot, leave his pack unguarded by the roadside to survey the fair prospects on either hand. Youth at its best is this constant susceptibility to the new, this constant eagerness to try experiments.

It is here that youth's quarrel with the elder generation comes in. There is no scorn so fierce as that of youth for the inertia of older men. The lack of adjustment to the ideas of youth's elders and betters, one of the permanent tragedies of life, is certainly the most sensational aspect of youth. That the inertia of the older people is wisdom, and not impotence, is a theory that you will never induce youth to believe for an instant. The stupidity and cruelties of their management of the world fill youth with an intolerant rage. In every contact with its elders, youth finds them saying, in the words of Kipling: —

> We shall not acknowledge that old
> stars fade and alien planets arise,
> That the sere bush buds or the desert
> blooms or the ancient well-head
> dries,
> Or any new compass wherewith new
> men adventure 'neath new skies.

Youth sees with almost a passionate despair its plans and dreams and enthusiasms, that it knows so well to be right and true and noble, brushed calmly aside, not because of any sincere searching into their practicability, but because of the timidity and laziness of the old, who sit in the saddle and ride mankind. And nothing torments youth so much as to have this inertia justified on the ground of experience. For youth thinks that it sees through this sophism of "experience." It sees in it an all-inclusive attempt to give the world a character, and excuse the older generation for the mistakes and failures which it has made. What is this experience, youth asks, but a slow accretion of inhibitions, a learning, at its best, not to do again something which ought not to have been done in the first place?

Old men cherish a fond delusion that there is something mystically valuable in mere quantity of experience. Now the fact is, of course, that it is the young people who have all the really valuable experience. It is they who have constantly to face new situations, to react constantly to new aspects of life, who are getting the whole beauty and terror and cruelty of the world in its fresh and undiluted purity. It is only the interpretation of this first collision with life that is worth anything. For the weakness of experience is that it so soon gets stereotyped; without new situations and crises it becomes so conventional as to be practically unconscious. Very few people get any really new experience after they are twenty-five, unless there is a real change of environment. Most older men live only in the experience of their youthful years.

If we get few ideas after we are twenty-five, we get few ideals after we are twenty. A man's spiritual fabric is woven by that time, and his "experience," if he keeps true to himself, consists simply in broadening and enriching it, but not in adding to it in arithmetical proportion as the years roll on, in the way that the wise teachers of youth would have us believe.

But few men remain quite true to themselves. As their youthful ideals come into contact with the harshnesses of life, the brightest succumb and go to the wall. And the hardy ones that survive contain all that is vital in the future experience of the man,—so that the ideas of older men seem often the curious parodies or even burlesques of what must have been the cleaner and more potent ideas of their youth. Older people seem often to be resting on their oars, drifting on the spiritual current that youth has set going in life, or "coasting" on the momentum that the strong push of youth has given them.

There is no great gulf between youth and middle age, as there is between childhood and youth. Adults are little more than grown-up children. This is what makes their arrogance so insulting,—the assumption that they have acquired any impartiality or objectivity of outlook, and have any better standards for judging life. Their ideas are wrong, and grow progressively more wrong as they become older. Youth, therefore, has no right to be humble. The ideals it forms will be the highest it will ever have, the insight the clearest, the ideas the most stimulating. The best that it can hope to do is to conserve those resources, and keep its flame of imagination and daring bright.

Therefore, it is perhaps unfair to say that the older generation rules the world. Youth rules the world, but only when it is no longer young. It is a tarnished, travestied youth that is in the saddle in the person of middle age. Old age lives in the delusion that it has improved and rationalized its youthful ideas by experience and stored-up wisdom, when all it has done is to damage them more or less—usually more. And the tragedy of life is that the world is run by these damaged ideals. That is why our ideas are always a generation behind our actual social conditions. Press, pulpit, and bar teem with the radicalisms of thirty years ago. The dead hand of opinions formed in their college days clutches our leaders and directs their activities in this new and strangely altered physical and spiritual environment. Hence grievous friction, maladjustment, social war. And the faster society moves, the more terrific is the divergence between what is actually going on and what public opinion thinks is actually going on. It is only the young who are actually contemporaneous; they interpret what they see freshly and without prejudice; their vision is always the truest, and their interpretation always the justest.

Youth does not simply repeat the errors and delusions of the past, as the elder generation with a tolerant cynicism likes to think; it is ever laying the foundations for the future. What it thinks so wildly now will be orthodox gospel thirty years hence. The ideas of the young are the living, the potential ideas; those of the old, the dying, or the already dead. This is why it behooves youth to be not less radical, but even more radical, than it would naturally be. It must be not simply contemporaneous, but a generation ahead of the times, so that when it comes into control of the world, it will be precisely right and coincident with the conditions of the world as it finds them. If the youth of to-day could really achieve this miracle, they would have found the secret of "perpetual youth."

In this conflict between youth and its elders, youth is the incarnation of reason pitted against the rigidity of tradition. Youth puts the remorseless questions to everything that is old and established,—Why? What is this thing good for? And when it gets the mumbled, evasive answers of the defenders, it applies its own fresh, clean spirit of reason to institutions, customs, and ideas, and, finding them stupid, inane, or poisonous, turns instinctively to overthrow them and build in their place the things with which its visions teem.

"This constant return to purely logical activity with each generation keeps the world supplied with visionaries and reformers, that is to say, with saviors and leaders. New movements are born in young minds, and lack of experience enables youth eternally to recall civilization to sound bases. The passing generation smiles and cracks its weather-worn jokes about youthful effusions: but this new, ever-hopeful, ever-daring, ever-doing, youthful enthusiasm, ever returning to the logical bases of religion, ethics, politics, business, art, and social life,—this is the salvation of the world."

This was the youthful radicalism of Jesus, and his words sound across the ages "calling civilization ever back to sound bases." With him, youth eternally reproaches the ruling generation,—"O ye of little faith!" There is so much to be done in the world; so much could be done if you would only dare! You seem to be doing so little to cure the waste and the muddle and the lethargy all around you. Don't you really care, or are you only faint-hearted? If you do not care, it must be because you do not know; let us point out to you the shockingness of exploitation, and the crass waste of human personality all around you in this modern world. And if you are faint-hearted, we will supply the needed daring and courage, and lead you straight to the attack.

These are the questions and challenges that the youth puts to his elders, and it is their shifty evasions and quibblings that confound and dishearten him. He becomes intolerant, and can see all classes in no other light than that of accomplices in a great crime. If they only knew! Swept along himself in an irrationality of energy, he does not see the small part that reason plays in the intricate social life, and only gradually does he come to view life as a "various and splendid disorder of forces," and exonerate weak human nature from some of its heavy responsibility. But this insight brings him to appreciate and almost to reverence the forces of science and conscious social progress that are grappling with that disorder, and seeking to tame it.

Youth is the leaven that keeps all these questioning, testing attitudes fermenting in the world. If it were not for this troublesome activity of youth, with its hatred of sophisms and glosses, its insistence on things as they are, society would die from sheer decay. It is the policy of the older generation as it gets adjusted to the world to hide away the unpleasant things where it can, or preserve a conspiracy of silence and an elaborate pretense that they do not exist. But meanwhile the sores go on festering just the same. Youth is the drastic antiseptic. It will not let its elders cry peace, where there is no peace. Its fierce sarcasms keep issues alive in the world until they are settled right. It drags skeletons from closets and insists that they be explained. No wonder the older generation fears and distrusts the younger. Youth is the avenging Nemesis on its trail. "It is young men who provide the logic, decision, and enthusiasm necessary to relieve society of the crushing burden that each generation seeks to roll upon the shoulders of the next."

Our elders are always optimistic in their views of the present, pessimistic in their views of the future; youth is pessimistic toward the present and gloriously hopeful for the future. And it is this hope which is the lever of progress,—one might say, the only lever of progress. The lack of confidence which the ruling generation feels in the future leads to that distrust of the machinery of social reform and social organization, or the use of means for ends, which is so characteristic of it to-day. Youth is disgusted with such sentimentality. It can never understand that curious paralysis which seizes upon its elders in the face of urgent social innovations; that refusal to make use of a perfectly definite programme or administrative scheme which has worked elsewhere. Youth concludes that its elders discountenance the machinery, the means, because they do not really believe in the end, and adds another count to the indictment.

Youth's attitude is really the scientific attitude. Do not be afraid to make experiments, it says. You cannot tell how anything will work until you have tried it. Suppose science confined its interests to those things that have been tried and tested in the world, how far should we get? It is possible indeed that your experiments may produce by accident a social explosion, but we do not give up chemistry because occasionally a wrong mixture of chemicals blows up a scientist in a laboratory, or medical research because an investigator contracts the disease he is fighting. The whole philosophy of youth is summed up in the word, Dare! Take chances and you will attain! The world has nothing to lose but its chains—and its own soul to gain!

I have dwelt too long on the conflicts

of youth. For it has also its still places, where it becomes introspective and thinks about its destiny and the meaning of its life. In our artificial civilization many young people at twenty-five are still on the threshold of activity. As one looks back, then, over eight or nine years, one sees a panorama of seemingly formidable length. So many crises, so many startling surprises, so many vivid joys and harrowing humiliations and disappointments, that one feels startlingly old; one wonders if one will ever feel so old again. And in a sense, youth at twenty-five is older than it will ever be again. For if time is simply a succession of incidents in our memory, we seem to have an eternity behind us. Middle-aged people feel no such appalling stretch of time behind them. The years fade out one by one; often the pressure of life leaves nothing of reality or value but the present moment. Some of youth's elders seem to enjoy almost a new babyhood, while youth has constantly with it in all its vividness and multifariousness that specious wealth of abrupt changes, climaxes and disillusions that have crowded the short space of its life.

We often envy the sunny noon of the thirties and forties. These elders of ours change so little that they seem to enjoy an endless summer of immortality. They are so placid, so robust, so solidly placed in life, seemingly so much further from dissolution than we. Youth seems curiously fragile. Perhaps it is because all beauty has something of the precarious and fleeting about it. A beautiful girl seems too delicate and fine to weather a long life; she must be burning away too fast. This wistfulness and haunting pathos of life is very real to youth. It feels the rush of time past it. Only youth can sing of the passing glory of life, and then only in its full tide. The older people's lament for the vanished days of youth may be orthodox, but it rings hollow. For our greatest fears are those of presentiment, and youth is haunted not only by the feeling of past change, but by the presentiment of future change.

Middle age has passed the waters; it has become static and placid. Its wistfulness for youth is unreal, and a forced sentimentality. In the same breath that it cries for its youth it mocks at youth's preoccupation with the thought of death. The lugubrious harmonies of young poets are a favorite joke. But the feeling of the precariousness of life gives the young man an intimate sense of its preciousness; nothing shocks him quite so much as that it should be ruthlessly and instantly snatched away. Middle age has acclimated itself to the earth, has settled down familiarly in it, and is easily befooled into thinking that it will live here forever, just as, when we are settled comfortably in a house, we cannot conceive ourselves as ever being dislodged. But youth takes a long time to get acclimated. It has seen so many mysteries and dangers about it, that the presence of the Greatest Mystery and the Greatest Danger must be the most portentous of things to it.

It is this sense of the preciousness of his life, perhaps, that makes a youth so impatient of discipline. Youth can never think of itself as anything but master of things. Its visions are a curious blend of devotion and egotism. Its enthusiasm for a noble cause is apt to be all mixed up with a picture of itself leading the cohorts to victory. The youth never sees himself as a soldier in the ranks, but as the leader, bringing in some long-awaited change by a brilliant *coup d'état*, or writing and speaking words of fire that win a million hearts at a stroke. And he fights shy of discipline in smaller matters. He does not submit willingly to a course of work that is not immediately appealing, even for the sake of the glorious final achievement. Fortunate it is for the young man, perhaps, that there are so many organs of coercion all ready in the world for him,—economic need, tradition, and subtle influence of family ambition,—to seize him and nail him fast to some profession or trade or activity, before he is aware, or has time to protest or draw back!

It is another paradox of youth that, with all its fine enthusiasm, it should accomplish so little. But this seeming aimlessness of purpose is the natural result of that deadly fear of having one's wings clipped by discipline. Infinitely finer, it seems to youth, is it to soar freely in the air, than to run on a track along the ground! And perhaps youth is right. In his intellectual life, the young man's scorn for the pedantic and conventional amounts almost to an obsession. It is only the men of imagination and inspiration that he will follow at all. But most of these professors, these lawyers, these preachers,—what has been their training and education, he says, but a gradual losing of the grip of life, a slow withdrawing into an ideal world of phrases and concepts and artificial attitudes? Their thought sees like the endless spinning out of a spider's web, or like the camel living upon the fat of his own hump. The youth fears this sophistication of thought as he would fear losing his soul. And this seeming perversity toward discipline is often simply his refusal to let a system submerge his own real and direct reactions to his observation and experience.

And yet as he studies more and more, and acquires a richer material for thought, a familiarity with words, and a skill in handling them, he can see the insidious temptation that comes to thinking men to move all their spiritual baggage over into that fascinating unreal world. And he admires almost with reverence the men who have been able to break through the terrible crust, and have got their thinking into close touch with life again; or, best of all, those who have kept their thinking constantly checked up with life, and are occupied with interpreting what they see about them. Youth will never be able to see that this is not the only true and right business of thought.

It is the glory of the present age that in it one can be young. Our times give no check to the radical tendencies of youth. On the contrary, they give the directest stimulation. A muddle of a world and a wide outlook combine to inspire us to the bravest of radicalisms. Great issues have been born in the last century, and are now loose in the world. There is a radical philosophy that illuminates our environment, gives us terms in which to express what we see, and coordinates our otherwise aimless reactions.

In this country, it is true, where a certain modicum of free institutions, and a certain specious enfranchisement of the human spirit have been achieved, youth may be blinded and drugged into an acquiescence in conditions, and its enthusiasm may easily run into a glorification of the present. In the face of the more urgent ideals that are with us, it may be inspired by vague ideas of "liberty," or "the rights of man," and fancy it is truly radical when it is but living on the radicalisms of the past. Our political thought moves so slowly here that even our radicalism is traditional. We breathe in with the air about us the belief that we have attained perfection, and we do not examine things with our own eyes.

But more and more of the clear-sighted youth are coming to see the appalling array of things that still need to be done. The radical young man of today has no excuse for veering round to the conservative standpoint. Cynicism cannot touch him. For it is the beauty of the modern radical philosophy that the worse the world treats a man, the more it convinces him of the truth of his radical interpretation of it. Disillusion comes, not through hard blows, but by the insidious sappings of worldly success. And there never was a time when there were so many radical young people who cared little about that worldly success.

The secret of life is then that this fine youthful spirit should never be lost. Out of the turbulence of youth should come this fine precipitate—a sane, strong, aggressive spirit of daring and doing. It must be a flexible, growing spirit, with a hospitality to new ideas, and a keen insight into experience. To keep one's reactions warm and true, is to have found the secret of perpetual youth, and perpetual youth is salvation.

John Dewey

EDUCATION AS GROWTH

Many of the ideas of John Dewey (1859–1952) have become commonplace in modern American life, whether in philosophy, psychology, or, above all, education. But we should not forget that his *Democracy and Education* (1916) was inextricably connected with the new conceptions of youth that were a significant part of the consciousness of the Progressive generation. The following chapter on "Education as Growth" from *Democracy and Education* contains the theory of child development on which Dewey's educational reforms were based.

THE CONDITIONS OF GROWTH

IN directing the activities of the young, society determines its own future in determining that of the young. Since the young at a given time will at some later date compose the society of that period, the latter's nature will largely turn upon the direction children's activities were given at an earlier period. This cumulative movement of action toward a later result is what is meant by growth.

The primary condition of growth is immaturity. This may seem to be a mere truism—saying that a being can develop only in some point in which he is undeveloped. But the prefix 'im' of the word immaturity means something positive, not a mere void or lack. It is noteworthy that the terms 'capacity' and 'potentiality' have a double meaning, one sense being negative, the other positive. Capacity may denote mere receptivity, like the capacity of a quart measure. We may mean by potentiality a merely dormant or quiescent state—a capacity to become something different under external influences. But we also mean by capacity an ability, a power; and by potentiality potency, force. Now when we say that immaturity means the possibility of growth, we are not referring to absence of powers which may exist at a later time; we express a *force* positively present—the *ability* to develop.

Our tendency to take immaturity as mere lack, and growth as something which fills up the gap between the immature and the mature is due to regarding childhood *comparatively*, instead of intrinsically. We treat it simply as a privation because we are measuring it by adulthood as a fixed standard. This fixes attention upon what the child has not, and will not have till he becomes a man. This comparative standpoint is legitimate enough for some purposes, but if we make it final, the question arises whether we are not guilty of an overweening presumption. Children, if they could express themselves articulately and sincerely, would tell a different tale; and there is excellent adult authority for the conviction that for certain moral and intellectual purposes adults must become as little children.

The seriousness of the assumption of the negative quality of the possibilities of immaturity is apparent when we reflect that it sets up as an ideal and standard a static end. The fulfillment of growing is taken to mean an accomplished growth: that is to say, an Ungrowth, something which is no longer growing. The futility of the assumption is seen in the fact that every adult resents the imputation of having no further possibilities of growth; and so far as he finds that they are closed to him mourns the fact as evidence of loss, instead of falling back on the achieved as adequate manifestation of power. Why an unequal measure for child and man?

Taken absolutely, instead of comparatively, immaturity designates a positive force or ability,—the *power* to grow. We do not have to draw out or educe positive activities from a child, as some educational doctrines would have it. Where there is life, there are already eager and impassioned activities. Growth is not something done to them; it is something they do. The positive and constructive aspect of possibility gives the key to understanding the two chief traits of immaturity, dependence and plasticity. (1) It sounds absurd to hear dependence spoken of as something positive, still more absurd as a power. Yet if helplessness were all there were in dependence, no development could ever take place. A merely impotent being has to be carried, forever, by others. The fact that dependence is accompanied by growth in ability, not by an ever increasing lapse into parasitism, suggests that it is already something constructive. Being merely sheltered by others would not promote growth. For (2) it would only build a wall around impotence. With reference to the physical world, the child is helpless. He lacks at birth and for a long time thereafter power to make his way physically, to make his own living. If he had to do that by himself, he would hardly survive an hour. On this side his helplessness is almost complete. The young of the brutes are immeasurably his superiors. He is physically weak and not able to turn the strength which he possesses to coping with the physical environment.

1. The thoroughgoing character of this helplessness suggests, however, some compensating power. The relative ability of the young of brute animals to adapt themselves fairly well to physical conditions from an early period suggests the fact that their life is not intimately bound up with the life of those about them. They are compelled, so to speak, to have physical gifts because they are lacking in social gifts. Human infants, on the other hand, can get along with physical incapacity just because of their social capacity. We sometimes talk and think as if they simply happened to be *physically* in a social environment; as if social forces exclusively existed in the adults who take care of them, they being passive recipients. If it were said that children are themselves marvelously endowed with *power* to enlist the cooperative attention of others, this would be thought to be a backhanded way of saying that others are marvelously attentive to the needs of children. But observation shows that children are gifted with an equipment of the first order for social intercourse. Few grown-up persons retain all of the flexible and sensitive ability of children to vibrate sympathetically with the attitudes and doings of those about them. Inattention to physical things (going with incapacity to control them) is accompanied by a corresponding intensification of interest and attention as to the doings of people. The native mechanism of the child and his impulses all tend to facile social responsiveness. The statement that children, before adolescence, are egotistically self-centered, even if it were true, would not contradict the truth of this statement. It would simply indicate that their social responsiveness is employed on their own behalf, not that it does not exist. But the statement is not true as a matter of fact. The facts which are cited in support of the alleged pure egoism of children really show the intensity and directness with which they go to their mark. If the ends which form the mark seem narrow and selfish to adults, it is only because adults (by means of a similar engrossment in their day) have mastered these ends, which have consequently ceased to interest them. Most of the remainder of children's alleged native egoism is simply an egoism which runs counter to an adult's egoism. To a grown-up person who is too absorbed in his own affairs

to take an interest in children's affairs, children doubtless seem unreasonably engrossed in *their* own affairs.

From a social standpoint, dependence denotes a power rather than a weakness; it involves interdependence. There is always a danger that increased personal independence will decrease the social capacity of an individual. In making him more self-reliant, it may make him more self-sufficient; it may lead to aloofness and indifference. It often makes an individual so insensitive in his relations to others as to develop an illusion of being really able to stand and act alone—an unnamed form of insanity which is responsible for a large part of the remediable suffering of the world.

2. The specific adaptability of an immature creature for growth constitutes his *plasticity*. This is something quite different from the plasticity of putty or wax. It is not a capacity to take on change of form in accord with external pressure. It lies near the pliable elasticity by which some persons take on the color of their surroundings while retaining their own bent. But it is something deeper than this. It is essentially the ability to learn from experience; the power to retain from one experience something which is of avail in coping with the difficulties of a later situation. This means power to modify actions on the basis of the results of prior experiences, the power to *develop dispositions*. Without it, the acquisition of habits is impossible.

It is a familiar fact that the young of the higher animals, and especially the human young, have to *learn* to utilize their instinctive reactions. The human being is born with a greater number of instinctive tendencies than other animals. But the instincts of the lower animals perfect themselves for appropriate action at an early period after birth, while most of those of the human infant are of little account just as they stand. An original specialized power of adjustment secures immediate efficiency, but, like a railway ticket, it is good for one route only. A being who, in order to use his eyes, ears, hands, and legs, has to experiment in making varied combinations of their reactions, achieves a control that is flexible and varied. A chick, for example, pecks accurately at a bit of food in a few hours after hatching. This means that definite co-ordinations of activities of the eyes in seeing and of the body and head in striking are perfected in a few trials. An infant requires about six months to be able to gauge with approximate accuracy the action in reaching which will co-ordinate with his visual activities; to be able, that is, to tell whether he can reach a seen object and just how to execute the reaching. As a result, the chick is limited by the relative perfection of its original endowment. The infant has the advantage of the *multitude* of instinctive tentative reactions and of the experiences that accompany them, even though he is at a temporary disadvantage because they cross one another. In learning an action, instead of having it given ready-made, one of necessity learns to vary its factors, to make varied combinations of them, according to change of circumstances. A possibility of continuing progress is opened up by the fact that in learning one act, methods are developed good for use in other situations. Still more important is the fact that the human being acquires a habit of learning. He learns to learn.

The importance for human life of the two facts of dependence and variable control has been summed up in the doctrine of the significance of prolonged infancy. This prolongation is significant from the standpoint of the adult members of the group, as well as from that of the young. The presence of dependent and learning beings is a stimulus to nurture and affection. The need for constant continued care was probably a chief means in transforming temporary cohabitations into permanent unions. It certainly was a chief influence in forming habits of affectionate and sympathetic watchfulness; that constructive interest in the well-being of others which is essential to associated life. Intellectually, this moral development meant the introduction of many new objects of attention; it stimulated foresight and planning for the future. Thus there is a reciprocal influence. Increasing complexity of social life requires a longer period of infancy in which to acquire the needed powers; this prolongation of dependence means prolongation of plasticity, or power of acquiring variable and novel modes of control. Hence it provides a further push to social progress.

HABITS AS EXPRESSIONS OF GROWTH

We have already noted that plasticity is the capacity to retain and carry over from prior experience factors which modify subsequent activities. This signifies the capacity to acquire habits, or develop definite dispositions. We have now to consider the salient features of habits. In the first place, a habit is a form of executive skill, of efficiency in doing. A habit means an ability to use natural conditions as means to ends. It is an active control of the environment through control of the organs of action. We are perhaps apt to emphasize the control of the body at the expense of control of the environment. We think of walking, talking, playing the piano, the specialized skills characteristic of the etcher, the surgeon, the bridge-builder, as if they were simply ease, deftness, and accuracy on the part of the organism. They are that, of course; but the measure of the value of these qualities lies in the economical and effective control of the environment which they secure. To be able to walk is to have certain properties of nature at our disposal—and so with all other habits.

Education is not infrequently defined as consisting in the acquisition of those habits that effect an adjustment of an individual and his environment. The definition expresses an essential phase of growth. But it is essential that adjustment be understood in its active sense of *control* of means for achieving ends. If we think of a habit simply as a change wrought in the organism, ignoring the fact that this change consists in ability to effect subsequent changes in the environment, we shall be lead to think of 'adjustment' as a conformity to environment as wax conforms to the seal which impresses it. The environment is thought of as something fixed, providing in its fixity the end and standard of changes taking place in the organism; adjustment is just fitting ourselves to this fixity of external conditions. Habit as *habituation* is indeed something *relatively* passive; we get used to our surroundings—to our clothing, our shoes, and gloves; to the atmosphere as long as it is fairly equable; to our daily associates, etc. Conformity to the environment, a change wrought in the organism without reference to ability to modify surroundings, is a marked trait of such habituations. Aside from the fact that we are not entitled to carry over the traits of such adjustments (which might well be called *accommodations*, to mark them off from active adjustments) into habits of active use of our surroundings, two features of habituations are worth notice. In the first place, we get used to things by *first* using them.

Consider getting used to a strange city. At first, there is excessive stimulation and excessive and ill-adapted response. Gradually certain stimuli are selected because of their relevancy, and others are degraded. We can say either that we do not respond to them any longer, or more truly that we have effected a persistent response to them—an equilibrium of adjustment. This means, in the second place, that this enduring adjustment supplies the background upon which are made specific adjustments, as occasion arises. We are never interested in changing the *whole* environment; there is much that we take for granted and accept just as it already is. Upon this background our activities focus at certain points in an endeavor to introduce needed changes.

Habituation is thus our adjustment to an environment which at the time we are not concerned with modifying, and which supplies a leverage to our active habits.

Adaptation, in fine, is quite as much adaptation *of* the environment to our own activities as of our activities *to* the environment. A savage tribe manages to live on a desert plain. It adapts itself. But its adaptation involves a maximum of accepting, tolerating, putting up with things as they are, a maximum of passive acquiescence, and a minimum of active control, of subjection to use. A civilized people enters upon the scene. It also adapts itself. It introduces irrigation; it searches the world for plants and animals that will flourish under such conditions; it improves, by careful selection, those which are growing there. As a consequence, the wilderness blossoms as a rose. The savage is merely habituated; the civilized man has habits which transform the environment.

The significance of habit is not exhausted, however, in its executive and motor phase. It means formation of intellectual and emotional disposition as well as an increase in ease, economy, and efficiency of action. Any habit marks an *inclination*—an active preference and choice for the conditions involved in its exercise. A habit does not wait, Micawberlike, for a stimulus to turn up so that it may get busy; it actively seeks for occasions to pass into full operation. If its expression is unduly blocked, inclination shows itself in uneasiness and intense craving. A habit also marks an intellectual disposition. Where there is a habit, there is acquaintance with the materials and equipment to which action is applied. There is a definite way of understanding the situations in which the habit operates. Modes of thought, of observation and reflection, enter as forms of skill and of desire into the habits that make a man an engineer, an architect, a physician, or a merchant. In unskilled forms of labor, the intellectual factors are at minimum precisely because the habits involved are not of a high grade. But there are habits of judging and reasoning as truly as of handling a tool, painting a picture, or conducting an experiment.

Such statements are, however, understatements. The habits of mind involved in habits of the eye and hand supply the latter with their significance. Above all, the intellectual element in a habit fixes the relation of the habit to varied and elastic use, and hence to continued growth. We speak of *fixed* habits. Well, the phrase may mean powers so well established that their possessor always has them as resources when needed. But the phrase is also used to mean ruts, routine ways, with loss of freshness, openmindedness, and originality. Fixity of habit may mean that something has a fixed hold upon us, instead of our having a free hold upon things. This fact explains two points in a common notion about habits: their identification with mechanical and external modes of action to the neglect of mental and moral attitudes, and the tendency to give them a bad meaning, an identification with "bad habits." Many a person would feel surprised to have his aptitude in his chosen profession called a habit, and would naturally think of his use of tobacco, liquor, or profane language as typical of the meaning of habit. A habit is to him something which has a hold on him, something not easily thrown off even though judgment condemn it.

Habits reduce themselves to routine ways of acting, or degenerate into ways of action to which we are enslaved just in the degree in which intelligence is disconnected from them. Routine habits are unthinking habits; "bad" habits are habits so severed from reason that they are opposed to the conclusions of conscious deliberation and decision. As we have seen, the acquiring of habits is due to an original plasticity of our natures: to our ability to vary responses till we find an appropriate and efficient way of acting. Routine habits, and habits that possess us instead of our possessing them, are habits which put an end to plasticity. They mark the close of power to vary. There can be no doubt of the tendency of organic plasticity, of the physiological basis, to lessen with growing years. The instinctively mobile and eagerly varying action of childhood, the love of new stimuli and new developments, too easily passes into a "settling down," which means aversion to change and a resting on past achievements. Only an environment which secures the full use of intelligence in the process of forming habits can counteract this tendency. Of course, the same hardening of the organic conditions affects the physiological structures which are involved in thinking. But this fact only indicates the need of persistent care to see to it that the function of intelligence is invoked to its maximum possibility. The short-sighted method which falls back on mechanical routine and repetition to secure external efficiency of habit, motor skill without accompanying thought, marks a deliberate closing in of surroundings upon growth.

THE EDUCATIONAL BEARINGS OF THE CONCEPTION OF DEVELOPMENT

We have had so far but little to say in this chapter about education. We have been occupied with the conditions and implications of growth. If our conclusions are justified, they carry with them, however, definite educational consequences. When it is said that education is development, everything depends upon *how* development is conceived. Our net conclusion is that life is development, and that developing, growing, is life. Translated into its educational equivalents, this means (*i*) that the educational process has no end beyond itself; it is its own end; and that (*ii*) the educational process is one of continual reorganizing, reconstructing, transforming.

1. Development when it is interpreted in *comparative* terms, that is, with respect to the special traits of child and adult life, means the direction of power into special channels: the formation of habits involving executive skill, definiteness of interest, and specific objects of observation and thought. But the comparative view is not final. The child has specific powers; to ignore that fact is to stunt or distort the organs upon which his growth depends. The adult uses his powers to transform his environment, thereby occasioning new stimuli which redirect his powers and keep them developing. Ignoring this fact means arrested development, a passive accommodation. Normal child and normal adult alike, in other words, are engaged in growing. The difference between them is not the difference between growth and no growth, but between the modes of growth appropriate to different conditions. With respect to the development of powers devoted to coping with specific scientific and economic problems we may say the child should be growing in manhood. With respect to sympathetic curiosity, unbiased responsiveness, and openness of mind, we may say that the adult should be growing in childlikeness. One statement is as true as the other.

Three ideas which have been criticized, namely, the merely private nature of immaturity, static adjustment to a fixed environment, and rigidity of habit, are all connected with a false idea of growth or development,—that it is a movement toward a fixed goal. Growth is regarded as *having* an end, instead of *being* an end. The educational counterparts of the three fallacious ideas are first, failure to take account of the instinctive or native powers of the young; secondly, failure to develop initiative in coping with novel situations; thirdly, an undue emphasis upon drill and other devices which secure automatic skill at the expense of personal perception. In all cases, the adult environment is accepted as a standard for the child. He is to be brought up *to* it.

Natural instincts are either disregarded or treated as nuisances—as obnoxious traits to be suppressed, or at all events to be brought into conformity with external standards. Since conformity is the aim, what is distinctively individual in a young person is brushed aside, or regarded as a source of mischief or anarchy. Conformity is made equivalent to uniformity. Consequently, there are induced lack of interest in the novel, aversion to progress, and dread of the uncertain and the unknown. Since the end of growth is outside of and beyond the process of growing, external agents have to be resorted to to induce movement towards it. Whenever a method of education is stigmatized as mechanical, we may be sure that external pressure is brought to bear to reach an external end.

2. Since in reality there is nothing to which growth is relative save more growth, there is nothing to which education is subordinate save more education. It is a commonplace to say that education should not cease when one leaves school. The point of this commonplace is that the purpose of school education is to insure the continuance of education by organizing the powers that insure growth. The inclination to learn from life itself and to make the conditions of life such that all will learn in the process of living is the finest product of schooling.

When we abandon the attempt to define immaturity by means of fixed comparison with adult accomplishments, we are compelled to give up thinking of it as denoting lack of desired traits. Abandoning this notion, we are also forced to surrender our habit of thinking of instruction as a method of supplying this lack by pouring knowledge into a mental and moral hole which awaits filling. Since life means growth, a living creature lives as truly and positively at one stage as at another, with the same intrinsic fullness and the same absolute claims. Hence education means the enterprise of supplying the conditions which insure growth, or adequacy of life, irrespective of age. We first look with impatience upon immaturity, regarding it as something to be got over as rapidly as possible. Then the adult formed by such educative methods looks back with impatient regret upon childhood and youth as a scene of lost opportunities and wasted powers. This ironical situation will endure till it is recognized that living has its own intrinsic quality and that the business of education is with that quality.

Realization that life is growth protects us from that so-called idealizing of childhood which in effect is nothing but lazy indulgence. Life is not to be identified with every superficial act and interest. Even though it is not always easy to tell whether what appears to be mere surface fooling is a sign of some nascent as yet untrained power, we must remember that manifestations are not to be accepted as ends in themselves. They are signs of possible growth. They are to be turned into means of development, of carrying power forward, not indulged or cultivated for their own sake. Excessive attention to surface phenomena (even in the way of rebuke as well as of encouragement) may lead to their fixation and thus to arrested development. What impulses are moving toward, not what they have been, is the important thing for parent and teacher. The true principle of respect for immaturity cannot be better put than in the words of Emerson: "Respect the child. Be not too much his parent. Trespass not on his solitude. But I hear the outcry which replies to this suggestion: Would you verily throw up the reins of public and private discipline; would you leave the young child to the mad career of his own passions and whimsies, and call this anarchy a respect for the child's nature? I answer,—Respect the child, respect him to the end, but also respect yourself. . . . The two points in a boy's training are, to keep his *naturel* and train off all but that; to keep his *naturel*, but stop off his uproar, fooling, and horseplay; keep his nature *and arm it with knowledge in the very direction in which it points*." And as Emerson goes on to show, this reverence for childhood and youth instead of opening up an easy and easy-going path to the instructors, "involves at once, immense claims on the time, the thought, on the life of the teacher. It requires time, use, insight, event, all the great lessons and assistances of God; and only to think of using it implies character and profoundness."

SUMMARY

Power to grow depends upon need for others and plasticity. Both of these conditions are at their height in childhood and youth. Plasticity or the power to learn from experience means the formation of habits. Habits give control over the environment, power to utilize it for human purposes. Habits take the form both of habituation, or a general and persistent balance of organic activities with the surroundings, and of active capacities to readjust activity to meet new conditions. The former furnishes the background of growth; the latter constitute growing. Active habits involve thought, invention, and initiative in applying capacities to new aims. They are opposed to routine which marks an arrest of growth. Since growth is the characteristic of life, education is all one with growing; it has no end beyond itself. The criterion of the value of school education is the extent in which it creates a desire for continued growth and supplies means for making the desire effective in fact.

III. THE CONFRONTATION OF GENERATIONS, 1945 TO THE PRESENT

Lawrence A. Cremin

THE CRISIS IN POPULAR EDUCATION

If political Progressivism suffered blows in the 1920's, it had also won several major victories. None was more important than the belief in young people and the triumph of its far-reaching institutional manifestation: progressive education. Though no victories are ever complete or final, the inter-war period saw the wide spread of many of the attitudes and proposals of G. Stanley Hall and John Dewey. Even during the darkest days of the Depression, Americans never lost faith in their children. The Progressives may simply have been making explicit what was always important in American thinking, but it is practically indisputable that their battles of the early twentieth century reaped significant harvests in the 1920's, 1930's, and beyond. By the 1940's, however, as Lawrence Cremin argues in the following selection, progressive child-rearing (a la Dr. Spock), progressive education, and the assumptions that underlay both, faced renewed attacks as, not coincidentally, did progressive reform in general. The final section of this volume furnishes some indication of the range and depth of these new inter-related challenges.

Cremin is a professor of education at Columbia University's Teachers' College in New York. Among all of the so-called "educationists" who write histories of education, it is Cremin whose work is valued most highly by professional historians.

THE attack on the life-adjustment movement was no isolated phenomenon; it came rather as part of a much larger crisis in American education that had been brewing at least since the early 1940's. There were, to begin, the prosaic problems of buildings, budgets, and enrollments created by the war: few schools had been built since 1941; teachers had deserted the profession in droves; inflation was rampant; and the first of a flood of "war babies" began to enter the elementary grades as early as 1946. Then too, there were the multifarious difficulties associated with deepening public concern over communist expansionism at home and abroad. And finally, though perhaps less visibly, there were the voracious demands of an expanding industrial economy for trained and intelligent manpower. Any one of these in and of itself would have loosed fantastic pressures on the schools. Taken together, however, and compounded by a growing dissatisfaction among the intelligentsia, they held the makings of the deepest educational crisis in the nation's history. A spate of books, articles, pamphlets, radio programs, and television panels burst upon the pedagogical scene, airing every conceivable ailment of the schools, real and imaginary. One result was the most vigorous, searching, and fundamental attack on progressive education since the beginning of the movement. . . .

The surprising thing about the progressive response to the assault of the fifties is not that the movement collapsed, but that it collapsed so readily. True, the Progressive Education Association had never been able to recoup its fortunes after the war, and slid steadily downhill after 1947. True, too, the phrase *progressive education* had itself fallen into disfavor among professionals, though progressive ideas continued to command wide assent. But even so, one is shocked by the rapidity of the decline. Why this abrupt and rather dismal end of a movement that had for more than a half-century commanded the loyalty of influential segments of the American public? A number of reasons suggest themselves.

First, distortion. As frequently happens with social movements, success brought schism in the ranks. The pluralism of the nineties became the bitter ideological fragmentation of the thirties and forties. Factions developed, and within the factions cults, cliques, and fanatics. The movement became strife-ridden, given to bandwagon behavior, dominated by the feuding of minorities. The strife made headlines, and within these headlines lay the seeds of many a cartoon version of progressive education.

Second, there was the negativism inherent in this and all social reform movements. Like many protestors against injustice, the early progressives knew better what they were against than what they were for. And when one gets a true picture of the inequities of American schools during the half-century before World War I, he realizes they had much to be against; the physical and pedagogical conditions in many schools were indescribably bad, an effrontery to the mildest humanitarian sentiments. Yet, granted this, a protest is not a program. Shibboleths like "the whole child" or "creative self-expression" stirred the faithful to action and served as powerful battering rams against the old order, but in classroom practice they were not very good guides to positive action. At least the generation that invented them had an idea of what they meant. The generation that followed adopted them as a collection of ready-made clichés—clichés which were not very helpful when the public began to raise searching questions about the schools.

Third, what the progressives did prescribe made inordinate demands on the teacher's time and ability. "Integrated studies" required familiarity with a fantastic range of knowledge and teaching materials; while the commitment to build upon student needs and interests demanded extraordinary feats of pedagogical ingenuity. In the hands of first-rate instructors, the innovations worked wonders; in the hands of too many average teachers, however, they led to chaos. Like the proverbial little girl with the curl right in the middle of her forehead, progressive education done well was very good indeed; done badly, it was abominable—worse, perhaps, than the formalism it had sought to supplant.

Fourth, and this too is a common phenomenon of social reform, the movement became a victim of its own success. Much of what it preached was simply incorporated into the schools at large. Once the schools did change, however, progressives too often found themselves wedded to specific programs, unable to formulate next steps. Like some liberals who continued to fight for the right of labor to organize long after the Wagner Act had done its work, many progressives continued to fight against stationary desks in schools where movable desks were already in use. For some young people in the post-World War II generation the ideas of the progressives became inert—in Whitehead's sense of "right thinking" that no longer moves to action. Dewey in the very last essay he ever published on education likened these progressive ideas gone stale to mustard plasters taken out of the medicine cabinet and applied externally as the need arose. Other young people of this same generation simply developed different preoccupations, different concerns, different rallying points. The old war cries, whatever their validity or lack of it, rang a bit hollow; they no longer generated enthusiasm. Like any legacy from a prior generation, they were too easily and too carelessly spent; rarely perhaps were they lovingly invested in something new. In the end, the result was intellectual bankruptcy.

Fifth, there was the impact of the more general swing toward conservatism in postwar political and social thought. If progressive education arose as part of Progressivism writ large, it should not be surprising that a reaction to it came as a phase of Conservatism writ large. When the reaction did come, too many educators thought they would be progressives in education and conservatives in everything else. The combination, of course, is not entirely impossible, though it may well be intellectually untenable. John Dewey addressed himself to the point in *Characters and Events.* "Let us admit the case of the conservative," he wrote; "if we once start thinking no one can guarantee what will be the outcome, except that many objects, ends and institutions will be surely doomed. Every thinker puts some portion of an apparently stable world in peril, and no one can wholly predict what will emerge in its place." Dewey's comment, by the way, makes incomparably clear what he thought was progressive about good education, and gives the lie to a good deal of nonsense about his philosophy being anti-intellectual.

Sixth, there was the price the movement paid for its own professionalization; for given the political realities of American education, no program can survive that ceases assiduously to cultivate lay support. Progressives were undoubtedly right in contending that teachers needed to be better educated and better paid, and that professionalization would ultimately serve these ends. And they were right, too, in assuming that once teachers had been converted to their cause, half the battle would be won. But they committed a supreme political blunder during the thirties when they allowed the movement itself to become professionalized; for in the process the political coalition of businessmen, trade unionists, farmers, and intellectuals that had supported them in their early efforts was simply permitted to crumble. The resultant lack of nonprofessional support during the fifties was a crucial factor in the high vulnerability of the movement to widespread criticism of its policies and procedures.

Seventh, and most important, progressive education collapsed because it failed to keep pace with the continuing transformation of American society. The ultimate enemy of the conventional wisdom, Galbraith points out, is not so much ideas as the march of events. For the conventional wisdom accommodates itself not to the world that it is meant to interpret, but to the audience's view of that world. And since audiences tend to prefer the comfortable and the familiar, while the world moves on, the conventional wisdom is ever in danger of obsolescence.

The fact is that postwar America was a very different nation from the one that had given birth to progressive education. The great immigrations were over, and a flow of publications by David Riesman, William H. Whyte, Jr., Will Herberg, and others wrestled insistently with a redefinition of community. The search for *Gemeinschaft* of the nineties had become the quest for pluralism of the fifties, while the rampant individualism that Dewey so earnestly feared was now widely applauded as nonconformity. The economy had entered upon an era marked by the harnessing of vast new sources of energy and the rapid extension of automatic controls in production, a prodigious advance that quickly outmoded earlier notions of vocational education. And new information was being generated at a phenomenal pace, thrusting to the fore the school's traditional responsibility for organizing and transmitting knowledge of every sort and variety.

Most fundamental of all, perhaps, the continued advance of the mass media, the proliferation of social welfare agencies under public and quasi-public sponsorship, and the rapid extension of industry-sponsored education programs—the "classrooms in the factories" that Harold Clark and Harold Sloan labelled the real pedagogical revolution of the time—had literally transformed the balance of forces in education. Whereas the central thrust of progressivism had been expansionist—it revolted against formalism and sought to extend the functions of the school—the central effort of the fifties was rather to define more precisely the school's responsibilities, to delineate those things that the school needed to do because if the school did not do them they would not get done. It was this problem more than any, perhaps, that stood at the heart of the argument over educational priorities that dominated the citizens' conferences of the decade.

Granted this, however, and granted the collapse of progressive education as an organized movement, there remained a timelessness about many of the problems the progressives raised and the solutions they proposed. John Dewey once wrote in the Preface to *Schools of To-Morrow:* "This is not a text book of education, nor yet an exposition of a new method of school teaching, aimed to show the weary teacher or the discontented parent how education should be carried on. We have tried to show what actually happens when schools start to put into practice, each in its own way, some of the theories that have been pointed to as the soundest and best ever since Plato, to be then laid politely away as precious portions of our 'intellectual heritage.' "

However much progressive education had become the conventional wisdom of the fifties, there were still slum schools that could take profitable lessons from Jacob Riis, rural schools that had much to learn from the Country Life Commission, and colleges that had yet to discover that the natural curiosity of the young could be a magnificent propellant to learning. Glaring educational inequalities along race and class lines cried out for alleviation, and the vision of a democracy of culture retained a nobility all its own—Lyman Bryson restated it brilliantly in *The Next America* (1953), a book that never received the attention it deserved. As knowledge proliferated, the need to humanize it only intensified; while the awesome imminence of atomic war merely dramatized the difference between knowledge and intelligence. Finally, the rapid transformation of the so-called underdeveloped nations lent new meaning and new urgency to Jane Addams's caveat that "unless all men and all classes contribute to a good, we cannot even be sure that it is worth having"—the point was compellingly made in C. P. Snow's widely read lecture, *The Two Cultures and the Scientific Revolution* (1959).

The Progressive Education Association had died, and progressive education itself needed drastic reappraisal. Yet the transformation they had wrought in the schools was in many ways as irreversible as the larger industrial transformation of which it had been part. And for all the talk about pedagogical breakthroughs and crash programs, the authentic progressive vision remained strangely pertinent to the problems of mid-century America. Perhaps it only awaited the reformulation and resuscitation that would ultimately derive from a larger resurgence of reform in American life and thought.

Richard Hofstadter

THE CHILD AND THE WORLD

Anti-Intellectualism in American Life earned for the late Richard Hofstadter his second Pulitzer Prize as well as several other awards. It did not, however, make the impact among historians equal to that of two of his earlier works—*The American Political Tradition* and *The Age of Reform*. Perhaps the main reason for this is that Hofstadter ranged far and wide over a large, somewhat amorphous subject. He made a variety of comments concerning all kinds of anti-intellectual manifestations in American society; he did not make a special attempt to relate one chapter to the next. But in taking the book for what it was intended to be, one comes across some unusually perceptive thinking about America, with no section being more rewarding than that which deals with American childhood. The excerpts below review much of the material that the reader has encountered so far in this volume, after which Hofstadter has reworked the data into a sophisticated and important commentary about childhood and about America.

1

THE new education rested on two intellectual pillars: its use, or misuse, of science, and its appeal to the educational philosophy of John Dewey. Of the two, Dewey's philosophy was much more important, for it embraced within it the belief in the power of science to illuminate educational thought, and yet went beyond this to give educators an inclusive and generous view of the world that satisfied their philanthropic sentiments and their urge to make education useful to democracy. Dewey's contribution was to take certain views of the child which were gaining force around the end of the nineteenth century, and to link them to pragmatic philosophy and the growing demand for social reform. He thus established a satisfying connection between new views of the child and new views of the world.

Anyone concerned with the new education must reckon with its use of Dewey's ideas. To consider this in a study of anti-intellectualism may unfortunately be taken as an attempt to characterize Dewey simply as an anti-intellectual—which hardly seems just toward a man who was so intent on teaching children how to think. It may also be taken as an attempt to locate the "blame" for the failings of American education—and will inevitably take on something of this color—but my purpose is quite otherwise: it is to examine the tendency and consequences of certain ideas to which Dewey gave by far the most influential expression.

An attempt to take account of the limitations and the misuse of these ideas should not be read as a blanket condemnation of progressive education, which, as Lawrence Cremin's discriminating history has shown, contained several streams of thought and a variety of tendencies. Although its reputation suffered unwarranted damage from extremists on its periphery, progressivism had at its core something sound and important. Today, partly because many "conservative" schools have borrowed discriminatingly from progressive innovations, we may easily forget how dismal and

From *Anti-Intellectualism in American Life*, by Richard Hofstadter, pp. 359–375, 383–386, 389–390.

self-satisfied the older conservative pedagogy often was, how it accepted, or even exploited, the child's classroom passivity, how much scope it afforded to excessively domineering teachers, how heavily it depended on rote learning. The main strength of progressivism came from its freshness in method. It tried to mobilize the interests of the child, to make good use of his need for activity, to concern the minds of teachers and educators with a more adequate sense of his nature, to set up pedagogical rules that would put the burden on the teacher not to be arbitrarily authoritative, and to develop the child's capacity for expression as well as his ability to learn. It had the great merit of being experimental in a field in which too many people thought that all the truths had been established. In an experimental school, where one can find picked pupils and teachers and instill in them a special ethos of dedication and excitement, one is likely to get extraordinary results, as many progressive schools did and still do. Unfortunately, one cannot expect to make universally applicable the results, however illuminating, which have been achieved in a special experimental situation.

The value of progressivism rested on its experimentalism and its work with younger children; its weakness lay in its efforts to promulgate doctrine, to generalize, in its inability to assess the practical limits of its own program, above all in its tendency to dissolve the curriculum. This tendency became most serious in the education of older children, and especially at the secondary level, where, as the need arises to pursue a complex, organized program of studies, the question of the curriculum becomes acute. Hitherto I have intentionally spoken not of progressivism in education, but of something still broader and more inclusive which I prefer to call "the new education." The new education represented the elaboration of certain progressive principles into a creed, the attempt to make inclusive claims for their applicability in a system of mass education, their extension from experimental work largely with very young children into a schematism for public education at all ages, and finally the development of an attack upon the organized curriculum and liberal education under the rubric of "progressivism." For all this, early and late, Dewey's thought was constantly invoked. His vocabulary and ideas, which were clearly evident in the *Cardinal Principles* of 1918, seem to appear in every subsequent document of the new education. He has been praised, paraphrased, repeated, discussed, apotheosized, even on occasions read.

It is commonly said that Dewey was misunderstood, and it is repeatedly pointed out that in time he had to protest against some of the educational practices carried on in his name. Perhaps his intent was widely, even regularly violated, but Dewey was hard to read and interpret. He wrote a prose of terrible vagueness and plasticity, which William James once characterized as "damnable; you might even say God-damnable." His style is suggestive of the cannonading of distant armies: one concludes that something portentous is going on at a remote and inaccessible distance, but one cannot determine just what it is. That this style is, perhaps symptomatically, at its worst in Dewey's most important educational writings suggests that his great influence as an educational spokesman may have been derived in some part from the very inaccessibility of his exact meanings. A variety of schools of educational thought have been able to read their own meanings into his writings. Although it is tempting to say that Dewey's work was crudely misread by the most anti-intellectual spokesmen of the new education, it seems fairer to admit that even the life-adjustment educators could have arrived at their use of Dewey through an honest and intelligent exegesis of the master. Lawrence Cremin has observed that, "however tortuous the intellectual line from *Democracy and Education* to the pronouncements of the Commission on Life Adjustment, that line can be drawn."

That it is in fact an unduly tortuous line one may be permitted to doubt. Serious faults in style are rarely, if ever, matters of "mere" style; they embody real difficulties in conception. Far more probable than the thesis that Dewey was perversely distorted by obtuse or over-enthusiastic followers is the idea that the unresolved problems of interpretation to which his work gave rise were tokens of real ambiguities and gaps in thought, which themselves express certain difficulties and unresolved problems in educational theory and in our culture. What many of Dewey's followers have done, with or without complete license from the master himself, is to attack the ideas of leadership and guidance, and the values of culture and reflective life, in favor of certain notions of spontaneity, democracy, and practicality. In this respect they repeat in education some of the themes that were sounded by the egalitarians in politics, the evangelicals in religion, and the prophets of practicality in business. Before attempting to see how Dewey's philosophy lent itself to these uses, let us first look at the essential argument of this philosophy and at the intellectual setting in which it emerged.

2

The objectives of Dewey's educational theory, which were closely knit into his general philosophy, comprise a high set of ambitions. In the first instance, Dewey was trying to devise a theory of education—of the development of intelligence and the role of knowledge—which would be wholly consistent with Darwinism. For a thinker born in the year in which *The Origin of Species* was published, and intellectually raised during the flowering of evolutionary science, modern education would be worth nothing if it were not scientific.

Dewey began by thinking of the individual learner as using his mind instrumentally to solve various problems presented by his environment, and went on to develop a theory of education conceived as the growth of the learner. The modern educational system, he saw, must operate in an age of democracy, science, and industrialism; education should strive to meet the requirements of this age. Above all, education should abandon those practices, based upon a pre-democratic and pre-industrial society, which accepted the leisured and aristocratic view that knowledge is the contemplation of fixed verities. Dewey felt that he and his contemporaries must now surmount a series of artificial dualisms inherited from past ages. Primary among these was the dualism between knowledge and action. For Dewey, action is involved in knowledge—not in the sense, as some of his uncomprehending critics charged, that knowledge is subordinated to action and inferior to "practice," but in the sense that knowledge is a form of action, and that action is one of the terms by which knowledge is acquired and used.

Dewey was also trying to find the educational correlates of a democratic and progressive society. How can one construct an educational system that will avoid perpetuating all the flaws of existing society at the root simply by molding children in its own image? If a democratic society is truly to serve all its members, it must devise schools in which, at the germinal point in childhood, these members will be able to cultivate their capacities and, instead of simply reproducing the qualities of the larger society, will learn how to improve them. It was in this sense that he saw education as a major force in social reconstruction. Plainly, if society is to be remade, one must above all look for the regenerative contribution the child is capable of making to society. And this cannot be done, Dewey thought, unless the child is placed at the center of the school, unless the rigid authority of the teacher and the traditional weight of the curriculum are displaced by his own developing interests and impulses. To mobilize these impulses and interests toward learning, under gentle adult guidance, is to facilitate the learning process and also to form a type of character and mind suitable to the work of social reform.

This is an excessively abbreviated statement of Dewey's theory, but it serves at least to show how he stated his problems and to turn attention to the central personage in their solution—the figure of the child. It is here that we may begin, for the conception of the child—no mere intellectual construct but the focus of a set of deep emotional commitments and demands—is at the core of the new education. To anticipate what must subsequently be elaborated at some length, I believe that the conception of the child formed by Dewey and his contemporaries, which later entered into the stream of the new education, was more romantic and primitivist than it was post-Darwinian. This conception of the child, and the related assumptions about his natural growth, made it all the more difficult for Dewey and his followers to resolve those dualisms which he felt should be resolved, and, despite his continuing efforts at clarification, made it difficult also to reconcile the central position of the child with what proved still to be necessary in the way of order and authority in education. Finally, the penumbra of sanctity with which the figure of the child was surrounded made it difficult to discuss with realism the role of democracy in education.

To understand the emotional commitment with which Dewey and his contemporaries approached the child, it is necessary to reconstruct to some extent the intellectual atmosphere around the turn of the century, when his generation began to work its transformation of American education. At this time, both in America and in Europe, there was a quickening of interest in the child and a new turn in sentiment among those professionally concerned with him. It was in 1909 that the Swedish feminist, Ellen Key, wrote her significantly titled book, *The Century of the Child*, which epitomized the expectations of of those who felt that the child had been newly rediscovered. But expressions of this order were becoming common coin. In 1900 the state superintendent of public instruction of Georgia presented at the annual meeting of the National Education Association an inspirational paper entitled "What Manner of Child Shall This Be?" In it he declared:

> If I were asked what is to be accounted the great discovery of this century, I would pass by all the splendid achievements that men have wrought in wood and stone and iron and brass. I would not go to the volume that catalogs the printing-press, the loom, the steam-engine, the steamship, the ocean cable, the telegraph, the wireless telegraphy, the telephone, the phonograph. I would not go among the stars and point to either one of the planets that have been added to our solar system. I would not call for the Roentgen ray that promises to revolutionize the study of the human brain as well as the human body. I would pass over all the labor-saving machines and devices by which the work of the world has been marvelously multiplied. Above and beyond all these the index finger of the world's progress, in the march of time, would point unerringly to the little child as the one great discovery of the century now speeding to its close.

Having thus stated what importance he attached to the discovery of the little child, the school official went on to summarize the progress of the previous century, from the days when, as he imagined, education had been "the exclusive privilege of an autocratic minority" and had been put at the disposal of "an all-powerful democratic majority." Freedom of opportunity had already been given to the American child, but further reforms were still in the making. "Already we Americans have discovered that the old system of education will not fit his case. . . . We have quit trying to fit the boy to a system. We are now trying to adjust a system to the boy." Turning to religious imagery, the official likened American teachers to Christ, in the sense that they were releasing the American child from shrouds and deathly cerements, as Christ released Lazarus, and turning him loose to grow. In the future, he predicted with remarkable prescience, the Christian challenge to the teacher would rise still higher, for the teacher would be expected to save the humblest of God's children: "Time was when the power of the teacher was measured by what he could do with a bright boy or a bright girl. From the beginning of this new century the power of the teacher will be measured by what he will be able to do with the dull boy, the defective child. More than ever before in the history of this world the real test of teaching power will be measured, not by what can be done with the best, but by what can be done with the worst boy in the school." The new educational psychology will be "the psychology of the prodigal son and the lost sheep." The "great rejoicings" in American life will come when child study is so mastered and the development of schools so perfected that the educational system touches and develops every American boy. "We shall come to our place of rejoicing when we have saved every one of these American children and made every one of them a contributor to the wealth, to the intelligence, and to the power of this great democratic government of ours."

I have chosen these remarks because, though written by a working educator rather than a theorist, they sum up in brief a number of the convictions prevalent in what was then up-to-date educational thinking. They reflect its Christian fervor and benevolence; its sense of the central place of the child in the modern world; its concern with democracy and opportunity as criteria of educational achievement; its conviction of the importance of the dull child and his demands on the educational system; its optimism about educational research and child study; its belief that education is to be defined essentially as growth; and its faith that a proper education, though focused on the self-realization of the individual child, would also automatically work toward the fulfillment and salvation of democratic society.

The Georgia school official may well have been reading the works of leading contemporaries in the field, for his view of the child is largely in accord with what they were then writing. Dewey, who was in his early forties and just beginning his work in education, was of course one of them; but it is desirable also to look for a moment at the influence, then more ponderable, of two older men who preceded him, the educator Francis Wayland Parker and the psychologist G. Stanley Hall. Parker, whom Dewey once called the father of progressive education, was a man of exceptional vitality, a remarkably effective pedagogue, and a distinguished school administrator. In the 1870's he remade the school system of Quincy, Massachusetts, achieving results that, by the most impeccably traditional criteria of educational performance, must be considered brilliant. Not long afterward, he went on to the principalship of the Cook County Normal School in Chicago, where he developed more fully his educational theories and his pedagogical techniques. There he undoubtedly set an important example for John Dewey, who was impressed by the Cook County Normal School before he set up his own "Laboratory School" in 1896, and for G. Stanley Hall, who for a time made annual visits to Parker's school "to set my educational watch."

The terms in which Parker cast his educational theory were in many respects too old-fashioned to be in tune with the new currents of thought. For example, they were altogether pre-Darwinian and had no trace of the more sophisticated functionalist psychology which made Dewey's writings so widely appealing. But Parker's view of the child, which was, to a great extent, patterned after Froebel's, was of capital importance. "The child," he said, "is the climax and culmination of all God's creations," and to answer the question: What is the child? is to approach a knowledge of God. "He put into that child Himself his divinity, and . . . this divinity manifests itself in the seeking for truth through the visible and tangible." "The spontaneous tendencies of the child are the records of inborn divinity," he asserted. "We are here, my fellow-teachers, for one purpose, and that purpose is to understand these tendencies and continue them in all these directions, following nature." If the child was the bearer of divinity and "the fruit of all the past and the seed of all the future," it was natural enough to conclude that "the centre of all movement in education is *the child.*" One may hazard the guess that Parker's concern with the spontaneous activities of the child were fruitful rather than stultifying partly because he also conceived of the child as omnivorously curious, as having a natural interest in all subjects, as being a sort of savant in the making, and a born artist and handicraftsman as well. Accordingly, he proposed a rather demanding curriculum, and unlike most later progressives, he believed even in teaching grammar in all grades of the elementary school, since he thought it should be "thoroughly mastered."

As Dewey did later, Parker stressed the school as a community: "A school should be a model home, a complete community and embryonic democracy." Properly used, it could be expected to achieve an extraordinary reformation: "We must believe that we can save *every child.* The citizen should say in his heart: 'I await the regeneration of the world from the teaching of the common schools of America.' "

The era in which these words were written was also the era in which G. Stanley Hall, the leader of the child-study movement, said: "The guardians of the young should strive first of all to keep out of nature's way. . . . They should feel profoundly that childhood, as it comes fresh from the hands of God, is not corrupt, but illustrates the survival of the most consummate thing in the world. . . . Nothing else is so worthy of love, reverence, and service as the body and soul of the growing child." It was the era in which Dewey himself said that "the child's own instincts and powers furnish the material and give the starting point for all education." Also: "We violate the child's nature and render difficult the best ethical results by introducing the child too abruptly to a number of special studies, of reading, writing, geography, etc., out of relation to [his] social life. The true center of correlation on the school subjects is not science, nor literature, nor history, nor geography, but the child's own social activities."

It will be apparent that the new education was presented to the world not simply as an instrumentality but as a creed, which went beyond the hope of this or that strictly educational result to promise some kind of ultimate salvation for individuals or for the race. We shall presently see, for example, how G. Stanley Hall foresaw that an education designed in accordance with the nature of child growth would rear the superman of the future. Dewey's early view of the possibilities of education were likewise exalted. Education, he said in his well-titled little pamphlet, *My Pedagogic Creed,* "is the fundamental method of social progress and reform." Hence the teacher must be seen as "engaged, not simply in the training of individuals, but in the formation of the proper social life." Every teacher should accordingly think of himself as "a social servant set apart for the maintenance of proper social order and the securing of the right social growth. In this way the teacher always is the prophet of the true God and the usherer in of the true kingdom of God." Plainly, high expectations like these put a staggering burden upon any proposal for educational reform.

This creed, this fighting faith, had to be put forward in the face of much stubborn resistance before it could be established as the reigning creed. Men who feel that they must engage in such a crusade are not likely to be greatly concerned with nuances, or with exploring the limits or dangers of their ideas. Unfortunately, what is important in a practical sphere like education is very often not so much the character of a philosophy or creedal commitment as certain questions of emphasis and proportion which arise in trying to execute it; and there is no automatic way of deriving a sense of proportion from a body of ideas. For example, the early spokesmen of the new education demanded that the child be respected, but it was difficult to say where respect might end and a kind of bathetic reverence might begin. Although Dewey himself began to warn in the 1930's against the overuse or the oversimplified use of his theories, he found it difficult to define, even in his later works, the points at which the lines of restraint could or should be drawn without at the same time abandoning certain of his essential commitments.

3

Here perhaps the romantic inheritance, quite as much or more than the appeal of post-Darwinian naturalism, may explain the charm of the concept of the child formulated by Dewey and his generation. The most elaborate statements of this concept come from European writers who applied romantic views to the child—on occasion Dewey referred respectfully to Rousseau, Pestalozzi, and Froebel, as he did to Emerson, whose essay "Culture" foreshadowed many of his ideas. The notion of education advanced at the turn of the century by these pedagogical reformers was romantic in the sense that they set up an antithesis between the development of the individual—his sensibility, the scope of his fancy, the urgency of his personal growth—and the imperatives of the social order, with its demand for specified bodies of knowledge, prescribed manners and morals, and a personal equipment suited to traditions and institutions. Theirs was a commitment to the natural child against artificial society. For them, the child came into this world trailing clouds of glory, and it was the holy office of the teacher to see that he remained free, instead of assisting in the imposition of alien codes upon him. They envisaged a child life engaged more or less directly with nature and with activity, and not with absorbing traditions meaningful only to adults or with reading books and mastering skills set not by the child's desires and interests but by adult society.

This view of education began once again to gain currency among Western thinkers at the turn of the century; the United States provided an unusually receptive soil. This country had always had a strong penchant for child-indulgence—it was an extremely common point of observation for nineteenth-century travelers in America. Moreover, American education, being in a singularly fluid state, offered less resistance to such attractive novelties than the tradition-encrusted educational systems of the European countries. The evangelical climate of this country was also a force: the new educators' rhetoric about "saving" every American child, and their implied promise that the child saved would himself redeem civilization, point to this conclusion. It was decades before even so secular a thinker as Dewey lost the confidence evident in the young educational reformer of 1897 who believed that the good teacher would usher in "the true kingdom of God."

If we attend carefully to the overtones of the new educators' pronouncements, with their stress on such terms as spontaneity, instinct, activity, and nature, we become aware of the way in which the problem of education is posed. The child is a phenomenon at once natural and divine—here post-Darwinian naturalism and the romantic heritage link arms—and the "natural" pattern of his needs and instincts becomes an imperative which it is profane for educators to violate.

We are now prepared to appreciate the significance of the central idea of the new educational thought: that the school should base its studies not on the demands of society, nor on any conception of what an educated person should be, but on the developing needs and interests of the child. This does not mean merely that the nature of the child imposes negative limits on the educational process and that it is vain to try to surmount them: to say this would be superfluous. It means that the nature of the child is a positive guide to educational procedure—that the child himself naturally and spontaneously generates the needs and impulses that should animate the educational process.

In a revealing article of 1901, "The Ideal School as Based on Child Study," G. Stanley Hall attempted to say what this guiding principle would entail. He would try, he said, "to break away from all current practices, traditions, methods, and philosophies, for a brief moment, and ask *what education would be if based solely upon a fresh and comprehensive view of the nature and needs of childhood.*" In short, he would strip away the inherited ideas of what education should be, which are the trappings of an outworn past, and assume that what modern child study has learned is of greater relevance to the purpose. Etymologically, Hall pointed out, the word for school meant leisure, "exemption from work, the perpetuation of the primeval paradise created before the struggle for existence began." Understood in this sense, the school stood for health, growth, and heredity, "a pound of which is worth a ton of instruction."

Because of the natural and sacred character of the child's health, leisure, and growth, every invasion of his time, every demand of the curriculum, must be doubly tried and conclusively justified before we subject him to it:

> We must overcome the fetichism of the alphabet, of the multiplication table, of grammars, of scales, and of bibliolatry, and must reflect that . . . the invention of Cadmus seemed the sowing of veritable dragon's teeth in the brain; that Charlemagne and many other great men of the world could not read or write; that scholars have argued that Cornelia, Ophelia, Beatrice, and even the blessed mother of our Lord knew nothing of letters. The knights, the elite leaders of the Middle Ages, deemed writing a mere clerk's trick beneath the attention of all those who scorned to muddle their wits with others' ideas, feeling that their own were good enough for them.

Of course no one will imagine that Hall, who had received one of the best educations of his generation—and a very traditional one—at Harvard and the German universities, thought that the new education would have as a goal the subversion of literacy. The importance of his views lay in the belief that there is a natural and normal course of child development to which bookish considerations should yield. Some of his particular suggestions were most sensible and some are still practiced to good effect. It is interesting, too, that just as Parker clung to the value of grammar, Hall did not think that the study of the classical languages had been altogether eliminated by this emphasis on natural development. At least some children might well study languages, Hall thought; what is especially interesting to a contemporary reader, looking back over the span of seventy years, is that Hall felt that he knew quite precisely at what points in a child's development the study of these subjects was "natural." "As to the dead languages, if they are to be taught, Latin should be begun not later than ten or eleven, and Greek never later than twelve or thirteen." A generation later, most proponents of the new education had no use for these languages, and they would have been horrified to see either of them begun in the primary grades.

Hall's hopes for what could be realized in education through the scientific study of the child were avowedly utopian. With a generous grant of funds and five years of experimentation, he had "no shadow of doubt or fear," it would be possible to work out a program that would satisfy educational prophets and even persuade conservatives, "because the best things established will be in it."

> But it will be essentially pedocentric rather than scholiocentric; it may be a little like the Reformation which insisted that the Sabbath, the Bible, and the Church were made for man and not he for them; it will fit both the practices and the results of modern science and psychological study; it will make religion and morals more effective; and, perhaps, above all, it will give individuality in the school its full rights as befits a republican form of government, and will contribute something to bring the race to the higher maturity of the superman that is to be, effectiveness in developing which is the highest and final test of art, science, religion, home, state, literature, and every human institution.

It will no doubt seem a far cry from Hall's hopes for ten-year-old Latinists and his call for the superman of the future to the work of the life-adjustment educators with their campaign against disciplinary subjects and their recommended class discussions on "How can I get everyone to participate in the activities at the party?" or "Should I have dates in junior high school?" But utopias have a way of being short-circuited under the very eyes of their formulators.

4

The romantic and Darwinian backgrounds of the new education make it easier to understand why Dewey should have chosen to define education as growth. In Dewey this conception that education is growth is no casual act of definition and no idle metaphor: it represents an attempt to locate and restate the very essence of the educational process. There is a frequently quoted passage in *Democracy and Education* which illustrates at once the disturbing quality of Dewey's style and the importance he attached to the conception of education as growth. There he wrote:

> We have been occupied with the conditions and implications of growth. . . . When it is said that education is development, everything depends upon *how* development is conceived. Our net conclusion is that life is development, and that developing, growing, is life. Translated into its educational equivalents, this means (*i*) that the educational process has no end beyond itself; it is its own end; and that (*ii*) the educational process is one of continual reorganizing, reconstructing, transforming. . . .
>
> Since in reality there is nothing to which growth is relative save more growth, there is nothing to which education is subordinate save more education. . . . Education means the enterprise of supplying the conditions which insure growth, or adequacy of life, irrespective of age. . . .
>
> Since growth is the characteristic of life, education is all one with growing; it has no end beyond itself. The criterion of the value of school education is the extent in which it creates a desire for continued growth and supplies means for making the desire effective in fact.

The implications of this must be reckoned with: we are not asked to consider that education resembles growth, or has something in common with growth, or may helpfully be thought of as a special form of growth. We are urged to consider that education *is* growth; that growth is life; that life is development; and above all that it is meaningless to try to provide ends for education, since it has no possible further end but more education. "The aim of education is to enable individuals to continue their education."

The idea that education is growth is at first blush all but irresistible. Certainly education is not a form of shrinkage. To say that it is growth seems to assert a desirable connection between the learning process and the world of nature. This concept is refreshingly unmechanical. It does justice to our sense that education is cumulative and self-enlarging and leads toward a mind and character which become larger, more complex, more powerful, and yet finer. But several critics have contended that the notion that education is growth was the source of endless difficulties; and I believe that in the hands of some of Dewey's followers this idea became one of the most mischievous metaphors in the history of modern education. Growth is a natural, animal process, and education is a social process. Growth in the child, taken literally, goes on automatically, requiring no more than routine care and nourishment; its end is to a large degree predetermined by genetic inheritance, whereas the ends of education have to be supplied. In contemplating a child's education we are free to consider whether he shall learn two languages, but in contemplating his natural growth we cannot consider whether he shall develop two heads.

Since the idea of growth is intrinsically a biological metaphor and an individualistic conception, the effect of this idea was of necessity to turn the mind away from the social to the personal function of education; it became not an assertion of the child's place in society but rather of his interests as against those of society. The idea of growth invited educational thinkers to set up an invidious contrast between self-determining, self-directing growth from within, which was good, and molding from without, which was bad. Students of Dewey's philosophy might readily object to any portrayal of his educational thought as oriented excessively toward the biological and individual and as insufficiently mindful of the collective and social. What writer on education, it might be asked, ever spoke more positively about the social character of the educational process and about its ultimate social function?

The problem, however, did not arise from any lack of awareness, on Dewey's part, of the social character of education; it arose from the fact that the concept of individual growth became a hostage in the hands of educational thinkers who were obsessed with the child-centered school. Although Dewey himself did not accept the antithesis between the child and society as a finality—indeed, he hoped to achieve a harmonious synthesis of the two—the historical effect of the conception of education as growth was to exalt the child and dismiss the problem of society, on the ground that the growth of the child stood for health, whereas the traditions of society (including curricular traditions) stood for outworn, excessively authoritative demands. "The authority of society," wrote a leading psychologist in this tradition, "or of any part of society is not presented to the child as a guide to conduct. Reliance is placed on the experience of each individual child. The experience of the race in discovering what line of conduct works out satisfactorily and what does not is utilized only in so far as the child sees fit to appeal to it."

Dewey himself never argued, as critics and followers have often thought, for a directionless education. On this point at least he was painfully clear. He often said in his early as well as his later educational writings that the child himself, unguided, is not capable of spinning out the proper content of his education; that every superficial act or interest, every stray impulse, of the child is not necessarily valuable; that the teacher must somehow, without imposing "external" ends, guide, direct, and develop those impulses of the child which are moving "forward."

Dewey's difficulty was of another order: having insisted that education, being growth itself, cannot have any end set for it save still more education, he was unable to formulate the criteria by which society, through the teacher, should guide or direct the child's impulses. The teacher was left with a firm mandate to exercise some guidance, to make some discriminations among the child's impulses and needs, but with no directional signposts. The child's impulses should be guided "forward"—but in which direction? Such a set of criteria presupposes an educational goal, an adult prevision of what the child should know and what he should be. "Let the child's nature fulfill its own destiny," Dewey urged, but the suggestion that the child has a destiny implied an end or goal somewhat removed in time and not envisaged by the child. For this reason, what came to be called progressive education, although often immensely fertile and ingenious concerning means, was so futile and confused about ends; much of what it had to say about teaching methods was of the highest value, but it was quite unclear, often anarchic, about what these methods should be used to teach. Remarkably effective beginnings were made at mobilizing the child's interests for learning, but often these interests simply displaced learning. The more certain progressive education was of its techniques, the less explicit it was about its goals—perhaps in this respect it offered a parable on American life.

Dewey was so concerned with adult authority as *the* threat to the child that it was hard for him to conceive of the child's peers as also constituting a threat. One can hardly believe that he really intended to liberate the child from the adult world only to throw him into the clutches of an even more omnivorous peer-culture. Yet there was very little place in Dewey's schoolroom for the contemplative or bookish child, for whom schooling as a social activity is not a thoroughly satisfactory procedure. "In social situations," Dewey approvingly wrote, "the young have to refer their way of acting to what others are doing and make it fit in." It was just this kind of activity that provided the participants with a common understanding. Was there not, in his view of the matter, more than a little suspicion of the child who remained aloof or hung back from social activity, who insisted on a singular measure of independence? "Dependence," Dewey wrote,

> denotes a power rather than a weakness; it involves interdependence. There is always a danger that increased personal independence will decrease the social capacity of an individual. In making him more self-reliant, it may make him more self-sufficient; it may lead to aloofness and indifference. It often makes an individual so insensitive in his relations to others as to develop an illusion of being really able to stand and act alone—an unnamed form of insanity which is responsible for a large part of the remediable suffering of the world.

These words are altogether intelligible against the background of nineteenth-century America. The rampant economic individualism that Dewey could see at work in his formative years had created a personal type which was indeed independent, if not to the point of insanity, at least to the point of being anti-social. And in the schoolroom the older education had given scope to the impulses of occasional teachers who who were harshly authoritarian. It would probably be too much to expect anyone in 1916 to anticipate the emergence among children of the kind of peer-group conformity that David Riesman has diagnosed in *The Lonely Crowd,* or the decline in adult authority that is observable both in the classroom and in the regulation of children's lives. Today, when we grow troubled about conformity in children, we are more often troubled about their conformity to the mandates of their peers and to directives from the mass media than we are by their conformity to parents or teachers. We are also aware of the possibility that excessive weakness in adult authority may even create difficulties for children quite as acute as those caused by adult tyranny.

These considerations did not enter into Dewey's world at the time he was formulating his educational theory; but it is possible that his theory itself has helped to bring about a state of affairs which he could hardly have desired. The core-curriculum educators invoke Dewey's principles of immediacy, utility, and social learning when they encourage children to discuss in school "How can I be popular?" or such implicit resistance to parental imperatives as "Why are my parents so strict?" and "What can I do with my old-fashioned parents?" and "Should I follow my crowd or obey my parents' wishes?" Such topics represent the projection of peer-conformity into the curriculum itself in a way that Dewey would surely have found offensive. The problem of conformity and authority was real enough, but it was not solved by reforming the old-fashioned classroom.

Perhaps Dewey somewhat overvalued the social side of learning. He and other thinkers of his generation, notably George H. Mead, were much concerned to establish the intrinsically social character of mind, an effort in which they were eminently successful. In a sense, however, this conception of mind proved almost too much to justify Dewey's view of education. If mental activity is intrinsically social, one may after all claim that the social prerequisities of learning can be met in a wide variety of types of learning, and not merely in the literal social co-operation of the classroom. As the new educators were somewhat reluctant to see, a child sitting alone and reading about Columbus's voyages is engaging in a social experience at least as complex, if of a different kind, from that of a child in the school workshop making model ships with other children. Yet in Dewey's work the important and persuasive idea that a thing gets its meaning from being a social object is at times transmuted into the more questionable idea that all learning has to be overtly shared in social action.

Even more important is a conception of the relationship between the educational process and its outcome which seems excessively mechanical, especially for one who, like Dewey, hoped always to do justice to the dialectical fluidity of life. The notion that the authoritative classroom would of necessity produce the conformist mind and that sociable learning would produce the ideally socialized personality is at first appealing, but there is about it a kind of rigid rationality of the sort that life constantly eludes. Did Dewey, for example, really imagine that traditional education had engendered in America, of all places, a mind notably characterized by "lack of interest in the novel, aversion to progress, and dread of the uncertain and the unknown"? Was it necessarily true that education founded upon authority invariably produces a conformist mind, and that there is a one-to-one relationship between the style of an educational system and the nature of its products? There hardly seems to be any place in Dewey's idea of the educational process for the fact that Voltaire was schooled by the Jesuits, or that the strong authoritative structure of the Puritan family should have yielded a personal type so important to the development of modern democracy. To expect that education would so simply produce a hoped-for personal type was to expect more than past experience warranted.

Finally, there are serious difficulties involved in living up to the idea that education should in no way be looked upon as a preparation for the child's future life—what Dewey always called a "remote future"—but rather as living itself, a simulacrum of life, or a sort of rehearsal in the experiences that make up life. The motive of achieving some continuity between school experience and other experiences seems altogether commendable. But Dewey not only held that education *is* life; he went on to say that the school should provide a *selective* environment for the child, an environment that represents so far as possible what is deemed good in society and eliminates what is bad. Yet, the more successful the school was in this task, the less it could live up to the ideal of representing or embodying life. The moment one admits that it is not all of life which is presented to children in school, one also admits that a selective process has been set up which is determined by some external end; and then one has once again embraced the traditional view that education is after all not a comprehensive attempt to mirror or reproduce life but a segment of life that is specialized for a distinct function.

If the new educators really wanted to reproduce life itself in the classroom, they must have had an extraordinarily benign conception of what life is. To every adult, life brings, in addition to some measure of co-operation, achievement, and joy, a full stint of competition, defeat, frustration, and failure. But the new educators did not accept the idea that these things too would be embodied in the little community that was to be organized for children in the school. Quite the contrary, their strongest impulse was to protect children from too acute an awareness of what their own limitations, under adult conditions, might cost them. They were much closer to the argument of Marietta Johnson, one of the pioneers of "organic education" and a founder of the Progressive Education Association, who said: "No child should ever know failure. . . . The school should *meet* the demands of the nature of childhood, not make demands. Any school system in which one child may fail while another succeeds is unjust, undemocratic, uneducational." In her experimental school at Fairhope, Alabama, which was described with enthusiasm by John and Evelyn Dewey in *Schools of To-Morrow*, there were therefore no examinations, no grading, no failures to win promotion; success was measured not by the amount of subject matter learned or the promotions earned but by the effort and joy of the work itself. This view of education may or may not have better affects on children than the traditional school, but that it bears a closer relation to "life" is eminently questionable. . . .

It is here that we must return again to the child, for the child is the key to the future; he has within himself the resources to liberate the world from the weight of its past. But before he can do this, the child himself must be freed—and under a proper educational regime really *can* be freed—from the oppressions of the world, from everything that is dead about the apparatus of culture, from the constricting effects of society on the school. Dewey himself was realistic enough to see, to assert and reassert, the limits of the child's spontaneous impulses as a guide to this process. But it was precisely these impulses that interested American educators. Since Dewey aimed at freeing the child from the shackles of the past to the point at which the child could make a reconstructive use of past culture, American educators seized upon his theory as having downgraded past culture and its merely ornamental and solacing "products" and as having finally produced a program to liberate the child for unimpeded growth. Having once put the child so firmly at the center, having defined education as growth without end, Dewey had so weighted the discussion of educational goals that a quarter century of clarificatory statements did not avail to hold in check the anti-intellectual perversions of his theory.

Like Freud, Dewey saw the process by which a society inculcates the young with its principles, inhibitions, and habits as a kind of imposition upon them. But Dewey's assumptions led to a more optimistic calculus of possibilities than that offered by Freud. Freud saw the process by which the individual is socialized as making genuinely impairing demands upon his instincts but also as being in some form tragically inevitable. Society, as Dewey saw it, spoiled the "plasticity" of children, which was the source of their "power to change prevailing custom." Education, with its "insolent coercions, insinuating briberies, and pedagogic solemnities by which the freshness of youth can be faded and its vivid curiosities dulled," had become "the art of taking advantage of the helplessness of the young," and education itself an art used by society to choke off the best part of its capacity for self-improvement. For Dewey, the world as a source of misery for the child is largely remediable through the educational process; for Freud the two are fixed in an opposition which, while alterable and even to a degree ameliorable in detail, is insurmountable in substance.

More than a generation of progressive educational experiment confirms Freud's view. Old educational failings have been remedied, often with much success, but other problems have been intensified by the new remedies. Conformity to arbitrary adult wishes has been diminished, but conformity to peers is now seen as a serious problem. The arbitrary authority of the teacher has been lessened, but a subtle manipulation, which requires self-deceit on the part of the teacher and often inspires resentment in the child, has taken its place. The fear of failure in studies has not been removed, but devices introduced to remove it have created frustrations arising from a lack of standards, of recognition, of a sense of achievement.

In his last significant statement on education, Dewey observed that "the drive of established institutions is to assimilate and distort the new into conformity with themselves." While commenting with some satisfaction on certain improvements introduced by progressive education, he ruefully remarked that the ideas and principles he had helped to develop had also succumbed to this process of institutionalization. "In teachers colleges and elsewhere the ideas and principles have been converted into a fixed subject matter of ready-made rules, to be taught and memorized according to certain standardized procedures. . . ." Memorization and standardized procedures once more! It did all too little good, he said, to train teachers "in the right principles the wrong way." With a hardy courage that can only inspire admiration, Dewey reminded progressive educators, once again and for the last time, that it is the right *method* of training which forms the character of teachers, and not the subject matter or the rules they are taught. Pursue the right methods, and a democratic society might yet be created; follow the "authoritarian principle" and education will be fit only to "pervert and destroy the foundations of a democratic society." And so the quest for a method of institutionalizing the proper anti-institutional methods goes on.

Bruno Bettelheim

THE PROBLEM OF GENERATIONS

There have been, generally speaking, two conceptual models for dealing with the unsettling assertiveness of young people in recent years. The first has dealt directly with the questions of value which have excited America: Vietnam, race, drugs, sex, rebellion, materialism, life-styles, life-purposes, ecology. Because this approach has taken seriously the arguments of the "rebels" and the "Establishment" it has frequently been a passionate approach. Most Americans have chosen sides in this debate; polar positions have been emphasized leading to a great deal of uncritical celebration and uncritical hostility. The final two essays of this volume, those by Theodore Roszak and Benjamin DeMott, suggest that the cultural-value approach need not be inflammatory, that it may indeed be a most fruitful way of understanding "where things are at."

Those who prefer more "objective" and abstract approaches, particularly the psychologists and the social scientists, have analyzed youth from a different, generational point of view. That is, they have attempted to discern universal and traditional patterns of child-parent relations and to apply somewhat abstract, general formulations to the American scene. The phrase "generation gap" has entered into common discourse through *Life* and the *Reader's Digest* as a kind of stock explanation for today's phenomena. Though it can be used in anger if one chooses to blame one or the other generation for America's distresses (note how the sociologist Edgar Friedenberg uses the concept to support a quasi-political sermon in a later essay), the "generation gap" has been generally used to soft-pedal the difficulties. After all, children grow up and become responsible. After all, the generation gap has always existed and still mankind survives. In this way the particular issues of the moment become less dramatic, less terrifying, less real.

While the final two essays in this volume take the cultural-value road, the next three, written typically enough by two psychologists and a sociologist, explore generational relationships. The message which most of the social scientists appear to be communicating, both in substance and in their often ponderoso-scientific prose, goes something like this: "Try to understand, dear readers, that the crises you face in your family have deep roots, that they are typical of most families that operate in

From "The Problem of Generations" by Bruno Bettelheim. Reprinted by permission from *Daedalus*, Journal of the American Academy of Arts and Sciences, Boston, Massachusetts, Vol. 91, No. I, pp. 77–80, 93–94.

your cultural milieu, and that not much can be done about them. Therefore be understanding. Be tolerant. Be patient, especially you parents who must realize that your children inevitably will challenge you as they seek their own way." Bruno Bettelheim, the distinguished psychologist who operates with modified Freudian categories, is more authoritarian than most of his colleagues. He feels that young people need and desire guidance and that the parental strategy that permits the child to "go his own way" does serious damage to both the parent and the child. Bettelheim's writings are important also because he pays special attention to the generational dilemmas of girls and mothers—dilemmas that will command further notice as the women's liberation movement gathers momentum and becomes the major social issue of the 1970's in America.

Since the analysts of generational conflict invoke historical precedents to justify their contentions, the reader might do well to think back to the first section of this volume in order to examine just which connections can be made and which cannot. The conclusions of the historians with regard to the "generation gap" seem to cut both ways. On the one hand, America did indeed spawn a youth culture. Children grew up in a different world from their parents—a world quite unlike the medieval European pattern of development. On the other hand, evidence indicates that American parents, by the mid-eighteenth century, understood this and applauded, rather than resented, the new departures of their children. Have American parents (compared to European) perhaps traditionally capitulated to their children and *avoided* generational conflicts which could be, at one and the same time, both dangerously divisive and richly creative? The following brief excerpt from Bettelheim permits such speculation.

MOST serious writers on the problem of youth have recognized that youth's present difficulties in Western society are closely related to changed social and economic conditions and to the ensuing difficulty for youth in finding self-realization in work. As Goodman observes: "It's hard to grow up when there isn't enough man's work," and he continues, "To produce necessary food and shelter is man's work. During most of economic history most men have done this drudging work, secure that it was justified and worthy of a man to do it, though often feeling that the social conditions under which they did it were not worthy of a man, thinking, 'It's better to die than to live so hard'—but they worked on. . . . Security is always first; but in normal conditions a large part of security comes from knowing your contribution is useful, and the rest from knowing it's uniquely yours: they need you."

Just as in this country an earlier generation needed youth because the economic security of the family depended on its contribution, so in Russia today youth is needed because only it can carry on the task of creating the new and better society; and in Africa because only it can move society from tribal confusion toward modern democracy. If the generations thus need each other, they can live together successfully, and the problem of their succession, though not negligible, can be mastered successfully. Under such conditions youth and age need each other not only for their economic but even more for their moral survival. This makes youth secure—if not in its position, at least in its self-respect. But how does the parent in modern society need the next generation? Certainly not for economic reasons any more, and what little expectation a parent may have had that his children would support him in old age becomes superfluous with greater social security. More crucially, the status-quo mood of the older generation suggests no need for youth to create a much different or radically better world.

In many respects youth has suddenly turned from being the older generation's greatest economic asset into its greatest economic liability. Witness the expense of rearing and educating youth for some twenty or more years, with no economic return to be expected. Youth still poses emotional problems to the preceding generation, as of old. But in past generations these emotional problems were, so to speak, incidental or subservient to economic necessity. What at best was once the frosting on the cake must now serve as both solid food and trimmings—and this will never work.

Thus the economic roles, obligations, and rewards are no longer clearly defined between the generations, if not turned upside down. Therefore, another aspect of the relation between the generations looms ever larger, in a balance sheet of interaction that is no longer economic but largely emotional. Modern man, insecure because he no longer feels needed for his work contribution or for self-preservation (the automatic machines do things so much better and faster), is also insecure as a parent. He wonders how well he has discharged that other great function of man, the continuation of his species.

At this point modern youth becomes the dreaded avenging angel of his parents, since he holds the power to prove his parents' success or failure as parents; and this counts so much more now, since his parents' economic success is no longer so important in a society of abundance. Youth itself, feeling insecure because of its marginal position in a society that no longer depends on it for economic survival, is tempted to use the one power this reversal between the generations has conferred on it: to be accuser and judge of the parents' success or failure as parents.

How new is all this? It is very hard to compare one age with another. But the Alcibiades or Catiline of antiquity would not have had their followings if the problem of youth having to test itself against an older generation had not existed in those times; nor do Plato's indictments of what he saw as obstreperous youth sound very different from those leveled at our young people today. I may be the victim of those distortions of perspective that make things distant seem far smaller than those looming in the foreground.

Whether this is error in judgment or not, the fact remains that the present problems of Western youth in finding self-definition, and with it security, seem more complex than those of other generations. I say Western youth because, while Russia appears to have its equivalent of the Teddy boys and while Israel does not seem altogether happy with all aspects of Kibbutz-reared youth, the problems there seem different not only in quantity but also in quality. The main difference lies not so much in the particular tasks society sets for its younger generation but in how clearly the latter realize that only they, the generation of the future, can achieve these tasks.

This difference is critical, for, contrary to some people's opinion, youth does not create its own cause for which it is ready to fight. All it can do is to embrace causes developed by mature men. But youth can only do this successfully if the older men are satisfied with providing the ideals and do not also wish to lead the active battle for reaching them. Or, to put it differently, a youth expected to fight for his personal place in a society of well-defined direction is not lost but on his way. A youth expected to create a new but not yet delineated society finds himself a rebel without a cause. Only when each group has its own important tasks, when one without the other cannot succeed, when age provides the direction but youth the leadership and the fighting manpower, is it clearly understood that whether the battle is won or lost depends on youth's fulfilling its all-important share of the total struggle. . . .

I have said before that for youth to come into his own means to a large degree his replacing the older generation, and that, whether the transition is smooth or hard-won, youth is still on its way. Thus the problem of the generations, when it goes wrong, may be characterized by saying that, whenever the older generation has lost its bearings, the younger generation is lost with it. The positive alternatives of emulation or revolt are then replaced by the lost quality of neither.

And this, I am afraid, is the situation in which large segments of American youth find themselves. They are unhappy when they settle down to continue in a pattern of life that their parents have arranged for them, because they know it to be an empty one. But they find it pointless to rebel, as do those others who, sensing emptiness in the lives prepared for them, fight against it but do not know what to fight for.

Old age is happiest when it can take youth up to the threshold of the good and the new and, like the mythical father of the West, point out the Promised Land to its children, saying: you and only you in a hard fight will have to make this your own; because what is handed down to you, what you have not won for yourselves, is never truly your own.

Youth, on the other hand, is happiest when it feels it is fighting to reach goals that were conceived of but not realized by the generation before them. What the older generation then urgently wished for itself, but had to acknowledge as the hope of the future—this is the legacy of youth. That the preceding generation wished to create such a better world makes it a worthy standard for youth. To come closer to achieving it through its own efforts proves to youth that it is gaining its own rich maturity.

Kenneth Keniston

YOUTH CULTURE AS ENFORCED ALIENATION

About thirty years ago Margaret Mead wrote that in America parents expect and desire that their children will surpass them in life. This is one form that the cult of youth takes. Kenneth Keniston develops that insight to indicate how this unusual regard for youth leads to a paradoxical sense of alienation—felt by young and old alike. In this way he can talk both about an American youth cult (which welcomes the creation of a separate youth culture) *and* about generational conflict. The essay that follows demands special attention because it deals with the apparently *un*alienated young people in America—the average, contented, well-adjusted youth rather than the obvious rebels. And yet his essay is about alienation. As was the case with Bettelheim, Keniston's model of generational conflict is far more complex and far more valuable than the popular view which simply sees young and old living in different worlds and adhering to differing views which must inevitably clash. (The article by Edgar Friedenberg offers an interesting variation of this simpler view.)

Kenneth Keniston is a psychologist at Yale who has written a great deal of consistently thoughtful and widely-respected commentary on American youth.

WHAT we call "youth culture"—the distinctive values, outlooks, manners, roles, activities, and behavior patterns of youth considered as a separate age group—is not a uniquely American phenomenon. In other technological societies, national variants of youth culture are increasingly visible.

But in America, the most advanced of the technological nations, youth culture shows its greatest scope and development. Here, youth culture involves not only the privileged and educated, but all sectors of society; it includes not only our "teenagers," but many who are advanced into their twenties. And though we commonly take it for granted that youths should exhibit special and often erratic, bizarre, and deviant behavior simply because of their age, not all societies make this assumption. On the contrary, in many, adolescents are seen primarily as young adults or as old children: they are expected to exhibit no distinctive behavior by simple virtue of their age. Even in our own country two generations ago, youth was largely defined as a time of apprenticeship: adolescence was a matter of "learning the ropes" and memorizing the map and the timetable for the road of success ahead. Gawky, awkward adolescence was a phase to be outgrown as quickly as possible.

Some few Americans still retain this view of youth, but most of us do not. Increasingly we expect that youth will have a special culture of its own, with characteristics that are those of neither childhood or adulthood. Our language reflects this expectation: we seldom speak colloquially of "youths" or "adolescents"—terms that implicitly suggest the transition to adulthood—but rather of "teenagers," "hoods," and "beatniks," all of whom are seen as ensconced in a world of their own with a world view of their own. Increasingly, we expect adolescents and young adults to behave in idiosyncratic ways which are symptomatic of their age.

The growth and dominance of youth culture in America means that most young Americans spend their formative years in a special culture only peripherally related to the adult world. We expect teenagers to be different, and they come to expect it of themselves as well. Most adults view a youth of seventeen with a firmly established adult outlook as someone who is "too old for his years." The values and behaviors of the youth culture are rarely explicitly anti-adult, but they are explicitly non-adult; and the dominant virtues of adolescent society are not those of the adult world. This means that the average young American must undergo two major transitions en route to adulthood: first he must move from childhood to the youth culture, learning its ways and adapting to its requirements; and later, when he "drops out" of the youth culture or is expelled by commencement, he must make a second transition into the "real" world of grownups.

To be precise, we should speak of many "youth sub-cultures" which share common characteristics rather than of one embracing youth culture, for under this rubric we must subsume a great many different groups, variously labeled "typical teenagers," "rock-and-rollers," "Joe College students," "youthful beatniks," and so on. F. Scott Fitzgerald's picture of Princeton before and after the First World War has come to epitomize one of the earliest American youth cultures, that of "flaming youth." In our own day, we have more various and contrasting versions, ranging to the black-jacketed delinquent to the oversensitive Catcher in the Rye, from the misunderstood James Dean to the fun-and-football fraternity man. A few of these sub-cultures are clearly alienated, like the delinquent gang or the youthful beat world; and if we are not to prejudge the issues of the tie of youth cultures with alienation, we must consider the other, more socially acceptable versions. Writing of these more than twenty years ago, Talcott Parsons suggested that they shared an emphasis on physical attractiveness, irresponsibility, lack of interest in adult things, and interest in athletics; but to this list we must now add further characteristics.

Let us take, then, as the most articulate form of the youth culture, the relatively unalienated group from which our alienated students were drawn, and attempt to characterize some of their dominant views and outlooks. And let us concentrate on those of their views which seem especially distinctive to this age group. This composite portrait, then, will be one of "elite youth," of those who have the ability to "fit in," of those whom society has fully embraced, of those from whom tomorrow's leaders will likely be drawn.

Few of these young men and women have any doubt that they will one day be part of our society. They do not actively or enthusiastically *choose* to be part; rather they will unreflectively assume that they *will* be part; and problems of "choosing" conventional adulthood, so central to the alienated, rarely even occur to them as such. They wonder about where they will fit, but not about whether. They take it for granted that they will one day "settle down"; and if it troubles them, they push it out of their minds or consider it a problem to be solved by finding a suitable wife and career. By and large they "approve" of American society if asked, though normally they do not think in these terms. Society is simply there.

But at the same time, these young men and women often show a lack of deep commitment to adult values and roles. They are not alienated as are beatniks, delinquents or our group of alienated students. Rather, they view the adult world they expect to enter with a subtle distrust, a lack of high expectations, hopes, or dreams, and an often unstated feeling that they will have to "settle" for less than they would hope for if they let themselves hope. A surprising number, despite their efforts to get good grades so that they can get into good graduate schools and eventually have good careers, despite their manifest desire to do well in the existing social order, nonetheless view it, in Paul Goodman's phrase, as "an apparently closed room with a rat race going on in the middle." Whether they call it a rat race or not is immaterial (though many half-jokingly do); the point is that they expect little in the way of personal fulfillment, growth, or creativity from their future roles in the public world. Essentially, they recognize that adulthood is a relatively cold, demanding, specialized, and abstracted world where "meaningful" work is so scarce they do not even ask for it. Thus, the majority stay "cool" when it comes to the "real world"; and "coolness" means above all detachment, lack of emotion, absence of deep commitment, not being either enthusiastic *or* rejecting of adulthood.

Toward their parents, who are psychologically the most crucial exemplars of adulthood, most students show a similar lack of conscious or articulate involvement. They are neither ardently devoted nor explicitly rebellious. Indeed, many a youth is so distant from his parents, in generational terms if not in affection, that he can afford to "understand" them and show a touching sympathy for their tentative efforts to guide and advise him. His parents, too, usually sense their distance, fear that they are "dated" or "square," and become reluctant to interfere by imposing their own values and styles of life where they might be inappropriate. The result is frequently an unstated gentleman's agreement between the generations that neither will interfere with the other. To be sure, beneath this agreement, most students are deeply and usually unconsciously involved in relinquishing their ties of personal dependency on their parents; and many of the 10 to 20 per cent of students who avail themselves of psychiatric help when it is available, are concerned with this problem. But dependency is not commitment; dependency *on* parents is often the greatest problem where commitment *to* what they stand for is impossible.

Most youths approach the wider world, social problems, political events, and international affairs with a comparable lack of deep involvement. There are notable exceptions in the civil rights movement, as among other student activists, but they are very few in number. The vast majority are well informed and uninvolved. Ultimately, most students feel a strong underlying sense of social powerlessness which dictates this lack of involvement. Few believe that society could, much less should, be radically transformed; most consider the world complex far beyond their power to comprehend or influence it; and almost all see the stage of history and social change as inhabited by vast impersonal forces which are quite beyond human control. The more sophisticated are sometimes drawn to Toynbeean or Spenglerian theories of the rise and fall of civilizations; the less sophisticated subscribe to theories of "the market"; and almost no one thinks that he, even in concert with his fellows, could alter the irrevocable course of events by so much as an iota.

The adult world, then, as seen from within the youth culture, inspires neither enthusiasm nor deep commitment. Most youths expect to be of it, but not for it or "with it." In fact, most do not expect very much at all of adulthood: they think about it rarely and ask little of it. Instead, their dominant focus is on the present, on the years of the youth culture itself, on high school or college life and on the pleasures to be derived therein. To be sure, many take courses whose goal is ultimately vocational: to become an engineer, a teacher, or a doctor; but most spend little time (as little as possible) thinking about what a career will involve. Instead they live within the present, for the present; the future will take care of itself.

Until that happens, the youth culture provides a distinctive and separate world, many of whose central themes are familiar from our survey of the motifs of alienation. One such theme is an emphasis on the present, on experience. In its most extreme form, this is the intense and obsessive alienated search for sentience; beatniks characteristically define experience as "kicks"—speed, sex, and stimulation. But most college students seek milder forms of experience: good times, girl friends, fun with the gang, the exploration of nature, happy days in summer, even art, music, and poetry. The American myth of "carefree college days" is dominated by an eternal present where things are done "just for the fun of it." For some students, the present means a bull session with the gang or a shopping expedition with the girls; for others, it means an opportunity to experiment, to make tentative commitments, to try on roles or selves with the option of returning them if they do not fit. The disappearance of the Protestant ethic among college students has entailed the demise of the concept of a "life work"; in place of yesterday's Horatio Algers are today's more easy-going, relaxed young men and women who are learning how to enjoy themselves.

Yet this cult of the present has a hidden rationale, the search for identity. Consciously, this search is usually defined as a question about "what to do with my life," that is, about careers and vocations. But less consciously the cult of the present, the freedom of the youth culture to experiment, and its authorization from adult society to postpone binding commitments—all allow young men and women time to confront the difficult freedoms, choices, and selections their society demands of them. Adolescence in America is considered a place for legitimate "role-playing," for testing alternatives, for provisional commitments followed by a loss of interest, for overwhelming enthusiasm followed by total apathy. In a few students, especially at the most demanding colleges, problems of choice and commitment may reach full consciousness; and there, many a graduating senior on the eve of graduation wonders "Who am I?" in a cosmic as well as a vocational sense. And at a few "elite" colleges, "I'm having an identity crisis," becomes the proud self-justification of any self-conscious youth. Though it can be exploited and caricatured, resolving this "identity crisis" is indeed a central function of the youth culture as a whole, which allows what Erik Erikson calls "a psychosocial moratorium" on adult commitments, and gives time and room for role-playing and experimentation.

The very discontinuity of the youth culture with the demands of adult society allows youth a "breathing space" between childhood and adulthood, time to try to resolve the developmental discontinuities between these two stages of life, and, above all, space to try to achieve some sense of inner unity, self-sameness, and continuity that promises to endure despite continual social change, to cohere despite the dissociative demands of our society. By providing a waiting room before adulthood, the youth culture offers a protected space in which to do the psychological work which adulthood presupposes. Most of this work is done unconsciously and quietly, "acted out" on the stage of college activities, summer jobs, going steady, and a continuing reassessment of one's links to the personal past. The youth culture permits experimentation in the service of unconscious choice, exposure to experience for the sake of selection, and trial commitment in the interest of future self-definition. Acute self-fragmentation, the alternative to success in these pursuits, only rarely occurs. But the problem of identity is there for all.

Much of this unconscious work ultimately involves redefining one's relationship to one's parents, to childhood, and to the childhood self. Those who founder often do so because the backward pulls of childhood are too strong. Like the alienated, they unconsciously find the fantasy of childhood embeddedness more compelling than the "cold adult world." Given the pull of childhood dependencies, alienation is but one possibility; others are so normal that we scarcely note them at all—the almost inevitable homesickness of freshmen, a tendency to alternate between nostalgic idealization of one's parents and acute embarrassment at their limitations, a readiness to plunge into some substitute and often premature intimacy with a girl, a reactive assertion of independence, masculinity, toughness, and autonomy from parents. College students are normally prone to become excessively dependent upon advisers, counselors, and even upon psychotherapists, who at best duplicate the role of the "good mother" by exploiting their patients' involvement with them in order to promote their eventual disengagement. The underlying fantasy of fusion often finds partial expression in fusion with some college group—a fraternity, a "crowd," a set of dorm mates, a sorority—all of which can inspire almost mystical feelings of solidarity, self-sacrifice, and devotion despite their actually limited goals and even meretricious values. At some colleges, this adolescent potential for self-surrender is channeled into "college spirit," which can bring unashamed tears to the eyes of a football player who would die rather than weep for his mother. The dependency and need for embeddedness fostered by our small intimate families must somehow be dislocated from mother, family, and childhood until it can be refocused on the second true love of one's life. The youth culture abets this rechanneling.

Though the youth culture permits narrowly defined forms of solidarity and surrender to a group, it enjoins against overt idealism, especially in any Utopian cause. It is normal to be loyal to college and fraternity, but not to an ideology. Even those who hanker after political careers rarely admit ideological commitment. To remain "popular" and "normal," they must avow a healthy cynicism, professing politics a "job like any other" and disavowing any intent to "change the world." Whatever one's real purposes (and these often are idealistic), the youth culture requires that one not admit to noble motives. Thus, young men and women who devotedly trudge each week to dismal mental hospitals to work with and sometimes save "hopeless" chronic patients will more often say that they "want the experience" or are "testing themselves" than they will confess to a genuine desire to help or serve. And a youth who joins the Peace Corps will often find it easier to term his decision a way of "solving his identity crisis" than to admit his Utopian hopes and goals. Idealistic motives and Utopian aspirations extend out of the youth culture into the wider society, and thus fall under the injunction to "coolness." Furthermore, because their childhoods often leave them so full of deep and sentimental nostalgias, American young men are fearful of all that might appear sentimental. Since once, in the distant and repressed past, it was so good to be cared for and enfolded, young Americans (and especially young men) are anxiously fearful of seeming "suckers," of being "taken in," of being embraced by any embracing cause.

Yet beneath this apparent cynicism there usually lies a deeper search for commitments of ultimate worth and value. When something like the Peace Corps comes along, a surprising number, disavowing idealism, are willing to join this idealistic cause. Philosophical or religious inquiry offers an avenue to commitment for a few; and others turn to the study of psychology, which seems to promise the "discovery" of positive values within the psyche. The arts, drama, poetry, music—all of which are undergoing a revival on better college campuses—also offer solace, if not purpose. And above all in the civil rights movement an increasing, though still small, number of students (most of whom are not ideologically alienated) can find a creative channel for their idealism. The struggle for equality for Negro Americans, like the Peace Corps, offers a vehicle for the expression of idealism without ideology, a simple moral commitment to work for the welfare of one's fellow men.

But for the great majority, commitment is sought and found in individual private experience—in leisure, in comradeship, in sports, in a girl. All of these commitments, which David Riesman calls "privatism," involve turning away from the wider social and public world toward the more manageable domain of personal life. Whatever dim glimmerings of Utopian spirit are visible in the youth culture can be seen largely as diffused through these privatistic pursuits. The Utopian quest, the search for positive values so clearly seen in the alienated, is here muted into the precursor of the ethic of family and fun in adulthood.

Yet we should recall that permission is granted to remain in the youth culture only so long as academic requirements are met. Those who quit, drop out, or are failed out, either enter adulthood forthwith or must enter upon serious delinquency or the "beat" world. The power of exclusion is a powerful sanction, and it is one reason Americans often prefer education to the "real world" for so many years. By indirectly encouraging prolonged education, this requirement also promotes the high-level ego training of precisely the kind our society requires: higher education is especially designed to inculcate and develop the specialized cognitive skills needed for success in American society. The price of admission and permission to stay in the youth culture is steadily rising academic performance: the most talented and hard-working can therefore stay the longest. The liberal arts colleges usually attended by such eager and able students explicitly disavow any intent at providing vocational training. They explicitly aim at training the mind, at developing powers of analysis, criticism, selection, and organization, at encouraging independent work and study—in short, at developing and defining ego skills that will be useful no matter what the job and even if its requirements change. The freedom of the youth culture is purchased at the price of the continuing acquisition of the ability to meet our society's ego demands.

The elite youth culture I have characterized is thus closely related to the major themes of alienation and to the central demands of American society. This group of talented young Americans, most of whom are not alienated, nonetheless show in their youth culture comparable themes to those found among the alienated: a preoccupation with the present, a concern with the search for identity, many symptoms of continuing problems of dependency, a quest for positive values which aborts in private commitment, and a preoccupation with the ego demands of our technological society. There are enormous differences between a college booster and an Inburn; but they have their underlying similarities as well.

More important, however, than any similarities between the themes of alienation and the motifs of the youth culture is the fact that the youth culture as a whole *requires* a refusal of conventional adulthood for the time one is in it. Its values are discontinuous with those of adulthood: it is not a simple transition or apprenticeship between the child and the man. In one sense, then, we normally *expect* its members to be alienated: not to undertake irrevocable adult commitments, to experiment and experience, to live in the present, to be irresponsible and carefree, to value and create color and excitement, to be physically daring and sexually attractive. All of these qualities are secondary, subordinated, or actively discouraged in adult society. Furthermore, youth culture and adulthood are defined as irreconcilable: any youth who is prepared to make an immediate commitment to adulthood *must* leave the youth culture, *must* stop his education, and *must* enter the world of grownups.

The youth culture therefore permits American youth as a whole to be "institutionally" alienated without having to be personally alienated. It provides a socially supported period when the average young man or woman simply finds it impossible to enter the adult world. It therefore points to the unreadiness, psychological and ideological, of most young Americans to accept adult commitments and to meet the difficult ego demands of our society. By "taking off the pressure" for a period ranging from five to fifteen years, the youth culture permits most youths to remain uninvolved in the adult world without having to take an open stand against it. By sanctioning and even requiring *de facto* alienation, it removes the need in most youths for a more focused and articulated alienation from adulthood. And it takes the pressure off longest for those on whom adult pressures will eventually be greatest: the highly educated, of whom most will be later required.

The relation of youth culture and alienation is therefore paradoxical. Youth is defined in America as a stage of systematic disengagement from conventional adulthood; the values of the youth culture involve a lack of any deep commitment to adult society, parents, and the adult world. But at the same time the socially supported alienation of the youth culture acts to absolve most young men and women of any need for personally repudiating conventional adulthood: their membership in the youth culture does it for them. During this long moratorium on adulthood, young Americans must undertake a series of major psychological transitions: they must attempt to abandon childhood identifications and commitments for the more selective and partial identifications of adulthood and for commitments that promise to weather the ravages of chronic social change. They must make the many choices our society demands and integrate them into one coherent sense of self. Perhaps most difficult psychologically, they must gradually renounce their ties of dependency on their first families and free themselves to form new ties to adult social groups and their own families. Somehow, usually without much conscious thought, they must find where they stand ideologically—*what* if anything they stand for, *how much* they will stand for, and *where* they stand. And simultaneously, they must develop to the limit of their ability and patience their capacity to meet the stringent demands of our society.

All of this means that most American youths have a double orientation to adulthood. On the one hand, they see themselves as free and feckless participants in the youth culture, by virtue of that fact committed (for the time being) to non-adult values and distrustful of the adult world. On the other hand, most take for granted that they will one day enter adulthood and see themselves as preparing themselves for it. Many of the controversies over the real nature of American youth—over whether it is irresponsible and hedonistic or sober and dedicated—stem from this double orientation. Some observers see one face of youth, and other observers the other; and both observers often mistake the part for the whole.

Such oversimplification is especially hard to avoid because young people themselves present now one and now another face, all the while maintaining there is no more than meets the eye. Not that they deliberately deceive older people as to what they are like—on the contrary, when a young man or woman is with representatives of the adult world (teachers, ministers, admissions officers, poll takers) he not only acts like a future citizen of America, he really *feels* that way. And the same youth under other circumstances—when with friends, at Daytona Beach or Newport, in campus coffee houses, fraternities, sororities, or dormitories—really *feels* like a hood, a beatnik, a college Joe or a Deke. But in each of these stances some of the same ambivalence exists, despite the frequent insistence of the young (with a characteristic adolescent combination of ambivalence and intolerance for ambivalence) that there is only one side of the coin.

Compared to the extreme group we have studied, then, their classmates are "alienated" as members of the youth culture but rarely as individuals. Our society evokes scant enthusiasm in them; but since it need not be actively confronted, it evokes little overt or articulate rejection. In many ways, the alienated are alienated because they have not been able to *use* the youth culture to escape the pressures of adult society. For them, there *is* no moratorium on the demands of adulthood; these demands continually push at them, epitomized by parents, teachers, and images of the "cold adult world." Paradoxically, though they vociferously reject conventional adulthood, the very act of rejection also makes them more continually concerned with it than are their less alienated fellows. . . .

Americans revere children and childhood for many reasons, not least because the young are the hope of parents the world over. But beneath the special American heightening of this universal hope there lies a deep if seldom voiced belief that children have the best of it, that childhood has qualities and joys for whose loss adulthood never really compensates. We love our children so well because in part we loved our lives as children best. Whatever the miseries of childhood in individual lives (and they are many), we view it in the image of happy irresponsibility, carefree play, and a ready shoulder to cry on. Perhaps we sacrifice so readily for children because by living on in them we hope we can spare them, our new selves, the adulthood we ourselves must live.

But of all the ages we most revere, youth is the foremost. We are a society that adds to its youth culture a cult of youth. No doubt, the capacities of youth for rapid growth and change again partly inspire our respect. But elsewhere, and even in our own American past, youth was largely laughable in its awkward imitation of adult things. What makes the modern difference in America is the inevitable incompleteness of our own adolescence. Psychologists have shown that we remember best the tasks we fail to finish. The tasks of youth in our own society are so overwhelming that most of us leave our adolescences with a vague sense of not being ready, of not having done, of having failed to finish some one or all of the crucial tasks of adolescence. As a consequence, we do not merely look back on our own youths fondly, as we would if youth were only a time of a job well done. Instead we weep for our lost youths, fear the gathering years that separate us from them, seek to preserve a "youthfulness" of outlook and visage which will belie these years, and warn our young against wasting their youths. Youth is not only a time of hedonism and irresponsibility which contrasts with adult cares and worries, but a stage we were not (and are still not) ready to abandon. Because we so often could not finish what we had to do, we view our own youths with an implicit "if only"—if only we had known then . . . , if only we had had time . . . , if only this instead of that. . . . The weeping of old grads at football games is both a mourning for what they had then but have lost, and a mourning for what they might have been but never became.

The idealization and mourning of childhood and youth, which is most common among the white, competent, "well-adjusted" middle-class, suggests that the typical quality of commitment to adulthood in America is at best halfhearted, that (at the very least) enthusiasm is scant, and that something more is involved than the simple fact that in no society do most men and women have a commitment to their adulthoods that is both deep and articulate. Our attitudes toward childhood and youth suggest that our commitment to our adulthood is not only shallow and inarticulate, but, at the deepest level, that it often gives way to a sense of historical loss, of developmental estrangement, of existential uprootedness, and of alienation.

Edgar Z. Friedenberg

THE GENERATION GAP

Of the mountain of material describing the aspirations and behavior of American youth, practically none of it is written by young people themselves. One cannot account for this by speaking of youthful bashfulness or lack of intelligence. Perhaps the chief reason lies in the preference young people have for expressing themselves in other media: in music, dance, film; and in behavior, drug-induced or politically motivated. The best way to approach the culture of youth is not by reading a book but by attending a performance given, let us say, by the Jefferson Airplane. With the lights low, the volume turned so high that the electric guitar vibrates through you, the bodies, exotically dressed (or undressed), moving freely and erotically, the suggestions of total sexual liberation, the smell of pot and incense, the light show producing weird, ever-changing and pulsating abstractions on a huge screen placed behind the performers, one begins to understand. But even here, understanding is hopelessly limited without participation by the observer, a participation which practically demands the surrender of consciousness. And how can one observe without consciousness?

Most sociologists, however, feel more comfortable with tangible materials than with these sensory perceptions. Edgar Friedenberg is a sociologist and he has little patience with those who blame the difference between the generations on imperfect communication, on affluence, on Dr. Spock or John Dewey, or on youthful folly. He emphasizes instead the notion of class conflicts—a special interest of his discipline—and argues that youth is (a) a class, and (b) an exploited one at that. His concentration on the specific deprivations experienced by young people offers a different perspective from that of other writers in this volume. His conclusions do not quite square with the commonly held view that most of the rebellion is led by privileged upper-middle-class youngsters who, because they do not have to worry about economic survival, open up for scrutiny questions concerning the largest purposes for living itself—questions which make those who spend most of their lives working hard to make a "good living" extremely uncomfortable. Friedenberg tries at the end of his essay to connect this notion with his apparently contradictory thesis concerning the bondage in which youth is held. His vigorous essay must be considered successful if that connection is well-made.

THE idea that what separates us from the young is something so passive that it may justly be called a "generation gap" is, I believe, itself a misleading article of middle-aged liberal ideology, serving to allay anxiety rather than to clarify the bases of intergenerational conflict. It is true, to be sure, that the phrase is strong enough to describe the barrier that separates many young people from their elders, for a majority still accept our society as providing a viable pattern of life and expectations for the future. Liberalism dies hard, and most young people, like some Negroes even today, are still willing to attribute their difficulties with their elders and society to mutual misunderstanding.

I believe, however, that this is a false position. Though most adults maintain a benevolent posture in expressing their public attitudes toward youth and—though, I think, steadily fewer—young people still accept this as what their elders intend in principle, both young and old seem trapped in a false view of what is actually a profound conflict of interest in our society. What appears to be a consequence of mere cultural lag in responding to a new social and political maturity in the young, with distressing but inintended repressive consequences, is rather the expression of what has become genuine class-conflict between a dominant and exploitive older generation and youth who are slowly becoming more aware of what is happening to them as demands on them are, in the language of the time, escalated.

DISCONTINUITY IN AN OPEN SOCIETY

In all societies, so far as I know, young people enter the social system in subordinate roles while older people run things. This is true even in technically primitive cultures where the crude physical strength of youth is still of real productive advantage. Is there always a generational conflict? And, if so, does it always reflect as profound a division, and as severe a conflict of interest, as generational conflict in America today?

There is, I believe, indeed an inherent basis for such a conflict in the fact that the old dominate the young and the young wish to replace them, but it is not as severe in most societies as in ours. Here, it has become different in kind, as the brightest and most articulate of the young declare that they will not even accept, when their turn comes, the kinds of roles—in the kind of society—which their parents have held. As Bruno Bettelheim pointed out in a classic paper some years ago, factors that have traditionally mitigated generational conflict have become feeble or inoperative even in this country. The family, for example, which is the context within which the strongest—albeit ambivalent—affectual ties between the generations are formed, plays a decreasing role in the lives of its members and, certainly, in the socialization of the young. It has less effect on their life-chances than it once had. If the Victorian father or the head of a traditional rural household was often a tyrant, and more or less accepted as such by his neighbors and his children, he was also a man who felt that he could transmit his wealth, his trade, and his position in the community, by inheritance. His relationship to his sons was not purely competitive but complementary as well: it was they who would have to carry on his work as his own powers failed, and on whom he was therefore ultimately dependent if his accomplishment in life was to lead to anything permanent. The proper attitude of father to son—both the authority and the underlying tenderness—took account of this mutual though unequal dependency. And while excessive and inconsiderate longevity in a father might make his son's position grotesque, as that of mad old George III did to the Prince Regent's position, the problems of succession were usually made less abrasive by the recognition of mutual need.

Moreover, so long as society changed slowly, elders really knew more that was useful than the young did; they were wiser; their authority was based on real superiority in the subtle techniques of living. This was never a very strong bond between the generations in America, where the sons of immigrants have always been as likely to find their greenhorn parents a source of embarrassment as of enlightenment; and generational conflict has probably always been more severe here than in more stable cultures—or would have been had there not also been a continent to escape into and develop.

But, today, the older generation has become not merely an embarrassment, but often an obstructive irrelevance to the young. We cannot even defend our former functions with respect to youth; for the ethos of modern liberalism condemns as inequitable, and a violation of equal opportunity, the arrangements on which continuity between the generations has been based. Bourgeois emphasis on private property and the rights of inheritance gave to the family the function of providing this continuity, which, under feudal conditions, would have been shared among several institutions—apprenticeship, for example. But the development of an open, bureaucratic society has weakened the influence of the family, and has transferred the task of distributing status among claimants primarily to the schools, which profess to judge them, so far as possible, without regard to their antecedents. . . .

YOUTH AS A DISCRIMINATED-AGAINST CLASS

I have already asserted that conflict between the generations is less a consequence of the ways in which old and young perceive, or misperceive, each other than of structurally created, genuine conflicts of interest. In this, as in other relationships, ideology follows self-interest: we impute to other people and social groups characteristics that justify the use we plan to make of them and the control over them that use requires. The subordinate group, in turn, often develops these very characteristics in response to the conditions that were imposed on them. Slaves, slum-dwellers, "teen-agers," and enlisted men do, indeed, often display a defensive stupidity and irresponsibility, which quickly abates in situations in which they feel to be free of officious interference, with which they can deal, by means of their own institutions, in their own way.

For American youth, these occasions are few, and have grown relatively fewer with the escalation of the war in Vietnam. The Dominican intervention, the scale and permanence of our military investment in Southeast Asia, and the hunch that our economic system requires the engagement of its youth at low pay, or none, in a vast military-academic complex, in order to avoid disastrously widespread unemployment—even under present circumstances far greater among youth than among older persons—suggest to thoughtful young people that their bondage may be fundamental to the American political system and incapable of solution within its terms.

That bondage is remarkably complete—and so gross, in comparison to the way in which other members of the society are treated, that I find it difficult to accept the good faith of most adults who declare their sympathy with "the problems of youth" while remaining content to operate within the limits of the coercive system that deals with them in any official capacity. To search for explanations of the problems of youth in America in primarily psychological terms while suggesting ways of easing the tension between them and the rest of society is rather like approaching the problem of "the American turkey in late autumn" with the same benign attitude. Turkeys would have no problem, except for the use we make of them, though I can imagine clearly enough the arguments that a cadre of specialists in poultry-relations might advance in defense of Thanksgiving, all of them true enough as far as they went: that wild turkeys could not support themselves under the demanding conditions of modern life; that there are now more turkeys than ever before and their general health and nutritional status, if not their life-expectancy, is much more favorable than in the past; that a turkey ought to have a chance to fulfill its obligations and realize the meaning of its life as a responsible member of society; that, despite the sentimental outcries of reformers, most turkeys seem contented with their lot—those that are not content being best treated by individual clinical means and, if necessary, an accelerated program; and that the discontented are not the fattest, anyway, only the brightest.

Young men in America, like most Negroes, are excluded from any opportunity to hold the kind of job or to earn the kind of money without which members of this society committed to affluence are treated with gross contempt. In a sense, the plight of youth is more oppressive, for the means by which they are constrained are held to be lawful, while discrimination against Negroes is now proscribed by law and what remains, though very serious indeed, is the massive toxic residue of past practice rather than current public policy.

Students are not paid for attending school; they are held to be investing in their future—though if, in fact, they invested as capital the difference between the normal wage of an employed adult high school graduate for four to seven years and what little they may have received as stipends during their academic careers for the same length of time, the return accrued to them might easily exceed the increment a degree will bring. But, of course, they have not got it to invest, and are not permitted to get it to live on. The draft siphons off working-class youth, while middle-class youth are constrained to remain in college to avoid it. If there were no draft, their impact on the economy would probably be ruinous. Trade-union restrictions and child-labor laws, in any case, prevent their gaining the kind of experience, prior to the age of eighteen—even as part of a high school program—that would qualify them for employment as adults by the time they reach their legal majority, though young workers could be protected by laws relating to working conditions, hours, and wage-rates, if this protection were indeed the intent of restrictive legislation, without eliminating his opportunity for employment.

Even the concept of a legal majority is itself a social artifact, defining the time at which the social structure is ready to concede a measure of equality to those of its members whom youthfulness has kept powerless, without reference to their real qualifications which, where relevant, could be directly tested. Nature knows no such sharp break in competence associated with maturation, except in the sexual sphere; and comparatively little of our economic and political behavior is overtly sexual. Perhaps if more were, we would be more forthright and less spiteful. Nor is there any general maturational factor, gradual but portentous in its cumulative effect, which is relevant to society's demands.

Neither wisdom nor emotional stability is particularly characteristic of American adults, as compared to the young; and where, in this country, would the electoral process become less rational if children were permitted to vote: southern California? Washington, D.C.? If there should be any age limitation on voting, it ought to apply, surely, to those so old that they may reasonably expect to escape the consequences of their political decisions, rather than to those who will be burdened and perhaps destroyed by them. Certainly, the disfranchisement of youth is impossible to square, morally, with the Selective Service Act—though politically, there is no inconsistency: the second implies the first. But the draft is pure exploitation, in a classical Marxian sense. The question of the need for an army is not the issue. A volunteer army could be raised, according to the conservative economist Milton Friedman, for from four to twenty billion dollars per year; and to argue that even the larger sum is more than the nation can afford is merely to insist that draftees support the nation by paying, in kind, a tax-rate several times greater than the average paid by civilian taxpayers in money, instead of being compensated for their loss in liberty and added risk. To argue that military service is a duty owed to one's country seems quite beside the point: it is not owed more by a young man than by the old or the middle-aged. And, at a time when a large proportion of enlisted military assignments are in clerical and technical specialties identical with those for which civilians are highly paid, the draft seems merely a form of involuntary servitude.

Without a doubt, the Selective Service Act has done more than any other factor not only to exacerbate the conflict between generations, but to make it clear that it is a real conflict of interest. The draft makes those subject to it formally second-class citizens in a way to which no race is subjected any longer. The arrogance and inaccessibility of Selective Service officials, who are neither elected nor appointed for fixed terms subject to review; the fact that it has been necessary to take court action even to make public the names of draft-board members in some communities; the fact that registrants are specifically denied representation by counsel during their dealings with the Selective Service System and can only appeal to the courts after risking prosecution for the felony of refusing induction—all this is without parallel in the American legal process.

But the laws of the land are, after all, what define youth as a discriminated-against class. In fact, it is their discrimination that gives the term "youth" the only operational meaning it has: that of a person who, by reason of age, becomes subject to special constraint and penalties visited upon no other member of the commonwealth—for whom, by reason of age, certain conduct, otherwise lawful, is defined as criminal and to whom special administrative procedures, applicable to no other member of the commonwealth, are applied. The special characteristics of "youth culture" are derived from these disabilities rather than from any inherent age-graded characteristics. "Youth culture" is composed of individuals whose time is pre-empted by compulsory school attendance or the threat of induction into the Armed Service, who, regardless of their skills, cannot get and hold jobs that will pay enough to permit them to marry and build homes, and who are subject to surveillance at home or in school dormitories if they are detected in any form of sexual activity whatever. Youth and prisoners are the only people in America for whom *all* forms of sexual behavior are defined as illicit. It is absurd to scrutinize people who are forced to live under such extraordinary disabilities for psychological explanations of their resistance or bizarre conduct, except insofar as their state of mind can be related to their real situation. . . .

BRINGING IT ALL BACK HOME

Finally, exacerbating the confrontations between youth and adults is the fact that the control of youth has largely been entrusted to lower-status elements of the society. Custodial and control functions usually are so entrusted, for those in subjection have even lower status themselves, and do not command the services of the higher grades of personnel that their society affords. Having low status, moreover, prevents their being taken seriously as moral human beings. Society tends to assume that the moral demands made on the criminal, the mad, and the young by their respective wardens are for their own good and to reinforce those demands while limiting the subjects' opportunities for redress to those situations in which the grossest violations of the most fundamental human rights have occurred. The reader's moral evaluation of the conflict that I have described will, therefore, depend very largely, I believe, on the degree to which he shares society's assumption.

As has surely been obvious, I do not share it. The process by which youth is brought into line in American society is almost wholly destructive of the dignity and creative potential of the young, and the condition of the middle-aged and the old in America seems to me, on the whole, to make this proposition quite plausible. Nevertheless, the violation of the young in the process of socialization fulfills an essential function in making our society cohesive. And curiously—and rather perversely—this function depends on the fact that custody and indoctrination—education is not, after all, a very precise term for it—are lower-status functions.

American democracy depends, I believe, on the systematic humiliation of potential elites to keep it going. There is, perhaps, no other way in which an increasingly educated middle class, whose technical services cannot be spared, can be induced to acquiesce in the political demands of a deracinated and invidious populace, reluctant to accept any measure of social improvement, however generally advantageous, which might bring any segment of the society slightly more benefits than would accrue to it. Teachers, police, and parents in America are jointly in the business of rearing the young to be frightened of the vast majority who have been too scarred and embittered by the losses and compromises which they have endured in the process of becoming respectable to be treated in a way that would enrage them. Anything generous—or perhaps merely civil, like welcoming a Negro family into a previously white community, or letting your neighbor "blow a little grass" in peace—does enrage them, and so severely as to threaten the fabric of society. A conference of recent American leaders associated with a greater measure of generosity toward the deprived—John and Robert Kennedy, Martin Luther King, Jr., and Malcolm X, for a start—might perhaps, agree, if it could be convened.

Many of today's middle-class youth, however—having been spared, by the prevailing affluence, the deprivations that make intimidation more effective in later life—are talking back; and some are even finding support, rather than betrayal, in their elders—the spectacle of older folks helping their radical sons to adjust their identifying armbands during the spring protests at Columbia University is said to have been both moving and fairly common. The protest, in any case, continues and mounts. So does the rage against the young. If the confrontation between the generations does pose, as many portentous civic leaders and upper-case "Educators" fear, a lethal threat to the integrity of the American social system, that threat may perhaps be accepted with graceful irony. Is there, after all, so much to lose? The American social system has never been noted for its integrity. In fact, it would be rather like depriving the Swiss of their surfing.

Theodore Roszak

THE MAKING OF A COUNTER CULTURE— TECHNOCRACY'S CHILDREN

There are those who stand convinced that when the war in Vietnam ends, the youthful rebellion will end with it. In this view, the events of the moment represent just another fad, and since fads come and go, why all the fuss? People who invoke the notion "a radical when young, a conservative when mature," who assert that each rebel will change when he reaches the age of 30, are making the same point. The upshot of this position is to dismiss the claims and activities of today's youth, and, not consciously, to imply that the idea of an historically high regard for young people in the United States is probably true, but that it probably is not very important, since, after all, the young grow up.

Published in late 1969, Theodore Roszak's new book, though it does not address itself explicitly to the historical dimension, may contain the most perceptive understanding of current events and future possibilities concerning youth written so far. As one may gather from the title of the book, Roszak does not believe the current phenomenon is ephemeral. The culture of youth represents, he thinks, no less than a new way of life and the most fundamental challenge to the twentieth-century American value system yet made. Much of the appeal of this book grows from the author's ability to criticize the counter culture while simultaneously finding in it the chief hope for mankind. Some biographical remarks about Roszak may help explain the duality: Roszak wrote the book when he was in his thirties, young but not that young; he is a University professor and historian, but he was an editor of a radical, pacifist British journal; he also edited a strong indictment of American universities (*The Dissenting Academy*), but has such a high respect for good thinking that his condemnation of the current drug mystique (not included in this excerpt) has unusual force.

If Roszak is right, then no subject is more important for the future than that discussed in this volume and for none is better understanding and perspective more needed.

THE struggle of the generations is one of the obvious constants of human affairs. One stands in peril of some presumption, therefore, to suggest that the rivalry between young and adult in Western society during the current decade is uniquely critical. And yet it is necessary to risk such presumption if one is not to lose sight of our most important contemporary source of radical dissent and cultural innovation. For better or worse, most of what is presently happening that is new, provocative, and engaging in politics, education, the arts, social relations (love, courtship, family, community), is the creation either of youth who are profoundly, even fanatically, alienated from the parental generation, or of those who address themselves primarily to the young. It is at the level of youth that significant social criticism now looks for a responsive hearing as, more and more, it grows to be the common expectation that the young should be those who act, who make things happen, who take the risks, who generally provide the ginger. It would be of interest in its own right that the age-old process of generational disaffiliation should now be transformed from a peripheral experience in the life of the individual and the family into a major lever of radical social change. But if one believes, as I do, that the alienated young are giving shape to something that looks like the saving vision our endangered civilization requires, then there is no avoiding the need to understand and to educate them in what they are about.

The reference of this book is primarily to America, but it is headline news that generational antagonism has achieved international dimensions. Throughout the West (as well as in Japan and parts of Latin America) it is the young who find themselves cast as the only effective radical opposition within their societies. Not all the young, of course: perhaps only a minority of the university campus population. Yet no analysis seems to make sense of the major political upheavals of the decade other than that which pits a militant minority of dissenting youth against the sluggish consensus-and-coalition politics of their middle-class elders. This generational dichotomy is a new fact of political life, one which the European young have been more reluctant to accept than their American counterparts. . . .

By the technocracy, I mean that social form in which an industrial society reaches the peak of its organizational integration. It is the ideal men usually have in mind when they speak of modernizing, up-dating, rationalizing, planning. Drawing upon such unquestionable imperatives as the demand for efficiency, for social security, for large-scale co-ordination of men and resources, for even higher levels of affluence and ever more impressive manifestations of collective human power, the technocracy works to knit together the anachronistic gaps and fissures of the industrial society. . . .

The great secret of the technocracy lies, then, in its capacity to convince us of three interlocking premises. They are:

1. That the vital needs of man are (contrary to everything the great souls of history have told us) purely technical in character. Meaning: the requirements of our humanity yield wholly to some manner of formal analysis which can be carried out by specialists possessing certain impenetrable skills and which can then be translated by them directly into a congeries of social and economic programs, personnel management procedures, merchandise, and mechanical gadgetry. If a problem does not have such a technical solution, it must not be a *real* problem. It is but an illusion . . . a figment born of some regressive cultural tendency.
2. That this formal (and highly esoteric) analysis of our needs has now achieved 99 per cent completion. Thus, with minor hitches and snags on the part of irrational elements in our midst, the prerequisites of human fulfillment have all but been satisfied. It is this assumption which leads to the conclusion that wherever social friction appears in the technocracy, it must be due to what is called a "breakdown in communication." For where human happiness has been so precisely calibrated and where the powers that be are so utterly well intentioned, controversy could not possibly derive from a substantive issue, but only from misunderstanding. Thus we need only sit down and reason together and all will be well.
3. That the experts who have fathomed our heart's desires and who alone can continue providing for our needs, the experts who *really* know what they're talking about, all happen to be on the official payroll of the state and/or corporate structure. The experts who

> count are the certified experts. And the certified experts belong to headquarters. . . .

In his analysis of this "new authoritarianism," Herbert Marcuse calls our attention especially to the technocracy's "absorbent power": its capacity to provide "satisfaction in a way which generates submission and weakens the rationality of protest." As it approaches maturity, the technocracy does indeed seem capable of anabolizing every form of discontent into its system.

Let us take the time to consider one significant example of such "repressive desublimation" (as Marcuse calls it). The problem is sexuality, traditionally one of the most potent sources of civilized man's discontent. To liberate sexuality would be to create a society in which technocratic discipline would be impossible. But to thwart sexuality outright would create a widespread, explosive resentment that required constant policing; and, besides, this would associate the technocracy with various puritanical traditions that enlightened men cannot but regard as superstitious. The strategy chosen, therefore, is not harsh repression, but rather the *Playboy* version of total permissiveness which now imposes its image upon us in every slick movie and posh magazine that comes along. In the affluent society, we have sex and sex galore—or so we are to believe. But when we look more closely we see that this sybaritic promiscuity wears a special social coloring. It has been assimilated to an income level and social status available only to our well-heeled junior executives and the jet set. After all, what does it cost to rent these yachts full of nymphomaniacal young things in which our playboys sail off for orgiastic swimming parties in the Bahamas? *Real* sex, we are led to believe, is something that goes with the best scotch, twenty-seven-dollar sunglasses, and platinum-tipped shoelaces. Anything less is a shabby substitute. Yes, there is permissiveness in the technocratic society; but it is only for the swingers and the big spenders. It is the reward that goes to reliable, politically safe henchmen of the status quo. Before our would-be playboy can be an assembly-line seducer, he must be a loyal employee.

Moreover, *Playboy* sexuality is, ideally, casual, frolicsome, and vastly promiscuous. It is the anonymous sex of the harem. It creates no binding loyalties, no personal attachments, no distractions from one's primary responsibilities—which are to the company, to one's career and social position, and to the system generally. The perfect playboy practices a career enveloped by noncommittal trivialities: there is no home, no family, no romance that divides the heart painfully. Life off the job exhausts itself in a constant run of imbecile affluence and impersonal orgasms.

Finally, as a neat little dividend, the ideal of the swinging life we find in *Playboy* gives us a conception of femininity which is indistinguishable from social idiocy. The woman becomes a mere playmate, a submissive bunny, a mindless decoration. At a stroke, half the population is reduced to being the inconsequential entertainment of the technocracy's pampered elite.

As with sexuality, so with every other aspect of life. The business of inventing and flourishing treacherous parodies of freedom, joy, and fulfillment becomes an indispensable form of social control under the technocracy. In all walks of life, image makers and public relations specialists assume greater and greater prominence. The regime of experts relies on a lieutenancy of counterfeiters who seek to integrate the discontent born of thwarted aspiration by way of clever falsification.

Thus:

We call it "education," the "life of the mind," the "pursuit of the truth." But it is a matter of machine-tooling the young to the needs of our various baroque bureaucracies: corporate, governmental, military, trade union, educational.

We call it "free enterprise." But it is a vastly restrictive system of oligopolistic market manipulation, tied by institutionalized corruption to the greatest munitions boondoggle in history and dedicated to infantilizing the public by turning it into a herd of compulsive consumers.

We call it "creative leisure": finger painting and ceramics in the university extension, tropic holidays, grand athletic excursions to the far mountains and the sunny beaches of the earth. But it is, like our sexual longings, an expensive adjunct of careerist high-achievement: the prize that goes to the dependable hireling.

We call it "pluralism." But it is a matter of the public authorities solemnly affirming everybody's right to his own opinion as an excuse for ignoring anybody's troubling challenge. In such a pluralism, critical viewpoints become mere private prayers offered at the altar of an inconsequential conception of free speech.

We call it "democracy." But it is a matter of public opinion polling in which a "random sample" is asked to nod or wag the head in response to a set of prefabricated alternatives, usually related to the *faits accompli* of decision makers, who can always construe the polls to serve their own ends. Thus, if 80 per cent think it is a "mistake" that we ever "went into" Vietnam, but 51 per cent think we would "lose prestige" if we "pulled out now," then the "people" have been "consulted" and the war goes on with their "approval."

We call it "debate." But it is a matter of arranging staged encounters between equally noncommittal candidates neatly tailored to fit thirty minutes of prime network time, the object of the exercise being to establish an "image" of competence. If there are interrogators present, they have been hand-picked and their questions rehearsed.

We call it "government by the consent of the governed." But even now, somewhere in the labyrinth of the paramilitary agencies an "area specialist" neither you nor I elected is dispatching "special advisors" to a distant "trouble spot" which will be the next Vietnam. And somewhere in the depths of the oceans a submarine commander neither you nor I elected is piloting a craft equipped with firepower capable of cataclysmic devastation and perhaps trying to decide if—for reasons neither you nor I know—the time has come to push the button.

It is all called being "free," being "happy," being the Great Society. . . .

Why should it be the young who rise most noticeably in protest against the expansion of the technocracy?

There is no way around the most obvious answer of all: the young stand forth so prominently because they act against a background of nearly pathological passivity on the part of the adult generation. It would only be by reducing our conception of citizenship to absolute zero that we could get our senior generation off the hook for its astonishing default. The adults of the World War II period, trapped as they have been in the frozen posture of befuddled docility—the condition Paul Goodman has called "the nothing can be done disease"—have in effect divested themselves of their adulthood, if that term means anything more than being tall and debt-worried and capable of buying liquor without having to show one's driver's license. Which is to say: they have surrendered their responsibility for making morally demanding decisions, for generating ideals, for controlling public authority, for safeguarding the society against its despoilers. . . .

The troubles at Berkeley in late 1966 illustrate the expansiveness of youthful protest. To begin with, a group of undergraduates stages a sit-in against naval recruiters at the Student Union. They are soon joined by a contingent of nonstudents, whom the administration then martyrs by selective arrest. A non-student of nearly thirty—Mario Savio, already married and a father—is quickly adopted as spokesman for the protest. Finally, the teaching assistants call a strike in support of the menaced demonstration. When at last the agitation comes to its ambiguous conclusion, a rally of thousands gathers outside Sproul Hall, the central administration building, to sing the Beatles' "Yellow Submarine"—which happens to be the current hit on all the local high-school campuses. If "youth" is not the word we are going to use to cover this obstreperous population, then we may have to coin another. But undeniably the social grouping exists with a self-conscious solidarity.

If we ask who is to blame for such troublesome children, there can be only one answer: it is the parents who have equipped them with an anemic superego. The current generation of students is the beneficiary of the particularly permissive child-rearing habits that have been a feature of our postwar society. Dr. Spock's endearing latitudinarianism (go easy on the toilet training, don't panic over masturbation, avoid the heavy discipline) is much more a reflection than a cause of the new (and wise) conception of proper parent-child relations that prevails in our middle class. A high-consumption, leisure-wealthy society simply doesn't need contingents of rigidly trained, "responsible" young workers. It cannot employ more than a fraction of untrained youngsters fresh out of high school. The middle class can therefore afford to prolong the ease and drift of childhood, and so it does. Since nobody expects a child to learn any marketable skills until he gets to college, high school becomes a country club for which the family pays one's dues. Thus the young are "spoiled," meaning they are influenced to believe that being human has something to do with pleasure and freedom. But unlike their parents, who are also avid for the plenty and leisure of the consumer society, the young have not had to sell themselves for their comforts or to accept them on a part-time basis. Economic security is something they can take for granted—and on it they build a new, uncompromised personality, flawed perhaps by irresponsible ease, but also touched with some outspoken spirit. Unlike their parents, who must kowtow to the organizations from which they win their bread, the youngsters can talk back at home with little fear of being thrown out in the cold. One of the pathetic, but, now we see, promising characteristics of postwar America has been the uppityness of adolescents and the concomitant reduction of the paterfamilias to the general ineffectuality of a Dagwood Bumstead. In every family comedy of the last twenty years, dad has been the buffoon.

The permissiveness of postwar child-rearing has probably seldom met A. S. Neill's standards—but it has been sufficient to arouse expectations. As babies, the middle-class young got picked up when they bawled. As children, they got their kindergarten finger paintings thumbtacked on the living room wall by mothers who knew better than to discourage incipient artistry. As adolescents, they perhaps even got a car of their own (or control of the family's), with all the sexual privileges attending. They passed through school systems which, dismal as they all are in so many respects, have nevertheless prided themselves since World War II on the introduction of "progressive" classes having to do with "creativity" and "self-expression." These are also the years that saw the proliferation of all the mickey mouse courses which take the self-indulgence of adolescent "life problems" so seriously. Such scholastic pap mixes easily with the commercial world's effort to elaborate a total culture of adolescence based on nothing but fun and games. (What else could a culture of adolescence be based on?) The result has been to make of adolescence, not the beginning of adulthood, but a status in its own right: a limbo that is nothing so much as the prolongation of an already permissive infancy.

To be sure, such an infantization of the middle-class young has a corrupting effect. It ill prepares them for the real world and its unrelenting if ever more subtle disciplines. It allows them to nurse childish fantasies until too late in life; until there comes the inevitable crunch. For as life in the multiversity wears on for these pampered youngsters, the technocratic reality principle begins grimly to demand its concessions. The young get told they are now officially "grown up," but they have been left too long without any taste for the rigidities and hypocrisies that adulthood is supposed to be all about. General

Motors all of a sudden wants barbered hair, punctuality, and an appropriate reverence for the conformities of the organizational hierarchy. Washington wants patriotic cannon fodder with no questions asked. Such prospects do not look like fun from the vantage point of between eighteen and twenty years of relatively carefree drifting.

Some of the young (most of them, in fact) summon up the proper sense of responsibility to adjust to the prescribed patterns of adulthood; others, being incorrigibly childish, do not. They continue to assert pleasure and freedom as human rights and begin to ask aggressive questions of those forces that insist, amid obvious affluence, on the continued necessity of discipline, no matter how subliminal. This is why, for example, university administrators are forced to play such a false game with their students, insisting on the one hand that the students are "grown-up, responsible men and women," but on the other hand knowing full well that they dare not entrust such erratic children with any power over their own education. For what can one rely upon them to do that will suit the needs of technocratic regimentation?

The incorrigibles either turn political or drop out. Or perhaps they fluctuate between the two, restless, bewildered, hungry for better ideas about grown-upness than GM or IBM or LBJ seem able to offer. Since they are improvising their own ideal of adulthood—a task akin to lifting oneself by one's bootstraps—it is all too easy to go pathetically wrong. Some become ne'er-do-well dependents, bumming about the bohemias of America and Europe on money from home; others simply bolt. The FBI reports the arrest of over ninety thousand juvenile runaways in 1966; most of those who flee well-off middle-class homes get picked up by the thousands each current year in the big-city bohemias, fending off malnutrition and venereal disease. The immigration departments of Europe record a constant level over the past few years of something like ten thousand disheveled "flower children" (mostly American, British, German, and Scandinavian) migrating to the Near East and India—usually toward Katmandu (where drugs are cheap and legal) and a deal of hard knocks along the way. The influx has been sufficient to force Iran and Afghanistan to substantially boost the "cash in hand" requirements to prospective tourists. And the British consul-general in Istanbul officially requested Parliament in late 1967 to grant him increased accommodations for the "swarm" of penniless young Englishmen who have been cropping up at the consulate on their way east, seeking temporary lodgings or perhaps shelter from Turkish narcotics authorities.

One can flippantly construe this exodus as the contemporary version of running off with the circus; but the more apt parallel might be with the quest of third-century Christians (a similarly scuffy, uncouth, and often half-mad lot) for escape from the corruptions of Hellenistic society: it is much more a flight *from* than *toward*. Certainly for a youngster of seventeen, clearing out of the comfortable bosom of the middle-class family to become a beggar is a formidable gesture of dissent. One makes light of it at the expense of ignoring a significant measure of our social health.

So, by way of a dialectic Marx could never have imagined, technocratic America produces a potentially revolutionary element among its own youth. The bourgeoisie, instead of discovering the class enemy in its factories, finds it across the breakfast table in the person of its own pampered children. To be sure, by themselves the young might drift into hopeless confusion and despair. But now we must add one final ingredient to this ebullient culture of youthful dissent, which gives it some chance of achieving form and direction. This is the adult radical who finds himself in a plight which much resembles that of the bourgeois intellectual in Marxist theory. In despair for the timidity and lethargy of his own class, Marx's middle-class revolutionary was supposed at last to turn renegade and defect to the proletariat. So in postwar America, the adult radical, confronted with a diminishing public among the "cheerful robots" of his own generation, naturally gravitates to the restless middle-class young. Where else is he to find an audience? The working class, which provided the traditional following for radical ideology, now neither leads nor follows, but sits tight and plays safe: the stoutest prop of the established order. If the adult radical is white, the ideal of Black Power progressively seals off his entree to Negro organizations. As for the exploited masses of the Third World, they have as little use for white Western ideologues as our native blacks—and in any case they are far distant. Unless he follows the strenuous example of a Regis Debray, the white American radical can do little more than sympathize from afar with the revolutionary movements of Asia, Africa, and Latin America.

On the other hand, the disaffected middle-class young are at hand, suffering a strange new kind of "immiserization" that comes of being stranded between a permissive childhood and an obnoxiously conformist adulthood, experimenting desperately with new ways of growing up self-respectfully into a world they despise, calling for help. So the radical adults bid to become gurus to the alienated young or perhaps the young draft them into service.

Of course, the young do not win over all the liberal and radical adults in sight. From more than a few their readiness to experiment with a variety of dissenting life styles comes in for severe stricture—which is bound to be exasperating for the young. What are they to think? For generations, leftwing intellectuals have lambasted the bad habits of bourgeois society. "The bourgeoisie" they have insisted, "is obsessed by greed; its sex life is insipid and prudish; its family patterns are debased; its slavish conformities of dress and grooming are degrading; its mercenary routinization of existence is intolerable; its vision of life is drab and joyless; etc., etc." So the restive young, believing what they hear, begin to try this and that, and one by one they discard the vices of their parents, preferring the less structured ways of their own childhood and adolescence—only to discover many an old-line dissenter, embarrassed by the brazen sexuality and unwashed feet, the disheveled dress and playful ways, taking up the chorus, "No, that is not what I meant. That is not what I meant at all."

For example, a good liberal like Hans Toch invokes the Protestant work ethic to give the hippies a fatherly tongue-lashing for their "consuming but non-contributing" ways. They are being "parasitic," Professor Toch observes, for "the hippies, after all accept—even demand—social services, while rejecting the desirability of making a contribution to the economy." But *of course* they do. Because we have an economy of cybernated abundance that does not need their labor, that is rapidly severing the tie between work and wages, that suffers from hard-core poverty due to maldistribution, not scarcity. From this point of view, why is the voluntary dropping-out of the hip young any more "parasitic" than the enforced dropping-out of impoverished ghetto dwellers? The economy can do abundantly without all this labor. How better, then, to spend our affluence than on those minimal goods and services that will support leisure for as many of us as possible? Or are these hippies reprehensible because they seem to enjoy their mendicant idleness, rather than feeling, as the poor apparently should, indignant and fighting mad to get a good respectable forty-hour-week job? There are criticisms to be made of the beat-hip bohemian fringe of our youth culture—but this is surely not one of them.

It would be a better general criticism to make of the young that they have done a miserably bad job of dealing with the distortive publicity with which the mass media have burdened their embryonic experiments. Too often they fall into the trap of reacting narcissistically or defensively to their own image in the fun-house mirror of the media. Whatever these things called "beatniks" and "hippies" originally were, or still are, may have nothing to do with what *Time*,

Esquire, Cheeta, CBSNBCABC, Broadway comedy, and Hollywood have decided to make of them. Dissent, the press has clearly decided, is hot copy. But if anything, the media tend to isolate the weirdest aberrations *and* consequently to attract to the movement many extroverted poseurs. But what does bohemia do when it finds itself massively infiltrated by well-intentioned sociologists (and we now all of a sudden have specialized "sociologists of adolescence"), sensationalizing journalists, curious tourists, and weekend fellow travelers? What doors does one close on them? The problem is a new and tough one: a kind of cynical smothering of dissent by saturation coverage, and it begins to look like a far more formidable weapon in the hands of the establishment than outright suppression.

Again, in his excellent article on the Italian students quoted above, Nicola Chiaromonte tells us that dissenters

> must detach themselves, must become resolute "heretics." They must detach themselves quietly, without shouting or riots, indeed in silence and secrecy; not alone but in groups, in real "societies" that will create, as far as possible, a life that is independent and wise. . . . It would be . . . a nonrhetorical form of "total rejection."

But how is one to develop such strategies of dignified secrecy when the establishment has discovered exactly the weapon with which to defeat one's purposes: the omniscient mass media? The only way anybody or anything stays underground these days is by trying outlandishly hard—as when Ed Saunders and a group of New York poets titled a private publication *Fuck You* to make sure it stayed off the newstands. But it can be quite as distortive to spend all one's time evading the electronic eyes and ears of the world as to let oneself be inaccurately reported by them.

Yet to grant the fact that the media distort is not the same as saying that the young have evolved no life style of their own, or that they are unserious about it. We would be surrendering to admass an absolutely destructive potential if we were to take the tack that whatever it touches is automatically debased or perhaps has no reality at all. In London today at some of the better shops one can buy a Chinese Army-style jacket, advertised as "Mao Thoughts in Burberry Country: elegant navy flannel, revolutionary with brass buttons and Mao collar." The cost: £28 . . . a mere $68. Do Mao and the cultural revolution suddenly become mere figments by virtue of such admass larks?

Commercial vulgarization is one of the endemic pests of twentieth-century Western life, like the flies that swarm to sweets in the summer. But the flies don't create the sweets (though they may make them less palatable); nor do they make the summer happen. It will be my contention that there is, despite the fraudulence and folly that collects around its edges, a significant new culture a-borning among our youth, and that this culture deserves careful understanding, if for no other reason than the sheer size of the population it potentially involves.

But there *are* other reasons, namely, the intrinsic value of what the young are making happen. If, however, we want to achieve that understanding, we must insist on passing over the exotic tidbits and sensational case histories the media offer us. Nor should we resort to the superficial snooping that comes of cruising bohemia for a few exciting days in search of local color and the inside dope, often with the intention of writing it all up for the slick magazines. Rather, we should look for major trends that seem to outlast the current fashion. We should try to find the most articulate public statements of belief and value the young have made or have given ear to; the thoughtful formulations, rather than the off-hand gossip. Above all, we must be willing, in a spirit of critical helpfulness, to sort out what seems valuable and promising in this dissenting culture, as if indeed it mattered to us whether the alienated young succeeded in their project.

Granted this requires a deal of patience. For what we are confronted with is a progressive "adolescentization" of dissenting thought and culture, if not on the part of its creators, then on the part of much of its audience. And we should make no mistake about how far back into the early years of adolescence these tastes now reach. Let me offer one illuminating example. In December of 1967, I watched a group of thirteen-year-olds from a London settlement house perform an improvised Christmas play as part of a therapeutic theater program. The kids had concocted a show in which Santa Claus had been imprisoned by the immigration authorities for entering the country without proper permission. The knock at official society was especially stinging, coming as it did instinctively from some very ordinary youngsters who had scarcely been exposed to any advanced intellectual influences. And whom did the thirteen-year-olds decide to introduce as Santa's liberators? An exotic species of being known to them as "the hippies," who shiva-danced to the jailhouse and magically released Father Christmas, accompanied by strobelights and jangling sitars.

However lacking older radicals may find the hippies in authenticity or revolutionary potential, they have clearly succeeded in embodying radical disaffiliation—what Herbert Marcuse has called the Great Refusal—in a form that captures the need of the young for unrestricted joy. The hippy, real or as imagined, now seems to stand as one of the few images toward which the very young can grow without having to give up the childish sense of enchantment and playfulness, perhaps because the hippy keeps one foot in his childhood. Hippies who may be pushing thirty wear buttons that read "Frodo Lives" and decorate their pads with maps of Middle Earth (which happens to be the name of one of London's current rock clubs). Is it any wonder that the best and brightest youngsters at Berkeley High School (just to choose the school that happens to be in my neighborhood) are already coming to class barefoot, with flowers in their hair, and ringing with cowbells?

Such developments make clear that the generational revolt is not likely to pass over in a few years' time. The ethos of disaffiliation is still in the process of broadening down through the adolescent years, picking up numbers as time goes on. With the present situation we are perhaps at a stage comparable to the Chartist phase of trade unionism in Great Britain, when the ideals and spirit of a labor movement had been formulated but had not reached anything like class-wide dimensions. Similarly, it is still a small, if boisterous minority of the young who now define the generational conflict. But the conflict will not vanish when those who are now twenty reach thirty; it may only reach its peak when those who are now eleven and twelve reach their late twenties. (Say, about 1984.) We then may discover that what a mere handful of beatniks pioneered in Allen Ginsberg's youth will have become the life style of millions of college-age young. Is there any other ideal toward which the young can grow that looks half so appealing?

"Nothing," Goethe observed, "is more inadequate than a mature judgment when adopted by an immature mind." When radical intellectuals have to deal with a dissenting public that becomes this young, all kinds of problems accrue. The adolescentization of dissent poses dilemmas as perplexing as the proletarianization of dissent that bedeviled left-wing theorists when it was the working class they had to ally with in their effort to reclaim our culture for the good, the true, and the beautiful. Then it was the horny-handed virtues of the beer hall and the trade union that had to serve as the medium of radical thought. Now it is the youthful exuberance of the rock club, the love-in, the teach-in.

The young, miserably educated as they are, bring with them almost nothing but healthy instincts. The project of building a sophisticated framework of thought atop those instincts is rather like trying to graft an oak tree upon a wildflower. How to sustain the oak tree? More important, how to avoid crushing the wildflower? And yet such is the project that confronts those of us who are concerned with radical social change. For the young have become one of the very few social levers dissent has to work with. This is that "significant soil" in which the Great Refusal has begun to take root. If we reject it in frustration for the youthful follies that also sprout there, where then do we turn?

Benjamin DeMott

THE SIXTIES—A CULTURAL REVOLUTION

Benjamin DeMott teaches English at Amherst College. He also writes novels and is a literary critic. He is best known, however, as an expert on "pop" culture. Unlike that other authority, Tom Wolfe, DeMott is not content simply to describe the culture: he evaluates it. In a sense his retrospective report of the 1960's which follows takes a less apocalyptic view of recent developments than does Theodore Roszak's. Rather than seeing two ways of life in dire opposition, DeMott writes of changes in view and in living which all Americans are experiencing together. But in another way he goes farther than Roszak in that he describes the triumph of the youth-oriented counter culture. The cultural revolution that DeMott says is occurring may be a more diffuse affair than the revolution which Roszak predicts and (with some reservations) advocates. But both writers are joined in their conviction that a new cultural revolution is occurring rather than a variation on traditional generational conflicts. There is a sense of drama, urgency, and an attention to definite questions of value one does not find in the analyses of Bruno Bettelheim and Kenneth Keniston. Is the urgency justified? Does the calmer, detached style and substance of the social scientists tell us more? Are the two approaches reconcilable?

Whatever the answers to these questions, there can be no doubt that DeMott's willingness and ability to examine the tenets of the new youth-stimulated culture on its merits is sorely needed. Americans today are generally uncritical in their hostility or uncritical in their capitulation to that culture. Clearly, much of what young people are saying and many people are doing is splendid. Just as clearly, much of it is garbage. Perhaps one reason for the lack of critical discrimination has been a too-easy acceptance of the cry: "I feel, therefore I am." The glorification of sensations, instant gratification, constant mind-blowing have discredited rationality. Many students will be impatient with a book such as this because they have learned, for good reasons, to distrust unwarranted faith in reason as symbolized by too many useless classes in college (the words "boring" and "irrelevant" representing the ultimate indictments). Can there be a bridge between feeling and thought? Is there any wisdom, any point in thinking beyond tomorrow? Is absorption in the moment, one of the greatest charms of youth, an adequate philosophy of living? Are there valid alternatives?

HARD times, confusing times. All at once—no warnings or trendy winks from the past—we were New People, putting demands to ourselves and to life in the large for which precedents didn't exist. And because the scale of our transformation caused inward ruptures, harried us into feelings and

From Benjamin DeMott, "The Sixties: A Cultural Revolution," *The New York Times Magazine*, December 14, 1969, pp. 28, 30, 122.

expectations that had no names, our nerves were shaky, we shuttled between nostalgia and a manic optimism—behaved always as though out at some edge.

If we grasped our situation, had a clear concept of where we were and why, we might have suffered less. But where could we turn for clarification? Among a thousand wonders, the period has been remarkable for the absence of a fully humane genius among those who represent us to ourselves. Vast stepups of production schedules have occurred in the art-and-culture-commentary industries, and substantial talents breathe among us, pump hard, fight for and win wide audiences. Yet no image or vocabulary adequate to the truth of the age has come forth. The need is for perspective and comparative evaluation, acts of consideration and assessment, and we've been offered instead—the notion of "blame" is irrelevant: the work produced probably could not have been otherwise, given the time—discreet patches of intensity, special pleading and description, and virtually no interpretation worth the name.

Wife-swapping (John Updike), protest marches (Norman Mailer), exotic theatrical and cinematic entertainments (Susan Sontag), acid-tripping and commune life (Tom Wolfe)—these and a hundred other "characteristic phenomena" of the years are evoked in exacting, often exciting detail and with superlative attentiveness to personal response. But the place of the phenomena in moral history; the interrelationships among them, the chief forces and principles determining the nature of the emergent new sensibility, are left undefined, as though they're "too important to matter." Often, in fact, the cant and jargon of the period—copywriters' tags like *The Scene . . . Baby, it's what's happening . . . encounter group . . . enter the dialogue . . . a piece of the action . . . with it . . . Now generation*—appear to contain better hints to our truth than does any novel, essay or play.

And from this failure of art and intellect to nourish and illuminate many problems flow. One is our readiness to accept "explanations" of the times that actually deepen the general confusion. There is, for instance, the hugely popular delusion that the central development of the sixties has been the widening of the gap between youth and everybody else. The yearly periodical indices disclose that three to four times as many words are now being written about youth as were written a decade ago. And the statistic reflects the growth of a superstition that the story of the age may simply be the simultaneous appearance of two ages, two decades, two worlds—one belonging to young people and the other to the rest of us—and that the prime influence on behavior and feeling in both worlds is the attitude of each toward the other.

A handy formula: it provides a means of organizing events, tastes, gestures. But if the order thus established is convenient, it's also primitive: you buy it only at the cost of blindness to the essential unity of the age. The college senior demanding the "restructuring" of his commencement ceremonies, the company president struggling to "involve" minor line executives in top echelon decisions, the guerrilla-theater propagandist sneering at old-style radicals for being "hung up on words and argufying"—these clearly aren't the same man. Yet ignoring the connections among their apparently disparate behaviors, pretending that the task of cultural inquiry amounts to finding out "what the young are thinking," as though the latter lived not among us but on remote, inaccessible islands, is a mistake. "The Sixties" is an age; what's happened, baby, has happened to men as well as babes; we can indeed say "we," and the sniffish fear of doing so continues to cost us to this day.

One other expensive delusion demands notice—namely, the view that our newness is a function of an unexampled fury of sensation-hunting. Easy to adduce evidence supporting this theory, to be sure. Sixties people have been trippers in many senses; the decade saw incredible expansions of air travel, motel chains, tourist agencies. The manufacture, on demand, of variety goes on without pause—"Hair," "Che," "Dionysus," Breslin, Crist, Rex Reed, Barbados, Eleuthera, the Algarve, Arthur, Trude's, Electric Circus, Beatles, Stones, Doors, topless, bottomless, bare . . . And it's undeniable that the age has created vehicles and instruments of sensation on an order of arousal power never before legitimized by the consent of an entire society. But we nevertheless simplify ourselves, enshroud our lives in a mist of moralizing, if we accept as an adequate perspective what in fact is no more than a style of self-laceration. We are not, in the broad mass, pure sensation lists, snappers-up of unconsidered kicks; without denying the chaos and the extravagance, it can still be claimed that the age has more dignity, promise and intellectual complication than any such formula allows.

Wherein lies the complication? If we aren't out for sensation alone, what are we after? Where is our center, what are our growing points, what actually has been happening in our lives?

Best to answer flatly: major changes have been occurring in our sense of self, time and dailiness. For one thing, we've become obsessed with Experience. (We behave, that is to say, as though we're determined to change our relation to our experience, or to have our "usual" experiences in new ways.) For another, we've come to relish plurality of self. (We behave as though impatient or bitter at every structure, form, convention and practice that edges us toward singleness of view or "option," or that forces us to accept this or that single role as the whole truth of our being.) For yet another, we seem to be striving to feel time itself on different terms from those hitherto customary. (We're anxious to shed ordinary, linear, before-and-after, cause-and-effect understandings of events even in our personal lives. We feel distaste for inward response that's insufficiently alive to The Moment, or that glides over each instant as a betweenness—in another minute it'll be time to go to work, go to dinner, write our brother, make love, do the dishes—rather than living into it, inhabiting it as an occasion, without thought of antecedents or consequences.) And finally, we've conceived a detestation of the habitual. (We are seeking ways of opening our minds and characters to the multiplicity of situations that are echoed or touched or alluded to by any one given situation. We hope to replace habit—"the shackles of the free," in Bierce's great definition—with a continually renewed alertness to possibility.)

As goes without saying, labeling and categorizing in this manner is presumptuous: the congeries of inexpressible attitudes and assumptions in question is dense, intricate, tightly packed—more so than any confident arbitrary listing can suggest. And, as also should go without saying, the vocabulary used here to name the assumptions isn't much favored by any of us who're just "getting through the days" called the sixties. We don't tell ourselves, "We must change our relation to our experience." We don't say, "I must find a new way of having my experience." We live by no abstract formulas, we simply express our preferences. We perhaps say, in planning a political meeting: "Let's not have so many speeches this time." We perhaps say, when serving on a parish committee to reinvigorate a WASP church: "Let's have a different kind of service at least once. . . . Once a month, maybe." We perhaps say at conferences: "When do we break into small groups?" We perhaps say, if we're a girl and boy preparing for a costume party (a girl in a mini did in fact say, Halloween night, at Hastings Stationery in Amherst, Mass., over by the greeting cards, to her date), "Look, why don't we just change clothes? I'll go in your stuff, you wear my mini." And it's clearly a jump from innocuous jokes of this sort to the solemn apparatus of historical statement.

On occasion, though, we ourselves do grow more explicit or theoretical. Certain exceptional situations—or community pressures—have drawn from some of us flat declarations that our aim is to change our relation to our experience. Middle-class drug users do say aloud, for example, that they use drugs, pot or acid, in order to create simultaneously a wholly new sense of personal possibility, and to alter the inner landscape of time so that experience can be occupied, known in its own moment-to-moment quality, texture, delight, rather than as a backdrop for plans, intentions, anxieties. And if the majority is vastly less explicit than this about its intentions, if the unity of our purposes escapes most of us, we nevertheless do venture forth, time and time over, old, young, middle aged, in situations of striking range, and do the thing itself—arrange, that is, to have our experience in new ways.

Some of our contrivances are mainly amusing—fit matter for *New Yorker* cartoons. They take the form of homely efforts at energizing recreation or casual relations with others, or at injecting the values of surprise—or even of moderated risk—into commonplace situations. The long-hair fad, feminization of costume and behavior, cosmetics for men, Unisex, etc.: here is an attempt to create a new way of having the experience of masculinity (or femininity). If freedom is most real when most on trial, then masculinity will be most piquantly masculine when set in closer adjacency to its "opposite": let me have my sexuality as conscious choice rather than as taken-for-granted, unopposable, unconfrontable bio-cultural conditiontioning. Or again: the taste of the sons and daughters of the middle class for tattered clothes, worn jeans, torn shoes, soul music, coarse language, rucksacks, thumbing—even for stripping to bare skin, as at Woodstock—is expressive of a yearning to have the experience of middle-class life in a fresh way, with an allusion to the life of the field hand or the workingman or the savage, and with a possibility vivid at every moment, at least in one's own fantasy, of being taken for something that (by objective definition) one isn't.

And there are countless comparable efforts—tentative, self-conscious, touching and hilarious by turns—to transform or ventilate familiar patterns of experience. The intimidated young grow beards and find a new way to have the experience of intimidation—as intimidators rather than as the initimidated. Men slightly older, stockbrokers or editors, grow beards and live for a moment, in a passing glance met on the street or subway, as figures momentarily promoted to eccentricity, individuality, mystery. The fashionably decorous find a new way of combining the experience of being fashionable with that of displaying sexual fury and abandon—The Scene, the pounding, raging discotheque. The experience of the theatergoer and moviegoer is complicated and "opened to possibility" by the invention of participatory theater and the art-sex film. (The routine moviegoing experience occurs in a new way at "I Am Curious (Yellow)" because of heightened consciousness among patrons of their adjacency to each other; the experience of theatergoing occurs in a new way at "Hair" or La Mama or the Living or Open Theaters because of heightened consciousness among the audience of its relations with the players.) Even the most ordinary activities—driving a car—are touched by the energizing spirit. And here as elsewhere risks are offered at a variety of levels. The timid can participate, while motoring, in the decade's decal dialogue—flags vs. flowers, patriots vs. hippies, on windshields and hoods. (The politicization of tourism.) The more daring can affix risqué bumper stickers and thereby possess an idea of themselves not merely as traveling or politicking but as, at any given moment, escalating to Don Juanism.

Predictably, the influence of the new impulses and assumptions has produced—even among "safe" middle-class people—behavior that's empty, ugly or pathetic: frivolous sexual indulgence, promiscuity, group sexual "experiments," attempts to restore lyric quality to humdrum domesticity by the gaudy device of The Affair. And predictably the influence of the new taste is easiest to read in the exotic trades and professions. The intellectual journalist seeks to change his relation to his work by crossing his objective function as a noter of external events with an enterprise in self-analysis—scrutiny of the unique intricacies of his own response to the occurrences "covered." Painters and sculptors for their part aim at altering their own and their audience's experience as gallery-goers by impacting that experience with the experience of the supermarket or with that of the toyshop or hobbyist's tool table. Directors like Julian Beck and Richard Schechner show actors how to alter the terms of their experience: no longer need the actor imitate another person, play a "role," learn a part. He can simultaneously act and *be:* by presenting his own nature, using his own language, setting forth his own feelings in a dynamic with an audience, establishing relations in accordance with momentary shifts of personal feeling, and thereby foreclosing no possibility within himself. And similar opportunities stem from the new terms of relatedness between performers and audience throughout the worlds of show-biz and sports—witness the example of the surprising intimacies of the amazin' Mets or the swinging Doors with their fans.

But it's not only in exotic worlds of work or leisure that men labor to invent new ways of having familiar experience. That effort has touched American culture in scores of unlikely places, from the condominium and the conglomerate to the Catholic nunnery and priesthood. And because the "movement," to speak of it as that, is universal, the economic consequences are overwhelming. The desire to combine plain locomotion with adventure, "engagement with reality," has recreated the family car as Mustang or Camaro and sold 10 million sports cars. The desire for access to a vision of self as speculator, as well as good provider, has sent millions of "little men" into the stock market and created that familiar but still surprising sight—letter carriers at rest before a brokerage-house window studying the noontime ticker. Corporations able to manufacture, for people immured in seemingly unchangeable situations, a means of moving toward an alternative experience, expand immensely—witness the growth of Avon Products, which sells the possibility of Fatal Womanhood to housewives unable to "get out." Everywhere the consumer pursues the means and images of another life, a different time, a strange new window on experience. And the supplier's ingenuity is breathtaking, as attested by Tom Wolfe's account of the contents of the novelist Ken Kesey's "house":

"Day-Glo paint . . . Scandinavian-style blonde . . . huge floppy red hats . . . granny glasses . . . sculpture of a hanged man . . . Thunderbird, a great Thor-and-Wotan beaked monster . . . A Kama Sutra sculpture . . . color film . . . tape recorders. . . ."

The range of materials manufactured in this country to meet the demand for self-transformation and extension of role has become so extraordinary, indeed, that a wholly new kind of mail-order catalogue has lately begun to appear. One such—the 128-page "Whole Earth Catalogue" (1969)—lists thousands of commercially produced products of use to ordinary men bent on moving beyond the limits of their training, job or profession in order to participate (by their own effort) in the life styles of others—farmers, geologists, foresters, you name it.

None of this would matter greatly, of course—much of it would seem eligible for only satiric regard—if it could be neatly separated from the major political events of the decade. But as is often true of alterations of sensibility, the new feeling for "possibility" and the new dream of plural selves can't be thus separated. Throughout the sixties these forces had measureless impact on public as well as upon private life, and their influence grows apace at this moment.

To speak of the influence with appropriate balance is difficult: political acts have political content—indefensible to propose some latter-day version of the old-style Freudian "medical egotism" which substituted chatter about neuroses and psychoses for political explanations of the course of national affairs. For that reason it needs to be said aloud once more—about, say, the teachers and students who participated in the first teach-ins against the Vietnam war in 1964 and '65, ventures whose consequences for men and nations still can't be fully accounted—that these were not trivial men acting out quirkish desires to escape into the Enveloping Scene, or into The Unpredictable. They and those who have since followed them were passionately concerned to alter what they regarded as a senseless, perilous, immoral course of adventurism.

But true as this is, the sixties behavior of teachers and students does have psychocultural as well as political ramifications. The "politically concerned" member of an American faculty knew in former days what his prescribed role was: to observe, to make amusing remarks. He might examine (ironically, in asides) the substance of his frustration or impotence—shrug it off in a glancing commentary in his classes, nothing more. During the teach-ins and in the earlier Cuban crisis he and many of his students stepped beyond these limits, reached out toward another self. No longer a teacher in the orthodox form, nevertheless he still taught; no longer a disseminator or accumulator of knowledge in the conventional frame, he still pursued understanding. He passed through the conventional frame with his students, advanced from the warehouse of reported experience—graphs, charts, texts—and appeared now as a grappler with immediacy, a man bidding for influence in the shaping of public policy even in the act of teaching, laboring to possess the teacher's experience in a new way.

And precisely this determination figured at the center of the major political event of the decade. It is the black man's declaration of his sense of possibility that, more than any other single force, has shaped these years. Whipped, lynched, scourged, mocked, prisoned in hunger, his children bombed, his hope despised, the American black was the archetypal "limited self": no movement feasible, seemingly, save from despair to a junkie's high. The glory and terror of the sixties is the awakened appetite for new selfhood, new understandings of time, new ground for believing in the pliancy of experience, on the part of 20 million black Americans. Their grasp of the meaning of "open" experience lends a color of dignity even to the most trivial venture in self-extension elsewhere in the culture. And nothing is more striking than that they truly are demanding multiplicity, will not trade off blackness for whiteness, will not substitute one simplicity for another. The aim is to add a new self and participate in a new life with no sacrifice of the old.

Everywhere in the culture, in sum, the same themes sound: the will to possess one's experience rather than be possessed by it, the longing to live one's own life rather than be lived by it, the drive for a more various selfhood than men have known before. Few efforts to summarize those themes convey the energy, excitement and intensity of the longing. ("There is an increased demand by all parts of the citizenry," says the Teachers College Center for Research and Education in American Liberties, in mild voice, "for participation in decision-making in all areas of public and private institutional life.") Few men can contemplate the new demands without contradictory responses, fear and trembling among them. But whatever the response, the unity of sensibility lies beyond denial. Young, old, black, white, rich and poor are pursuing the dream of a more vital experience. Propelled often by the belief that if we know the good, then we must act the good, we're moving from passive to active, from "package to prove." And at the root of our yearning stand the twin convictions: that we can be more, as men, than we're permitted to be by the rule of role and profession, and that the life of dailiness and habit, the life that lives us, precedes us, directs us to the point of suppressing moral conscience and imagination, is in truth no life at all.

Fine, fine, says a voice: it's a way of describing a cultural change. But why did the change occur in the first place? All that fifties' agonizing about Conformity, Silent Generation, etc. And then this sudden outbreak, this demand (if you will) for more life, more selves, the open sense of time and the rest: how and why did it happen? Surely not a simple cyclical process. . . .

For philosophers of the media the question holds no mysteries. Nothing more natural, they consider, than for people to ask more of themselves now; men *are* more, as men, than they used to be. Through the centuries we've been extending ourselves steadily, touching and comprehending life at ever-greater distances from our immediate physical environment. Lately we press a button and a world of hot events pours into our consciousness—at peace we know war; in the clean suburb we know the blighted ghetto; sober and rational we watch doomed men turn on; law-abiding and confident, we watch the furtive cop collect his grease. As we hold the paper in our hands we know that somewhere on earth an excitement yet undreamed is tracked for us: hijackers whirled across the sky are tied to us with umbilical cables. And the knowledge quickens our belief in a fascinating otherness that could be, that will be, momentarily ours. Why would we rest content in mere is-ness? What can our experience be but a ceaseless prodding by the demons of Possibility?

Nor do the philosophers stop here. Marshall McLuhan argues that, because of its low-definition picture, TV has restructured the human mind, remade mental interiors in the Kantian sense, creating new aptitudes, new schema of perception, which in turn foster generalized enthusiasm for "involvement and participation" throughout the culture. . . . "TV has affected the totality of our lives, personal and social and political," he writes. "If the medium is of high definition, participation is low. If the medium is of low intensity, the participation is high. . . . In 10 years the new tastes of America in clothes, in food, in housing, in entertainment and in vehicles [will] express the new pattern of . . . do-it-yourself involvement fostered by the TV image."

A match for the ingenuity of this sort of explanation is found in the writings of some who propose existential philosophy as a Key Influence on the age. Since the philosophy asserts the precedence of the person over the culturally fixed function or situation (so runs the argument), and since its themes are well diffused, is it not reasonable to feel its presence in the new insistence on a man's right to break free of the constraints of special social or professional roles?

Perhaps—but the likelihood is strong in any case that the engulfing public events of the decade have had a shade more to do with our new attitudes and psychology than the line count in the boob tube or the essays of Merleau-Ponty. A powerful lesson taught by the Vietnam war, from the mid-sixties onward, for example, was that bureaucrats, diplomats, generals and presidents who allow themselves to be locked into orthodox, culturally sanctioned patterns of thought and assumption make fearful mistakes. Men came to believe that it was because General Westmoreland *was* a general, a military man to the core, that he could not admit to scrutiny evidence that challenged his professional competency. No event in American history cast sterner doubt on the efficacy of the limited professional self—on the usefulness of clear-eyed, patent-haired, inhumanly efficient defense secretaries, technicians, consultants, advisers, military spokesmen—than the disasters that followed every official optimistic pronouncement about Vietnam from the middle sixties onward.

Because men of authority were inflexible, locked into Chief-Executivehood, because they couldn't bring themselves to believe in the upsurges of The Scene that destroy careful, sequential, cause-and-effect narratives, human beings by the tens of thousands were brutally slaughtered. What good therefore was the perfected proficiency that took a man to the top? We had begun learning, in the fifties, to say the phrase "The Establishment" in a tone of contempt. In those early days the chief target was a certain self-protectiveness, caution—and snootiness—in the well placed. But the war showed The Establishment forth as a particular style of intellectual blindness and emotional rigidity: those black suits, high-rise collars, unctuous assurances, fabled undergraduate distinctions at Harvard and Yale, 19-hour days, those in-group back-patting sessions, at length came to appear, in the eyes of people at every level of life, as a kind of guarantee of self-loving self-deception. Lead us not into that temptation, so went the general prayer: give us back our flexibility.

And the prayer for variousness, for a way out of "structured experience," was hugely intensified in the sixties by the national traumas through which we passed. In the moments of national shame and grief and terror—the killing of the Kennedys, of Martin Luther King, Malcolm X—a new truth came belatedly but fiercely home. Our fixities weren't objectionable simply because they were fixities: they carried within them, unbeknownst to the generations that kept faith with them, a charge of human unconcern and viciousness that positively required a disavowal of the past—flat rejection of past claims to value, principle or honor. For the seed of our traumas, whether assassinations or riots, seemed invariably to lie in racism, in a willful determination to treat millions of human beings as less than human. The contemplation of the deaths of heroes, in short, opened a door for us on our own self-deceit and on the self-deception practiced by our fathers. Neither they nor we had told it like it was. And they were apparently all unaware that because of their fantasies and obliviousness millions suffered. They spoke of goodness, of social and family values, of man's responsibility to man, they spoke of community, fidelity, ethics, honor before God, and never obliged themselves to glance at the gap between their proclamations and the actualities their uncaringness created. Their way of inhabiting doctordom, lawyer-dom, sober citizenhood, their ways of having the experience of respectable men, shut them in a prison of self-love and unobservance: who among us could bear so airless, priggish, mean a chamber?

Had we had no help in ascertaining the relevant facts, had the discoverers and representatives of the Black Experience not written their books, we might have been slower to ask such questions. Dr. King's dream might have moved us less, and lived less vividly in memory, had James Baldwin not written "The Fire Next Time," or had there been no successors—no Cleaver, no LeRoi Jones—or had we been unprepared by the struggles, marches, rides of the fifties.

But what matters here is that the discovery of the Black Experience filled us with a sense that, if we were connected with the history that shaped that experience, then the connection should be broken. Let us no longer dress or act or feel as our predecessors had done, let us no longer be educated passively in lies as we had done, let us no longer listen politely to the "authorities" sanctimoniously assuring us that history is "important" or that the great writers "must be mastered" or that truth is tradition or that virtue equals a stable self. Our obligation to the past, the credibility of those who spoke of the dignity of the departed—blind men, crude unbelievers in the human spirit—these vanished, leaving us freer of the hand of the past than any before us had been. Faith of our fathers—what God could sponsor that faith? How could we *be* men and go on living in the old ways in the old house?

And then over and beyond all this, though entangled with it in subtle potent ways, there arose an unprecedented outcry against human dailiness itself. The outcry I speak of isn't rationalized as an onslaught against moral obliviousness. It appears also to be beyond politics, domestic or foreign, and without philosophical content. Its single thrust is the claim that middle-class life is unredeemable not by virtue of its being evil but because it is beyond measure boring.

The decade opened with pronouncements by Norman Mailer against the dreariness of safe, habitual life and for violence and brutality, even when practiced by mindless teen-agers murdering a helpless old man, as an escape from deadly dailiness. Well before the middle of the decade, a chorus of sick comics and "black-humor" novelists were being applauded for social commentary issuing directly from professed disgust with every aspect of habit-ridden middle-class life.

And, arguably more important, whenever middle-class experience was represented at any length and with any care in our period, the artist obdurately refused to include a detail of feeling that would hint at imaginative satisfactions—or openings of possibility feasible within the middle life. Teaching a toddler to swim, for instance—a familiar cycle. Coaxed and reassured, my child at length jumps in laughing from poolside, absolute in trust of my arms; a second later she discovers that by doing my bidding she can "stay up," move; watching in delight, I'm touched and freshened. I see I'm trusted and worth trusting, emulated and worth emulating. . . . What a drag, says mod fiction, what sentimentality, how trivial . . . In the domestic pages of John Updike's "Couples," no mother is radiated by the beauty of her child bathing in the tub. No father learns, with a thrust of pride, of his son's meeting a hard responsibility well and tactfully. The insistence on boredom, weariness, repetitiveness, burdensomeness is unrelenting; crankiness, leftovers, nagging, falsity, insufferable predictability—these are presented as the norms of the workaday-weekend cycle. Grown men join together for a recreational game of basketball in Mr. Updike's novel—but, although the author is a master at rendering sensation, he creates no pleasure of athletic physicality, nor even the act of slaking decent thirst. Everywhere his talk assures the reader There Must Be More Than This, nowhere in the texture of dailiness can he find a sudden, sweet increment of surprise, a scene that permits "modest, slow, molecular, definitive, social work," or any other hope for renewal:

> Foxy . . . was to experience this sadness many times, this chronic sadness of late Sunday afternoon, when the couples had exhausted their game, basketball or beach-going or tennis or touch football, and saw an evening weighing upon them, an evening without a game, an evening spent among flickering lamps and cranky children and leftover food and the nagging half-read newspaper with its weary portents and atrocities, an evening when marriages closed in upon themselves, like flowers from which the sun is withdrawn, an evening giving like a smeared window on Monday and the long week when they must perform again their impersonations of working men, of stockbrokers and dentists and engineers, of mothers and housekeepers, of adults who are not the world's guests but its hosts.

Whether the writers of this commitment and assumption were creators of the age less than they were its victims can't be known. Whether their voices would have sufficed to persuade us of the uselessness of sequential, predictable, "closed-self" ways of having our experience, had there been no war and no black rebellion, we can't be certain. It's clear, though, that a man who sought, in the popular literature of the sixties, an image of his life that allowed for possibility and freshening within the context of dailiness, and without loss of stable selfhood, could not have found it: in that world, so said the official word, it's quite impossible to breathe.

But, says another voice, is it impossible? Or, asking the question in a different way, can we truly survive if we persist in our present direction? Suppose we continue on our sixties course, pressing for new selves and new ways of experiencing. Will we be nourishing a growing point for humanness? Can a humane culture rise on any such foundations?

For pessimists several reminders are of use. One is that the taste for Immediate Experience and Flexible Selves is deeply in the American grain. The belief in the power of unmediated experience to show men where they err—and how to cope—was powerful on the American frontier, and survives in the writings of virtually every major American thinker in our past. Again and again in the pages of Thoreau, Emerson, William James, Peirce and Dewey "pure" Experience is invoked as teacher, and again and again these sages set forth a demand for Openness. Habit, routinized life, fixed manners, conventions, customs, the "usual daily round"—these block us off from knowledge and also from concern for the lives of those different from ourselves. Therefore (our native sages concluded) therefore, shake free of the deadening job or ritual, escape into the grace of wholeness, fly in the direction of surprise and the unknown—in that direction lie the true beginnings of a man.

And there is far more to the return to the ideal of open experience than the ineluctable American-ness of the thing. The return is itself a symbol of an awakened awareness of the limits of reason and of the danger that constant interventions of intellect between ourselves and experience hide from us the truth of our natural being, of our deep connectedness with the natural world that the technological mind has been poisoning. And, more important than any of this—for reasons already named—there is a moral and spiritual content to the rejection of the structures of the past which, though now deprecated by everyone chic, has unshakable vigor and worth.

There are, however, immense problems. The immediate experience, multiple-selves cause contains within it an antinomian, anti-intellectual ferocity that has thus far created fears only about the safety of institutions—universities, high schools, legislatures, churches, political conventions. But the serious cause for alarm is the future of mind. The love of the Enveloping Scene as opposed to orderly plodding narratives, fondness for variety of self rather than for stability, puts the very idea of mind under extraordinary strain. It is, after all, by an act of sequential reasoning that Norman O. Brown and many another characteristic voice of the sixties arrived at their critique of the limits of consecutive thought. Once inside the scene, utterly without a fixed self, will our power to compare, assess and choose survive?

Toward the close of the sixties men began thinking purposefully on these problems, aware that "planning" would necessarily henceforth be in bad odor, yet unconvinced that the future could be met with any hope whatever minus the resources of intellect. One question addressed was: Can society be reorganized in a manner that will accommodate the appetite for self-variousness and possibility—without insuring the onset of social chaos? (Among the most brilliant suggestions were those advanced by Profs. Donald Oliver and Fred Newmann in a Harvard Education Review paper (1967) that looked toward the invention of a world in which men may move freely at any point in their post-pubescent lives into and away from the roles of student, apprentice and professional.) Another question addressed was: Can society be so organized as to permit genuine simultaneities of role? Is it possible to create situations in which we can simultaneously engage our resources as domestic man, political man, inquiring man? (The most imaginative effort in this direction in the sixties is a two-year-old Office of Education venture in educational reform—Triple T, Training of Teacher-Trainers. The scheme has enlisted scholars, professional instructors in pedagogy and a significant segment of tives—barbers to bankers—in coopera-laymen and minority group representa-tive planning and carrying out of experimental teaching programs in dozens of local communities around the nation.)

These were small beginnings—but already some significant truths appeared. It was clear that men on the conservative side, "defenders of orthodox values" (professional, social or academic), needed to be disabused of the wishful notion that heroic, do-or-die Last Stands for tradition might still be feasible. The movement of culture, what "had happened in the sixties," had happened so irreversibly, the changes of assumption and of cultural texture were so thoroughgoing, that the idea of drawing a line—thus far and no farther—was at best comic. The option of Standing Pat was foreclosed; there is no interest on the part of the "opposition" in face-to-face struggle; when and if traditionalists march forth to an imagined Fateful Encounter, they'll find only ghosts and shadows waiting.

And on the radical side, it became clear that the task is somehow to establish that the reason for rehabilitating the idea of the stable self, and the narrative as opposed to the dramatic sense of life, is to insure the survival of the human capacity to *have* an experience. For as John Dewey put it years ago:

> Experiencing like breathing is a rhythm of intakings and outgivings. Their succession is punctuated and made a rhythm by the existence of intervals, periods in which one phase is ceasing and the other is inchoate and preparing. [We compare] the course of a conscious experience to the alternate flights and perchings of a bird. The flights are intimately connected with one another; they are not so many unrelated lightings succeeded by a number of equally unrelated hoppings. Each resting place in experience is an undergoing in which is absorbed and taken home the consequences of prior doing, and, unless the doing is that of utter caprice or sheer routine, each doing carries in itself meaning that has been extracted and conserved. . . . If we move too rapidly, we get away from the base of supplies—of accrued meanings—and the experience is flustered, thin and confused. If we dawdle too long after having extracted a net value, experience perishes of inanition.

Despite the cultural revolution, we still possessed, for most of the sixties, a poet of "perchings," a believer in human rhythms who was capable of shrewd distinctions between caprice and routine, and firm in his feeling for the ordinary universe—and for the forms of ordinary human connectedness. Randall Jarrell (1914–1965) could write of ordinary life that it was a matter of errands generating each other, often a tiresome small round, the pumping of a rusty pump, water seeming never to want to rise—and he could then add that within the round, to alert heads, came a chance to act and perceive and receive, to arrive at an intensity of imaginative experience that itself constitutes an overflowing and a deep release:

> . . . *sometimes*
> *The wheel turns of its own weight, the rusty*
> *Pump pumps over your sweating face the clear*
> *Water, cold, so cold! You cup your hands*
> *And gulp from them the dailiness of life.*

The shadow over us is that we seem, at the end of the sixties, too disposed to disbelieve in that nourishment—almost convinced it can't be real. But we nevertheless possess some strength, a possible way forward. We know that within the habitual life are a thousand restraints upon feeling, concern, humanness itself: our growing point is that we have dared to think of casting them off.

SUGGESTIONS FOR ADDITIONAL READING

THE form of bibliographies is such that the average reader is usually impressed by the wealth of published material extant on any given subject. Before listing titles concerning childhood in America, the major historiographical generalization must be made with some force before it is submerged in a thicket of titles, authors, places and dates of publication. That point is that we know relatively little about childhood and family practices in the American past; historians have neglected the subject. Arthur W. Calhoun wrote the last comprehensive history of American family life, *A Social History of the American Family: From Colonial Times to the Present* (Cleveland, 1917–1919, 3 vols.), fifty years ago. These are serviceable volumes, but they were written without the benefit of the methodology and insights of the behavioral sciences, and they do not probe very deeply.

The field of general studies of the family has been left to the sociologists and anthropologists. This means, among some assets, an encounter with the jargon, the one-dimensional time perspective, and the unreal "ideal types" that scholars in these "sciences" sometimes are unable to avoid. Whatever their limitations, these writers merit gratitude for daring to till the field. The best results include Talcott Parsons and Robert F. Bales, *Family Socialization and Interaction Processes* (Glencoe, 1955); Ruth N. Ashen, ed., *The Family: Its Function and Destiny* (New York, 1949); W. Allison Davis and Robert J. Havighurst, *Father of the Man* (Boston, 1947); Andrew G. Truxal and Francis E. Merrill, *The Family in American Society* (New York, 1947); Willard Waller, *The Family: A Dynamic Interpretation* (New York, 1938); and J. Piaget, *The Child's Conception of the World* (New York, 1929). Useful statistics are contained in Paul C. Glick, *American Families* (New York, 1957). Recent textbooks used for sociology courses on the family are too numerous and too conventional to mention.

In addition to Erik Erikson's seminal studies, other widely-read social scientists have paid some attention to the American family. Margaret Mead has written a great deal on the subject, and some of her best insights on America are obtainable in *And Keep Your Powder Dry: An Anthropologist Looks at America* (New York, 1943). Geoffrey Gorer makes some fanciful, but provocative comments in *The American People* (New York, 1948). Most influential has been David Riesman, *The Lonely Crowd: A Study of the Changing American Character* (New Haven, 1950). Riesman claims that Americans and their family patterns were inner-directed in the nineteenth century and are other-directed today. His generalization concerning the nineteenth century has stirred some historians to comment, most notably Carl N. Degler in "The Sociologist As Historian: Riesman's *The Lonely Crowd*," *Amer. Quar.*, XV (Winter, 1963), 483–497. Degler thinks American children and adults have *always* been other-directed, but Cushing Strout, also an historian, disagrees in "A Note on Degler, Riesman and Tocqueville," *Amer. Quar.*, XVI (Spring, 1964), 100–102. For the most thorough investigation into Riesman's ideas, see Seymour Lipset and Leo Lowenthal, eds., *Culture and Social Character: The Work of David Riesman Reviewed* (Glencoe, 1961). The works listed in this paragraph indicate the close relationship between studies of American child-rearing habits and those of the American character.

Although works dealing specifically with the child and his family are rare, the schooling of the American child has received exhaustive treatment. Most of this work has been carried on by the educationists and products of the teachers' colleges, with the consequence that concentration has not been on the child and the society, but upon the institutions of instruction themselves. Bailyn remarks upon this in *Education in the Forming of American Society*, and upon the narrow definition of education as formal schooling in our histories. He recalls favorably Edward Eggleston's *The Transit of Civilization from England to America in the Seventeenth Century* (New York, 1900), a book which treated curricula and formalized school learning as a small part of a much larger process in which the child picks up the values of his culture. The study of the transmission of values as a complex process involving community, church, family, government, and peers as well as schools sheds far more light upon the society than do the strictly institutional analyses of public education with which we are surrounded. The educationists have tended to write about elementary and secondary education, frequently celebrating the evolutionary growth of public schools. The best of these books are R. Freeman Butts and Lawrence A. Cremin, *A History of Education in the United States* (New York, 1953); Sidney Jackson, *America's Struggle for Free Schools* (Washington, D.C., 1941); and Cremin's *The American Common School* (New York, 1951). Some standard, though perhaps less valuable studies include H. G. Good, *A History of American Education* (New York, 1956); Paul Monroe, *Founding of the American Public School System* (New York, 1940); Charles Franklin Thwing, *A History of Education in the United States since the Civil War* (Boston, 1910); and, most widely read in this genre, Elwood P. Cubberley, *Public Education in the United States* (rev. ed. Boston, 1934). Analyses of the content of the schoolbooks, such as Ruth Elson's, attempt more consciously to relate schooling to the interest of the society at large. Also useful, in this vein, is Richard Mosier, *Making the American Mind: McGuffey Readers* (New York, 1947). Less specific, but no less valuable, is Paul Goodman's popular critique, *Growing Up Absurd* (New York, 1960).

Since most historians are college professors, it is not surprising that many historians have written, and written well, about higher education in the United States. Among the best general works are Frederick Rudolph, *The American College and University: A History* (New York, 1962); Richard Hofstadter and C. De Witt Hardy, *The Development and Scope of Higher Education in the United States* (New York, 1952); D. G. Tewksbury, *The Founding of American Colleges and Universities before the Civil War* (New York, 1932); and Richard Hofstadter and Walter P. Metzger, *The Development of Academic Freedom in the United States* (New York, 1955). Histories of particular colleges and universities are quite illuminating for the way they recreate the temper and tone of various periods of the past through personal glimpses of students and through the special perspectives of the undergraduates themselves. There are a multitude of these frequently outstanding studies. See, especially, George Wilson Pierson, *Yale: College and University, 1871–1937* (New Haven, 1952–55, 2 vols.); Frederick Rudolph, *Mark Hopkins and the Log; Williams College, 1836–1872* (New Haven, 1956); George E. Peterson, *The New England College in the Age of the University* (Amherst, 1964); Hugh Hawkins, *Pioneer: A History of the Johns Hopkins University, 1874–1889* (Ithaca, N.Y., 1960); Thomas Le Duc, *Piety and Intellect at Amherst College, 1865–1912* (New York, 1946); Carl Becker, *Cornell University: Founders and the Founding* (Ithaca, N.Y., 1943); Merle Curti and Vernon Carstensen, *The University of Wisconsin: A History, 1848–1925* (Madison, 1949, 2 vols.); and, above all, the many volumes on Harvard by Samuel Eliot Morison, most comprehensive of which is *Three Centuries of Harvard 1636–1936* (Cambridge, Mass., 1936).

But one can write about schools without touching upon the students. This is especially the case with the books dealing with primary and secondary schools. The outpouring of educational history should not obscure the fact that the American child has been neglected by historians. Among the major exceptions are those historians who appear in this volume: Tocqueville, Hofstadter, Bailyn,

Potter. It is encouraging that the latter two rank at the top of the guild of living American historians and it is possible that their interest in the subject may spur other historians into action. Instead of merely hoping, however, it would be more useful to indicate some of the kinds of sources that might aid those who become interested in the future study of the relationship between the American child and his nation. Another top-flight historian, Edmund S. Morgan, furnishes a starting point in the bibliography of his *The Puritan Family: Essays on Religion and Domestic Relations in Seventeenth Century New England* (Boston, 1944). Note the range of sources he used in this book and in his somewhat less successful *Virginians at Home: Family Life in the Eighteenth Century* (Chapel Hill, 1952). Two types of materials abound. First are the official public documents—the records of counties and towns, of the courts, the schools, the churches, and the statistical figures. They document the nature, the problems, and the alterations in American family life. Second are the indefinite, but perhaps more suggestive, literary documents. These include the abundant diaries, letters, and autobiographies of various individuals; the popular novels which invariably picture scenes of family life; travel accounts; songs; schoolbooks; paintings; guidebooks to childrearing; sermons; the numerous commentaries on childhood in popular magazines and in newspapers. Almost any of the materials of cultural, social, and intellectual history bear on childhood; the richness of data for our own time is overwhelming. For the period 1830–1900, see Bernard Wishy, *The Child and the Republic: The Dawn of Modern American Child Nurture* (Philadelphia, 1968). This monograph is the most recent and rigorous study of the American child before the twentieth century. Wishy's bibliography is especially valuable.

The intellectual wealth to be exploited by the historical study of the child may be gleaned from some of the questions proposed by various sociologists and anthropologists who, while turning their imaginations loose on American family life, have bewailed the lack of historical analysis they feel they need for their own benefit. See, for example, Donald Young, ed., "The Modern American Family," *Annals of the American Academy of Political and Social Science,* CLX (March, 1932); Margaret Mead, "The Implications of Culture Change for Personality Development," *American Journal of Orthopsychiatry,* 17 (1947), 633–646; Talcott Parsons' influential "The Kinship System of the Contemporary United States," in *Essays in Sociological Theory* (Glencoe, 1949); and John Sirjamaki, *The American Family in the Twentieth Century* (Cambridge, 1953). The study of the American family is significant, and the historical sources for such study abound. Bernard Bailyn, whose splendid critical bibliographical essay in *Education in the Forming of American Society* is a first stop for would-be researchers, is nonetheless forced to conclude, after listing a few scattered historical works on the subject: "Aside from these writings, limited either in locality or approach, the history of the family in America is completely unexplored."

The books that have inundated the country in the late 1960's in response to student unrest, have been, therefore, essentially one-dimensional. Most of the studies lack the perspective that can be furnished by a solid understanding of both American history and the history of the American family. Until historians do their job, writers must do their best to grapple with the problems dramatized by the emergence of the "counter culture" of youth. Although an inordinate amount of nonsense has been published, a list of some useful works written in just the past two years (1968 and 1969) dealing with student disquiet as an international phenomenon is witness to its enormous impact. Among the best are: Tariq Ali, *The New Revolutionaries* (New York, 1969); Herve Bourges, ed., *The French Student Revolt: The Leaders Speak* (New York, 1968); Alexander Cockburn and Robin Blackburn, eds., *Student Power: Problems, Diagnosis, Action* (Baltimore, 1969); Lewis

S. Feuer, *The Conflict of Generations: The Character and Significance of Student Movements* (New York, 1969); Kenneth Keniston, *Young Radicals: Notes on Committed Youth* (New York, 1968) [See also Keniston, *The Uncommitted: Alienated Youth in American Society* (Boston, 1969)]; Armstead L. Robinson, Craig C. Foster and Donald H. Ogilvie, *Black Studies in the University: A Symposium* (New Haven, 1969); Jerome H. Skolnick, *The Politics of Protest* (New York, 1969); Kerry G. Smith, ed., *Stress and Campus Response* (San Francisco, 1968); Stephen Spender, *The Year of the Young Rebels* (New York, 1968); Harold Taylor, *Students Without Teachers: The Crisis in the University* (New York, 1969); and United Nations Economic and Social Council, *Preliminary Report on Long-Term Policies and Programmes for Youth in National Development* (New York, 1969). The most valuable student-written book, James Simon Kunen's *The Strawberry Statement—Notes of a College Revolutionary* (New York, 1969), made into a most uneven movie, reminds us that many students, were they pressed into accounting for the anger of their generation, would be unlikely to lay it to generational difficulties or class conflict or faulty communication. Like Kunen, they would talk about the "racism" of Americans, their "hypocritical" life-style, and the "aggressiveness" of their country's foreign policy, as in the case of Vietnam.

Three scholarly journals are among many that devoted their entire issues recently to such topics, as "Students and Politics" *Daedalus, Journal of the American Academy of Arts and Sciences*, Vol. 97, No. 1 (Winter 1968); "Protest in the Sixties," *Annals of the American Academy of Political and Social Science*, Vol. 382 (March 1969); and "Alienated Youth," *The Journal of Social Issues*, Vol. CXXV, No. 2 (Spring 1969). It is certain that we will see youth analyzed inside out in the 1970's. One of the best recent works is Urie Bronfenbrenner, *Two Worlds of Childhood: U.S. and U.S.S.R.* (New York, 1970). Even historians will join in the hunt.

This volume adds to the numbers but it may be worth it if it leads readers to look back into time in addition to being fixed on the moment. This perspective will add greatly not only to our comprehension of youth but to our understanding of America as well. As an illustration of how analysis of childhood in the past can aid in cultural analysis, readers should note the stimulating, general account of childhood in European civilizations since the Middle Ages contained in P. Aries, *Centuries of Childhood* (New York, 1962). For the future, Charles Reich, *The Greening of America: How the Youth Revolution Is Trying to Make America Livable* (New York, 1970), is arresting and popular, but perhaps sentimental, innocent, and already outdated in its warm-hearted Utopianism.

1 2 3 4 5 6 7 8 9 10